Sams **Teach Yourself**

Minecraft™

Mod Development

in 24 Hours

SAMS   800 East 96th Street, Indianapolis, Indiana, 46240 USA

Sams Teach Yourself Minecraft™ Mod Development in 24 Hours

ISBN-13: 978-0-672-33719-2
ISBN-10: 0-672-33719-3

Library of Congress Control Number: 2014943465

Printed in the United States of America

First Printing: September 2014

Trademarks

All terms mentioned in this book that are known to be trademarks or service marks have been appropriately capitalized. Sams Publishing cannot attest to the accuracy of this information. Use of a term in this book should not be regarded as affecting the validity of any trademark or service mark.

Minecraft is a registered trademark of Mojang.

Warning and Disclaimer

Every effort has been made to make this book as complete and as accurate as possible, but no warranty or fitness is implied. The information provided is on an "as is" basis. The author(s) and the publisher shall have neither liability nor responsibility to any person or entity with respect to any loss or damages arising from the information contained in this book.

Special Sales

For information about buying this title in bulk quantities, or for special sales opportunities (which may include electronic versions; custom cover designs; and content particular to your business, training goals, marketing focus, or branding interests), please contact our corporate sales department at corpsales@pearsoned.com or (800) 382-3419.

For government sales inquiries, please contact governmentsales@pearsoned.com.

For questions about sales outside the U.S., please contact international@pearsoned.com.

Editor-in-Chief
Greg Wiegand

Executive Editor
Rick Kughen

Development Editor
Mark Renfrow

Managing Editor
Kristy Hart

Senior Project Editor
Betsy Gratner

Copy Editor
Karen Annett

Indexer
Erika Millen

Proofreader
Katie Matejka

Technical Editors
LexManos
Boris Minkin

Publishing Coordinator
Kristen Watterson

Cover Designer
Mark Shirar

Senior Compositor
Gloria Schurick

Contents at a Glance

Table of Contents

Part VI: Final Pointers

About the Author

Jimmy Koene maintains one of the world's most popular Minecraft mod websites (www. wuppy29.com/minecraft/modding-tutorials/forge-modding/). He is one of the only Minecraft modders who consistently maintains and updates his online tutorials. Also an expert Java and C++ programmer, he has written an Android Minecraft app that has been downloaded more than 30,000 times along with various other smaller apps. He also maintains several Minecraft mods that cover many different aspects of Minecraft, ranging from slight changes to how food works to mods that completely change the way you play.

Dedication

To the Minecraft mod community, who make Minecraft one of the best-selling and amazing games there is. Thanks to the community I started modding, which led to the writing of this book.

Acknowledgments

First of all, I want to thank Rick Kughen, who was the one who approached me about writing a book about Minecraft mod development. Before he mailed me with his ideas, I never thought this would be possible. One of the biggest problems with developing mods for a game such as Minecraft is that the code you are working with will constantly change. Every update of Minecraft or Forge, which is the application programming interface (API) used in this book, may change quite a lot of the code. Thankfully, eBooks can be easily updated and Rick told me about the possibility of having an online database where I could add updates and changes to the book frequently. This made it possible to write this book.

Some other people I should thank are Markus "Notch" Persson, who created Minecraft. Without his idea, I would never have started programming and this book would never have been written. There are many others who helped create Minecraft and the modding community. Some of those people are Jeb, Dinnerbone, Searge, ProfMobius, R4wk, CodeWarrior, ZeuX, Risugami, cpw, AbrarSyed, and LexManos. These are the creators of MCP, MCEdit, Techne, ModLoader, and Forge. All of these things are (indirectly) used in this book. Finally, I would like to thank everybody who worked on the book. This includes the editors, Mark Renfrow and Rick Kughen, the reviewers, and everybody else who did anything related to the book. Without all of these people, this book would never have been possible. I especially want to thank LexManos, the creator of Forge. His expertise in this field helped a lot to improve this book.

We Want to Hear from You!

As the reader of this book, *you* are our most important critic and commentator. We value your opinion and want to know what we're doing right, what we could do better, what areas you'd like to see us publish in, and any other words of wisdom you're willing to pass our way.

We welcome your comments. You can email or write to let us know what you did or didn't like about this book—as well as what we can do to make our books better.

Please note that Pearson cannot help you with technical problems related to the topic of this book. However, the author has a Google User Group for this. You can access this group using the following link: http://bit.ly/1wpMwef.

When you write, please be sure to include this book's title and author as well as your name and email address. We will carefully review your comments and share them with the author and editors who worked on the book.

Email: consumer@samspublishing.com

Mail: Sams Publishing
         ATTN: Reader Feedback
         800 East 96th Street
         Indianapolis, IN 46240 USA

Reader Services

Visit our website and register this book at informit.com/register for convenient access to any updates, downloads, or errata that might be available for this book.

Introduction

Minecraft is a great game. It's one of the best-selling PC games, and it's exceedingly popular. One of the many reasons why it is so popular is because there are mods. If you picked up this book, you likely already have an interest in Minecraft and you might have already played with some mods. This book teaches you how to create these mods yourself.

Creating mods yourself has two big advantages. First, you can improve the game in the way you want, shaping the mod to exactly fit your needs and making the game more fun for you to play. Second, modding is an easy way to get into programming, which is a booming industry, and, according to many people (including me), modding is a really interesting thing to do.

By the end of this 24-hour book, you will be able to create your own mods and be well on your way to programming with Java. Each hour covers an important aspect of Minecraft mod development, including various items, blocks, and entities. You will learn a lot about each of these subjects by following along with each hour, actively participating in the hands-on Try It Yourself activities, and completing the Workshops and Exercises at the end of each hour. You will also gain more information on how to use your development environment, learn things by yourself, and many other topics provided in various Notes and Tips sprinkled throughout the book.

Who Should Read This Book

This book is written for anyone who likes Minecraft and isn't afraid to learn a thing or two about programming and Minecraft.

If you expect a full guide on how to start programming, this book isn't for you. However, if you want to get into programming or already know how to program, this book will certainly help. Creating mods for Minecraft is how I got started with programming and the same goes for many other mod creators.

It might be helpful to have some familiarity with Java before beginning this book; however, the Java basics are explained as they are used throughout the book. Therefore, it isn't necessary to have prerequisite programming knowledge. It is helpful if you have experience playing Minecraft, though, because many terms used in the game are also used in the book.

Additionally, playing Minecraft gives you an insight into how certain aspects of the game work, which makes it easier to understand what you are creating. When you get to the last hour of this book, it is suggested that you learn Java, but by that time you should already have a reasonable understanding of it, which makes it easier to learn. After the last hour is an appendix that contains even more code, which you will likely need in your own mod.

How This Book Is Organized

Learning everything Minecraft has to offer in just 24 hours might seem like a lot to learn—and it is. This book doesn't cover the creation of every single thing in Minecraft. Instead, it covers creating the most commonly used parts, which gives you the knowledge to make the more specific things. The following breakdown contains the details of what you will learn in each of the hours:

▶ In Hour 1, "Setting Up the Minecraft Development Environment," you set up the environment in which you will start developing your Minecraft mods. In this hour, you learn about most of the programs you will be using throughout the book.

▶ In Hour 2, "Creating the Basics for Forge," you start coding things. In this hour, you create the framework of your mod, which you will build on in all the other hours.

▶ Hour 3, "Working with Recipes and Other Small Modifications," is the first hour where you add custom content to Minecraft in the form of crafting and smelting recipes and more.

▶ In Hour 4, "Making Your First Item," you create your first item. Starting in this hour, you add the first truly unique and interesting content to your mod. Four hours until you start adding unique content is a long time, but it is required, because you can't mod without the code or a mod class.

▶ In Hour 5, "Creating Multiple Items in a Smart Way," you expand the code you made in Hour 4 to make sure your mod looks clean and works well with other mods.

▶ In Hour 6, "Cooking Up a Food Item," your goal is to create an item that the player can eat and that heals the player. This is one of the many custom item types you can create.

▶ Hour 7, "Making Your Own Tools," is another hour containing a custom item type. This time, you learn how to make custom pickaxes, shovels, and completely new tools.

▶ In Hour 8, "Creating Armor," you learn about another custom item type—armor. You learn how to create armor and then you learn how to customize it.

▶ In Hour 9, "Making Your First Block," similar to Hour 4, you learn about another important aspect of Minecraft. In this hour, you learn about the things the world is made of—blocks.

▶ In Hour 10, "Creating Multiple Blocks in a Smart Way," you learn the same thing you learned in Hour 5 about items, but for blocks.

- In Hour 11, "Making Your Blocks Unique," you learn various ways to make your blocks interesting. You learn how to make half blocks, plants, and several other items.

- In Hour 12, "Creating a Tile Entity," you learn about one of the most complicated parts of Minecraft—a tile entity.

- Hour 13, "Generating Ores," is the first hour in which you generate something. In this hour, you learn how to create a class that will do all the world generation for you. It uses premade code to generate your ores.

- In Hour 14, "Generating Plants," you take what you learned in Hour 13 one step further. You now learn how to create custom code to generate things in the world.

- In Hour 15, "Using MCEdit," you learn how to use a program called MCEdit to create a structure that will be generated in your mod in Hour 16.

- In Hour 16, "Generating Your Structure," you make the structure created in the previous hour generate in the world of Minecraft.

- In Hour 17, "Learning About Entities," you learn what entities are, which kind of entities there are, and how to create the fundamentals for an entity.

- In Hour 18, "Creating an Entity Model Using Techne," you learn how to create a model for the entity you will create in Hour 19. This uses a tool called Techne, which is a piece of modeling software created specifically for Minecraft mods.

- In Hour 19, "Coding a Mob," you use the model you created in Hour 18, combine it with code from Hour 17, and then add some more code to create something similar to a zombie, but slightly different.

- In Hour 20, "Creating a Throwable," you learn about a different kind of entity that can be thrown by the player.

- In Hour 21, "Editing Vanilla Minecraft," you learn how to edit Minecraft in such a way that multiple mods can edit the same thing without it breaking the game.

- In Hour 22, "Structuring Your Mod," you learn how to clean up your mod a little. At this point, several files will look quite crowded, which can be harmful to your experience. After this hour, you should be able to continue coding in an environment that is much easier to use.

- Hour 23, "Releasing Your Mod," is a very important hour. In this hour, you learn how to use your mod outside of your development environment and how to distribute it to users.

- In Hour 24, "What's Next," you learn how to continue working with Minecraft mod development after completing this book. The intent of this book is not just to be a guide for copying what it has to say. The intent is that you learn how to create things yourself.

Conventions Used

This book uses several conventions to make it easier for you to understand what is being explained.

Try It Yourself

The Try It Yourself activities are one of the most important conventions in this book. The Try It Yourself activities provide hands-on opportunities to actively experience and engage in the topic covered in that hour. These hands-on activities provide an opportunity to "learn by doing." This is the best way to learn Minecraft modding.

Notes

The Note elements provide extra tidbits of information. These interesting tidbits provide supplemental content or expand the information given in the nearby text.

Tips

A Tip element provides extra information that can be useful when you are modding. This information can range from tips on how to better use a program to certain things you might want to change in the code. Tips identify handy tricks or expert advice that will help you along the way.

Cautions

The Caution element is used to warn you when an action you might take could have dire consequences later. This cautionary text warns you of potential hazards and provides advance warning of outcomes you want to avoid.

Code Listings

Code listings are another helpful element you'll find in this book. Code listings provide sample snippets of code that relate to the topic at hand. You'll be able to examine the sample code to get a feel for how your code should be written.

In this book, formal code listings are always surrounded by two lines to show where the code starts and where it ends. The text surrounding the listing explains where this code should be placed, if this isn't clear from the code itself.

When a line of code is too long to fit on one line of text, it is wrapped to the next line. In that case, the continuation is preceded with a code-continuation arrow (➡).

Downloading the Code and Resources

Sometimes your mod will just not work, and no matter how much you look at it, you just can't find the error. In this case, it might be helpful to copy the code used in this book directly into your workspace. Examining the sample code and comparing it with the code you have written might help you locate and correct the error in your code. Additionally, not everyone is good at making textures, so you might want to obtain the textures used in this book. Both of these things can be accessed by registering your book:

1. Go to www.informit.com/title/9780672337192.

2. Click Register Your Product and log in or create a new account.

3. Enter this ISBN: 9780672337192. This is the ISBN of the print book and must be used to register every edition.

4. Click the Access Bonus Content link in the Registered Products section of your account page, which will take you to the page where your downloadable content is available.

Furthermore, as mentioned in the Acknowledgments, the code used to make mods for Minecraft can change quite often. To make sure this book will remain useful in the future, there are online updates and errata, which can be found at www.informit.com/title/9780672337192 on the Updates tab.

Setting Up the Minecraft Development Environment

What You'll Learn in This Hour:

▶ Understanding how Minecraft is written and what you will do with it

▶ Learning about Forge

▶ Setting up the JDK

▶ Setting up Eclipse

▶ Setting up Forge

In this hour, you learn how Minecraft is written and what you need before you can start coding in Minecraft. This includes the programming language it was written in, a new program that you'll use to write your code, as well as some information on the application programming interface (API), which will be used to write mods. Finally, you learn how to set up your development environment.

Understanding How Minecraft Is Written and What You Will Do with It

If you have ever played Minecraft before, you know that Minecraft is written in Java. Java is a programming language that works on every type of computer. It does not matter if you have a Mac or a PC, or if you run Linux or Windows. It will work regardless of your operating system. This also means you can work on Minecraft mods on any operating system.

NOTE

About Java

Because Minecraft is written in Java, you will be writing in Java as well. Some modders think you need to already know Java to write even the most basic kind of mod. However, that isn't required for this book. It is still a smart idea to learn it, but you can follow the entire book without any prerequisite knowledge of Java.

It also means you will have to set up some things related to Java. If you want to play Minecraft, you need the Java Runtime Environment (JRE), but most computers have this installed anyway because it's used in many programs. For mod writing, you need the development side from the JRE, which is called the Java Development Kit (JDK). This is a bit more work to set up, but you learn how to do this in this hour.

In addition to the JDK, you also need a place to write the code in. You can write code in Word, Notepad, or any other text editor. However, there are many Integrated Development Environments (IDEs) that can be used to increase your coding speed. The IDEs provide tools such as code formatters and word auto completion. There are many different IDEs for almost any programming language. Because you are writing in Java, several IDEs are available to choose from. In this book, the setup for Eclipse is covered, which is the most commonly used Java IDE.

NOTE
_____

Other IDEs

There are more IDEs than just Eclipse. There is also the IntelliJ IDEA and Oracle NetBeans. Alternatively, you could use a basic text editor or NotePad++. However, only Eclipse and IDEA come with ready-to-use development environments. For the others, you have to set it up yourself.

_____

Getting the Source Code

To get started with Minecraft mod development, you need one other thing in addition to the programming language and the program used to write it in: You also need a way to change the Minecraft code into readable source code. This can be done using the Mod Coder Pack (MCP), which is written by the Minecraft community. Before the modding community was as large as it is now, Minecraft mods were written using this set of utilities. However, if you write code like this, users can't use multiple mods in the same Minecraft. To enable users to use multiple mods at once, an API was written. For the current version of Minecraft, there is only one API that is still updated regularly. This API is called Forge. Almost always when Minecraft is run with mods, Forge is installed.

Learning About Forge

Forge is an API that, as mentioned earlier, makes it possible for multiple mods to work in the same game. However, Forge goes much further than just that, making modding much easier and giving you many tools to change certain aspects of Minecraft (that can only be changed with Forge).

Forge is a very well-written program. What Forge does can be compared with trying to gather up everyone in a group, without knowing everyone's names. It can locate and load mods without having Minecraft explicitly know about them. To make this possible, Forge requires users and mod writers to do several things to make mods recognizable. For users, this means you have to put the `.jar` file from the mod into the mods folder. For mod developers, this means you have to follow several rules about how your mod must be written. Most of these rules are covered in Hour 2, "Creating the Basics for Forge."

NOTE

Other Options

There are other ways to write mods for Minecraft. Forge is not required, but it ensures mods can be written as easily as possible. It also ensures multiple mods can be used at the same time.

Setting Up the JDK

The setup must be done in a specific order. First, you set up the requirements for the programming language, then the IDE, and finally what you want to program in. This means that you start with installing the JDK. First, download the JDK by going to the Oracle website at the following URL: www.oracle.com/technetwork/java/javase/downloads/index.html. Select the JDK version for your system. But be sure to download the JDK version 7. If you try to use JDK 8, it will likely not work.

The JDK is set up differently for every operating system (OS). Be sure to read the instructions based on your OS.

CAUTION

Accuracy

Follow these next steps very carefully. If you make even a minor mistake in one of these steps, none of the steps after this point will work.

Windows

Setting up the JDK for Windows entails the most work. What you downloaded from Oracle is an executable, which installs most of the JDK, but there is a little bit more setup involved in getting it to actually work. To set up the JDK, follow these steps:

1. Run the executable for the JDK to install. Follow the instructions given in the installer. When prompted to select which components to install, simply click Next. The install path does not really matter, but the standard location is advised.

2. Next, navigate to the folder where you just installed the JDK. With the standard path, this should be C:/Program Files/Java. If you have installed the 32-bit version of Java on a 64-bit machine, you have to go to C:/Program Files (x86)/Java. In this folder, you might find several versions of Java. There likely is a JRE folder and a JDK folder. Enter the JDK folder and then go into the bin folder. Now click on the path at the top of Windows Explorer and copy the file path. You will need this path later.

3. Now you have to navigate through a few windows, starting with Figure 1.1.

FIGURE 1.1
Navigating to Computer Properties.

First click the Windows icon (callout 1 in the figure). Then right-click Computer, as shown by number 2 in the figure. Finally, click Properties at the bottom of the context menu that appears (number 3).

4. After doing this, a new window opens, as shown in Figure 1.2.

FIGURE 1.2
Control Panel, System Properties.

In this window, click the Advanced System Settings on the left, highlighted in Figure 1.2.

5. Next, the System Properties window opens, as shown in Figure 1.3.

FIGURE 1.3
System Properties window, Advanced tab.

In this window, make sure you are on the Advanced tab, which should be the default. Now click the Environment Variables button highlighted in the figure.

6. The Environment Variables window opens once you do this, as shown in Figure 1.4.

FIGURE 1.4
Environment Variables window.

In this window, you only have to worry about the settings in the top section. The bottom section is not important for setting up the JDK. The User Variables, box 1 in the figure, shows all of the variables your PC has up to this point. You can add a new variable in there by clicking the New button (box 2 in the figure).

7. The New User Variable window opens, in which you add the new variable. Figure 1.5 shows this window.

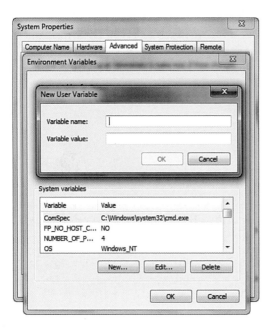

FIGURE 1.5
Adding a user variable.

To add a new user variable, enter a Variable Name as well as a Variable Value. For the name, enter **PATH**. For the value, paste in the path from Java you copied earlier followed by ;%PATH%. This is important because it combines the new variable PATH with the systemwide variable PATH, which has important locations, such as where Windows is installed.

If you already have a PATH value, highlight it and click Edit. Then go to the end of the variable and add a semicolon (;), after which you paste the path from earlier.

CAUTION

Adding a Second PATH Value

Be very careful that you don't make a second PATH variable. If you already have one, edit that one. When you are editing one, make sure there is no space between the first value, the semicolon (;), and the new value, or neither of them will work.

8. Finally, click OK in the New User Variable window, the Environment Variables window, and the System Properties window, and then close the Control Panel, System Properties window. Your Java JDK should be installed correctly now.

9. To check if the JDK works properly, open up a command prompt anywhere and run the `javac` command. This command should print out a bunch of information starting with the following lines:

```
C:\Users\Jimmy>javac
Usage: javac <options> <source files>
where possible options include:
```

And then a list of options starting with a `-`.

If this does not print out, you have done something wrong during the installation of Java or the creation of the PATH variable. When this happens, remove what you made in the PATH variable, uninstall the JDK, and restart from step 1. Also make sure you downloaded the right version of the JDK.

Another thing you could do is check the Java version to make sure you have the right one. This can be done by running `javac -version` and then comparing the output with the version number you downloaded.

Mac

1. Double-click the `.dmg` file to launch the JDK.

2. A Finder should appear with an icon of an open box and the name of the `.pkg` file. Double-click the package to launch the installer.

3. Follow the instructions on the installer.

Linux

If you have the `.tar.gz` file, complete the following steps:

1. Cut and paste the `.tar.gz` file in the location where you want the JDK to be installed.

2. Unpack the tarball and install the JDK using the following command in your Terminal:

```
% tar zxvf jdk-7u<version>-linux-x64.tar.gz
```

If you downloaded the `.rpm` file instead, run this and JDK will be installed.

Setting Up Eclipse

Setting up Eclipse is far less work than setting up the JDK. Eclipse can be downloaded on eclipse.org. On the download page, make sure you get the Eclipse IDE for Java EE Developers version for your operating system. The file you download from the website is an extractable file. When you extract it using Winrar, 7Zip, or a similar program, it is immediately installed and will work. Because of this, it is suggested to extract it in a place where you will be able to find it. The ideal way to do this is to create a Programming folder somewhere on your computer. This folder should contain not only your Eclipse but also your Minecraft code.

The file you use to launch Eclipse is the `eclipse.exe` in the folder you just extracted. It could be a good idea to create a shortcut to this file on your desktop, Quick Launch menu, or another place you can find easily.

Setting Up Forge

The final step in the setup is to download Forge and install it. To do this, go to the minecraftforge.net website. Navigate to the download page (http://files.minecraftforge.net/) and get the src version of the version of Forge you want. When you click the src version, it takes you to an adf.ly link. Make sure to wait five seconds and click the large button on the top right, which downloads Forge. Any of the other buttons might contain spyware. Generally, the best version to take is the most recent release for the version of Minecraft you will be developing for. At the time of writing, this is 10.13.0.1152 for Minecraft 1.7.10. If you are writing mods for a newer version of Forge, things may work slightly differently. If this happens, an update to this information may be available on this book's website (www.informit.com/title/9780672337192), so be sure to register your book to get the most recent information.

NOTE

Adfly and Modders

As you will find out when you work through this book, making mods can take a long time. Often modders want a small bit of money for their work. This can be done through donations, which almost every modder has on their mod pages, but donations hardly ever come in. Because of this, many modders put their mod downloads behind an adf.ly link. This is a website with ads where you have to wait five seconds, after which you can move on and download the mod. You should be careful on an adf.ly website because the only good link is on the top right. All others are ads and could potentially be harmful to your PC.

Once you have the src file downloaded from the Forge download website, open the `.zip` file with winRar, 7Zip, or another program that can open this type of file. Now go to the folder where you extracted Eclipse earlier and make a forge folder in the same parent folder. In this folder, paste all the files in the Forge `.zip` file. Among these files should be `gradlew.bat`. If the file is not there, you didn't download the correct version of Forge.

Next, you run two commands using your command prompt or Terminal.

The first command is as follows:

```
gradlew setupDecompWorkspace
```

On a Mac, preface all the commands with `./`. This takes a few minutes to finish up depending on your Internet speed. After that, run the following command:

```
gradlew eclipse
```

Once the command prompt is finished, Forge will be ready for use. The only thing left to do is open up your development environment (Eclipse) to start coding. After starting Eclipse, a window opens. This window starts up Eclipse for you. After a short amount of time, the Workspace Launcher window opens over it with a Browse button. It should look like Figure 1.6.

FIGURE 1.6
The startup for Eclipse.

After clicking the Browse button, as shown in Figure 1.6, the Select Workspace Directory window opens, as shown in Figure 1.7.

Select the Eclipse folder in your Forge.

Click OK.

FIGURE 1.7
The Select Workspace Directory window in Eclipse.

Now navigate to the folder where you installed Forge and select the Eclipse folder within it. Finally, click OK once more on the Workspace Launcher window shown in Figure 1.6. Once you have finished, Eclipse will load what it needs and then open up a window in which you will write all of your code. On the left, you see a Project called Minecraft. Click the little down arrow to the left of this. When you do this, it shows a lot of files and folders, but you don't have to worry about most of these. The only thing you have to do is navigate to the src/main/java folder and click the arrow to the left of that. This opens another drop-down menu in which you should see a brown package with the name `com.example.examplemod`. Once again, click the arrow to the left of it, which shows you a file called `ExampleMod`. Double-click this one and the middle window displays the code in that file. It should look like Listing 1.1.

LISTING 1.1 The `ExampleMod` in the Setup

```
package com.example.examplemod;

import net.minecraft.init.Blocks;
import cpw.mods.fml.common.Mod;
import cpw.mods.fml.common.Mod.EventHandler;
import cpw.mods.fml.common.event.FMLInitializationEvent;

@Mod(modid = ExampleMod.MODID, version = ExampleMod.VERSION)
public class ExampleMod
{
    public static final String MODID = "examplemod";
    public static final String VERSION = "1.0";
```

```
@EventHandler
public void init(FMLInitializationEvent event)
{
    // some example code
    System.out.println("DIRT BLOCK >> "+Blocks.dirt.getUnlocalizedName());
}
}
```

This is the sample mod for Forge. Hour 2 explains the way this file works.

TRY IT YOURSELF ▼

Start Minecraft

After the setup is done, you might want to start Minecraft in your development environment and check if the `ExampleMod` works.

1. Start Minecraft by clicking the green arrow at the top of the Eclipse interface, which should start Minecraft as you are used to.

2. Click the mod window at the bottom of the main menu.

3. Search for the Example Mod in the list.

Summary

In this hour, you learned what the requirements are and what you need to know before you can start coding. You learned that Minecraft is written in Java, which can be run on any operating system. This hour also covered several programs you will use to write your code, including the IDE Eclipse as well as the API Forge. Finally, you set up the required elements to start coding.

Q&A

Q. Why do we have to use Eclipse?

A. You don't have to use Eclipse. However, Eclipse and Intellij IDEA are the only two IDEs that have everything set up for you. With all the others, you will have to do this manually. This doesn't mean you have to use them, but it's highly suggested. NetBeans or basic text editors can also be used, but Forge doesn't have useful workspace settings for those.

Q. **Why Forge?**

A. Forge is the most frequently updated API that strives to be compatible with as many mods as possible. In addition, it is open source, which allows the community to submit feedback, bug fixes, and new feature requests. It also provides the easiest setup for the end modder and tries to steer the community toward using the industry-standard forms of programming.

Workshop

Now that the setup is completed, you will soon start coding. However, first there are some questions you should answer.

Quiz

1. **In what language is Minecraft written?**

2. **What is the name of the API used?**

   A. Modloader

   B. Forge

   C. Eclipse

   D. Java

Answers

1. Java.

2. The answer is B. Eclipse is the IDE used, and Java is the programming language. Answer A is the name of a different, no longer updated API, but it is also a description of what Forge does.

Exercises

Try to change some of the code in the `ExampleMod` class to find out what does what. You might find this information useful in the next hour.

HOUR 2
Creating the Basics for Forge

What You'll Learn in This Hour:

▶ Understanding the Java in the `ExampleMod`
▶ Creating your own package
▶ Creating your own class file
▶ Creating the mod file

In this hour, you first learn some basic Java. All the lines of code used in the `ExampleMod` are explained. Once you understand all of this code, it is time to first create your custom *package*. A package is basically a folder for Java code. It can be used to structure your code a little better. However, it also applies certain rules about which pieces of code can and can't be accessed. When you have made a package according to the current conventions, it's time to create your own *mod file*. Your mod file is the most important file in your code. For simple mods, it contains all of the code, but for even the biggest mods, a small mistake in the mod file disables the entire mod.

Understanding the Java in the `ExampleMod`

At the end of Hour 1, "Setting Up the Minecraft Development Environment," the setup for Forge was finished. In this setup was an example mod. The `ExampleMod` file looked like Listing 2.1.

LISTING 2.1 The `ExampleMod` in the Setup

```
package com.example.examplemod;

import net.minecraft.init.Blocks;
import cpw.mods.fml.common.Mod;
import cpw.mods.fml.common.Mod.EventHandler;
import cpw.mods.fml.common.event.FMLInitializationEvent;

@Mod(modid = ExampleMod.MODID, version = ExampleMod.VERSION)
public class ExampleMod
{
```

```
public static final String MODID = "examplemod";
public static final String VERSION = "1.0";

@EventHandler
public void init(FMLInitializationEvent event)
{
    // some example code
    System.out.println("DIRT BLOCK >> "+Blocks.dirt.getUnlocalizedName());
}
}
```

Before writing your own mods, it would be useful to know what all of the code actually does. This way, writing mods can be done much faster and more effectively later. In Hour 3, "Working with Recipes and Other Small Modifications," you create your first custom code.

Packages and Imports Explained

The top line in the ExampleMod is a package line. As explained in the introduction to this hour, a package is basically a folder for Java. The code is as follows:

```
package com.example.examplemod;
```

This isn't the complete file path for the ExampleMod, but just a part of it. That is because this Java code should work everywhere regardless of the path it is in. However, the three folders in the package will stay the same no matter what. Usually, having the right path is taken care of by your Integrated Development Environment (IDE). In Eclipse, you make a package for this.

The way a folder path becomes a package in code is very simple. In the File Explorer window, folders in folders are generally separated by a /. In Java, this is done with a dot. In this case, the ExampleMod file will be in the .../com/example/examplemod folder, which is com.example.examplemod in Java, where ... is any folder it may be located in. If you go to the place where you installed Forge, you will find out this folder structure is located in src/main/java. In Eclipse, you will see a folder with a package icon in it with this location. A folder like that is called a *source folder*. Whenever you change the folders inside of a source folder, the package will change and you will have to take care of that in your code.

TIP

Renaming in Eclipse

You can easily change the package a folder is in by clicking on the package in the Package Explorer on the left in Eclipse and pressing Alt+Shift+R. This brings up a window where you will be able to change the package name. It automatically changes the line with the package in the code for every file in the changed package.

The next thing you should be familiar with in the ExampleMod is a group of four lines. All of the lines start with import, and in the ExampleMod, they look like this:

```
import net.minecraft.init.Blocks;
import cpw.mods.fml.common.Mod;
import cpw.mods.fml.common.Mod.EventHandler;
import cpw.mods.fml.common.event.FMLInitializationEvent;
```

All these lines import a class, which is used later in the file. If you look one line below the import lines, you see a line starting with @Mod (which is explained in just a bit). This line refers to a file called Mod. The second import in this list is the Mod file. Imports are useful because they allow programmers to more fluently refer to other classes and files. Take Blocks.dirt, for example. Without the import, the code must be written as net.minecraft.init.Blocks.dirt. Think of an import as saying, "I am familiar with this person, so from now on, I will only use their first name."

Whenever you use a new class, which you will do very frequently, you must add an import for it; otherwise, it will give you errors. Usually, the IDE also takes care of this. As soon as you use code that refers to a different file that is not yet imported, it may import it for you without any further work. If it doesn't do that for you, there are several things you could do:

▶ Write the import line yourself, which is always the package name followed by the filename you want to have.

▶ Hover your mouse over the new file, which will now be underlined in red because Java doesn't know what you mean, and select Import for the file. If there are multiple files with the same name, make sure you select the one in the right package.

▶ Press Ctrl+Shift+O, which imports the file you require. If there are multiple files with the same name, it shows you a screen where you have to choose which one you want to import. This command also removes any unused imports.

▶ Right-click anywhere in the source code, select Source, and then select Organize Imports. This does the same thing as Ctrl+Shift+O.

When selecting the right import over the course of this book, the right choice is always one of the Minecraft-related packages, such as net.minecraft, cpw.mods.fml, or net.minecraftforge unless specified differently. The last two package names come with Forge, and the first is standard in Minecraft.

The @Mod and the Class

Next up is the @Mod line, as shown here:

```
@Mod(modid = ExampleMod.MODID, version = ExampleMod.VERSION)
```

This line is a little more complicated than the others up to this point. Therefore, it has to be cut up into pieces for it to become clear to understand. The first piece is @Mod. This part is an annotation. An annotation in Java is a feature that allows coders to attach extra information to methods, classes, and fields that other programs can read. This feature can be used in code by preceding the filename with an @. The annotation generally adds some information to the file. In this case, the @Mod part makes sure Forge recognizes this file as a mod. Annotations can be used above almost everything in Java. It works for classes, variables, and methods, which are covered soon. If you have several annotations above each other, Java finds the code below that it references to.

The @Mod requires two parameters. In Java, *parameters* are groups of information that get sent with something. In this case, it requires two parameters that will be sent to Mod to be used by Forge. Both parameters are a String. A String in Java is a class used to store a group of characters. To declare a String, you simply type the characters you want, surrounded by quotes. A String is an example of a *constant* in Java. Constants can be assigned to *variables*. The code used to declare a variable is explained shortly. First, it's important to understand the code in the @Mod line.

Inside of the parentheses after the annotation are several things. The first thing in there is modid. This is a variable in Mod that is used to track a *mod ID*. In Forge, every mod has a mod ID. This is a String that has to be different for every single mod. It is used in many different places, most of which are taken care of by Forge to make sure this mod will work with others. To set the modid, this variable is followed by an equal sign. On the right side of the equal sign is what it will be set to. In this case, it looks in the ExampleMod file and selects the MODID variable. It might seem weird that it has to specify to look in the ExampleMod file even though the code is in this file. However, according to Java, when it reads the @Mod line, it isn't in the ExampleMod file just yet.

In Java, the actual ExampleMod class starts beyond the brace below the line starting with public class. Anything before that isn't considered part of the class. However, the package, imports, and sometimes annotations are placed above this and are just as important. The start of the class looks like this:

```
public class ExampleMod
{
```

Even though the actual class line is only a single line, the line just below it is also included in the preceding code snippet. That is because of the way Java works. As you might have noticed—and will definitely find out when programming yourself—Java uses different kinds of brackets very frequently. Code between brackets can be considered a group of code. In the case of ExampleMod, you can call all of the code between the opening bracket below ExampleMod and the closing bracket at the bottom a single group of code, which can be referred to as the

ExampleMod class group. There are smaller groups of code in there, which are methods. Those are explained shortly. Coding in this way is called object-oriented programming (OOP). Because Java is an OOP language, the code will always have this.

The public class line is very important for Java. It defines where the class starts and what the class is called. One important thing to note is that if you ever change the name of the file ExampleMod is in, the public class ExampleMod name has to change into the new filename.

Fields in a Class

Now that you have a basic understanding of a class and how it's created, you need to understand what a class is made up of. In Java, there are several things that can be in a class file. These are *fields*, *methods*, and potentially other classes. All of these are in the ExampleMod. The following code snippet shows fields in the ExampleMod:

```
public static final String MODID = "examplemod";
public static final String VERSION = "1.0";
```

In the preceding code snippet are two different fields, variables or *objects*. Both of them have a lot in common. The first three words are attributes you give to the field in Java. Public means the field can be accessed in every other Java file. This book basically always uses a public field. Public makes the field visible and, more importantly, usable everywhere. Alternative variable visibility names are protected, which are only package and subclasses, and private, which makes it only visible in the class itself.

After public is the word static. That means you can refer to the object by using ExampleMod.MODID. If a field is not static, you can't use the field in that way. If it's not static, which doesn't require a word, you can only refer to it using the object of the file. An example is the event parameter from the init method, which is covered soon. If you use event, followed by a dot, you can access any nonstatic fields and methods. You can't use static methods and fields that way. Static fields always have to be preceded by the full class name. As you might expect, Minecraft doesn't have a different file for every single dirt block in the game. It uses the same file for every block. This is also part of the OOP style of code.

If you have a static field in the class for the dirt block, this field will be the same for every single dirt block. Nonstatic fields can be different for all the dirt blocks. An example of a possible static field in a dirt block could be the texture, because every dirt block has the same texture. An example of a possible nonstatic field in a dirt block is the x coordinate, because that is different for every single block.

After static is the word final. Final means the field can be initialized once and never changed after that. The name of a final field should always be in all caps. Your code will not crash if it isn't, but it's a Java convention, which should always be followed.

To the right of the three purple words is the word `String`. This word is the actual object used. In this case, it creates an object of the `String` class, which is a standard Java class for words.

Once you have written what kind of field it has to become, it requires a name. The top field has the name `MODID`. After the name, you set the field to something using the = sign. What comes after the equal sign may be different for any object. In the case of a `String`, you use a pair of quotation marks with the word you want to store in it.

Methods in a Class

The next and final few lines in the `ExampleMod` have to be explained as a group:

```
@EventHandler
public void init(FMLInitializationEvent event)
{
    // some example code
    System.out.println("DIRT BLOCK >> " + Blocks.dirt.getUnlocalizedName());
}
```

This code is a method. The method name is `init`. It takes one parameter and it contains two lines of code. Finally, it also has an annotation above it. Just like variables, methods can be static as well as nonstatic. The behavior of these keywords on methods is the same as for variables. The `init` method doesn't have the `static` keyword. Therefore it's nonstatic, which means it is different for each instance of the `ExampleMod` class.

The annotation is for Forge. Along with the parameter, it makes sure Forge reads this method during setup. `@EventHandler` is used to register every `FMLInitializationEvent`. There are three types of initialization events. There is `PreInit`, `Init`, and `PostInit`. All the code you will be writing has to go in a specific initialization event. Most mods will only require a `PreInit` and `Init`. Both are written in different methods. At which point during initialization the method is run is dictated by the parameter in the method; `@EventHandler` only makes sure Forge knows which methods to search for.

After the annotation is the line that specifies what kind of method it is. The purple names are, just like with variables, certain attributes you give to the method. `Public`, `protected`, `private`, and `static` work exactly the same as with variables. For methods, there is one other thing you must take care of, which is called the return type. Every method has the option to return something. This can be a number, a `String`, a `Block`, or nothing. In this case, the return type is `void`, which means nothing. If your method has a return type of anything but `void`, you must end the method with a return statement. Later you will find methods that require this, in which case you simply return whatever the method requires.

In this case, there are two purple keywords, after which is the method name. The method name is `init`. After the method name is a parenthesis. In this round bracket are the parameters of the method. The first word in this bit is a class called `FMLInitializationEvent`; the second word is the variable name used to refer to it. The variable name in the preceding code snippet is event.

After this line is a brace, which defines the start of the method. Three lines down is a closing bracket, which defines the end of the method. This method includes two lines, but only one of those is code. The first is a comment. Comments are useful things you can write in your files. Comments state what something does, if there is anything broken that has to be fixed, and so on. You can write anything in these comments and Java will never use them. In Java, comments can be created by entering `//`. This turns everything to the right of this into a comment.

Sometimes you might want to have either a longer comment, or only want a small part of the line to be a comment. This can be done by using `/*` and `*/`. Anything between the first and the second comment sign is not used by Java.

The second line in this method actually does something. It is also a line similar to something you will be writing very frequently. `System.out.println` prints out the `String` you write in the brackets behind it to the *console*. In Eclipse, the console is at the bottom. Another example of the console is the command prompt.

This *syso,* as a `System.out.println` is commonly referred to in programming, consists of two parts. The first part is `DIRT BLOCK >>`, which will be printed exactly like that in the console. After this `String` is a `+`, which means there is going to be a second `String` that has to be added to the first to be printed out together. The second `String` here is the unlocalized name of a dirt block. This name is accessed by using `Blocks.dirt.getUnlocalizedName()`. `Blocks` is a file that contains all of the `Block` objects. One of those `Block` objects is `dirt`. From this `dirt` object, the unlocalized name is returned by using the `getUnlocalizedName` method. This method is an example of a return type, which is a `String`.

In this case, `System` is the class, `out` is a static field, and the `println` is a nonstatic method.

TIP

Eclipse Typing Shortcut

You can easily type a `System.out.println` in Eclipse by typing **syso** and then pressing Ctrl+Space. This automatically changes the `syso` into `System.out.println`.

Creating Your Own Package

Now that you know the basics of Java and understand the code in the `ExampleMod`, it is time to create your own mod. Before you can start creating your own mod, you need a package that will contain all of your mod files and code. To create your own package, you need to understand the Project Explorer on the left in Eclipse and shown in Figure 2.1.

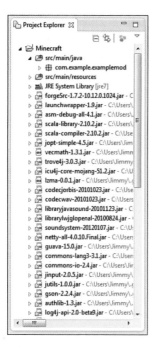

FIGURE 2.1
The Eclipse Project Explorer.

This is one of the windows in Eclipse you will be using very often. In this window, you can create new files, packages, or anything else you need to write code. You can also find already created files. After finishing the setup in Hour 1, there should already be quite a lot of things in the Package Explorer. When modding, you will always be working in the Minecraft Project shown at the top. In there are two source folders. *Source folders* contain all of the code and resources for a program or, in this case, a mod. The top source folder called src/main/java is where you will be placing all of your code. The other source folder, which is src/main/resources, is where you will be placing all of your resources. Right now there is a single file in the resources folder called mcmod.info. This file will be covered in Hour 23, "Releasing Your Mod." In short, this file is used to provide what you see in the Mods tab of the Minecraft menu. In this hour, the focus is on the src/main/java folder, where all of the mod code is. Right now, there already is a package in there, which contains the `ExampleMod`.

Below the two source folders is a green icon, which contains Java. Below that is a long list with white icons to the left of them. All of these are JAR files containing code required to run Minecraft. Except for the top JAR file starting with forgeSrc, these are not important when making not-too-complicated mods. forgeSrc is a very important library, though. This library, which is saved as a JAR, contains all of the Minecraft source code. The code isn't changeable, but you can read through it and copy anything you want.

Next, right-click src/main/java and create a new package, as shown in Figure 2.2.

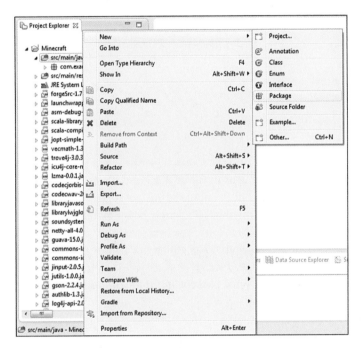

FIGURE 2.2
Creating a new package.

When you right-click src/main/java, a menu should open with a large list of options. The option you want is New. Hover your mouse over this option, which opens up another list of options. Navigate to and select the Package option on the submenu, which closes the lists and opens up a window similar to Figure 2.3.

FIGURE 2.3
The New Java Package window.

In this window, you enter the name of the package and the source folder (where it should be located). First, make sure the source folder is the same as in Figure 2.3. Next, it's time to write the name of the package. It might not seem like it, but the name of this package is quite important. Your mod won't break if you don't follow the rules, but it's simply better to follow them. Whenever I am writing mods, the package name is as follows: com.wuppy. [mod name]. The first word generally is either com or net. The second word is something like your own name or username. The final word is generally the mod name. Once you have finished your package name, click the Finish button. This creates a grey-colored package in the src/main/java source folder.

NOTE

Properly Naming Packages

If you have a domain name (email addresses are also commonly used for this, in case you don't have a domain), you could follow the name of that backward (for example, google.com into com. google), which is commonly done. Then follow it up with the mod name—unless your domain is already similar to that name.

Creating Your Own Class File

Next, right-click the grey package to create your first class. Again navigate to New and this time Class, as shown in Figure 2.4.

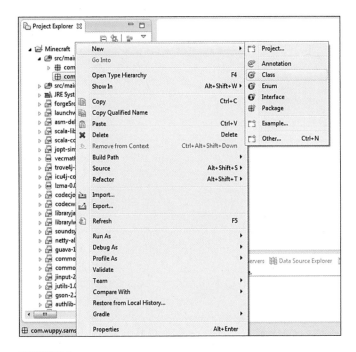

FIGURE 2.4
Creating a new class.

When you click the Class option, the New Java Class window opens, where you enter the name of the class. This window is shown in Figure 2.5.

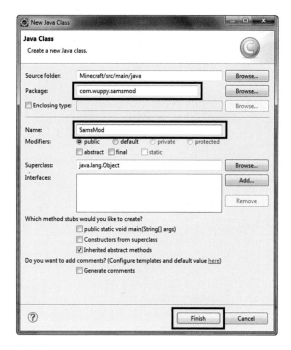

FIGURE 2.5
The New Java Class window.

There are a lot of options on this screen, but the only three things you need to worry about are highlighted in black in the figure. First, make sure the package name is the same as the one you just created. Next, enter the name of the class you are going to make. Because this is going to be the base class of your mod, the name is generally the same as the mod. As is visible in Figure 2.5, in this book the mod class is called SamsMod. From now on, if this book mentions main class, mod file, or the SamsMod file, it will be this main file. When you have selected the name for your class, simply click Finish and don't worry about all of the other options. Figure 2.6 shows the complete Eclipse program with the SamsMod class open.

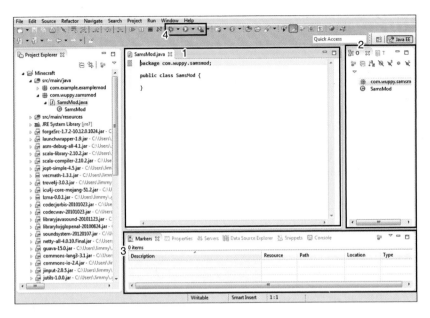

FIGURE 2.6
Eclipse with the mod file opened.

The following list references the numbers shown in Figure 2.6 and explains what those areas are:

1. This is the area you will be spending most of your time in. It is the code window in which you will be writing and reading all of your code.

2. This area contains the outline of a file. An outline contains all of the important Java parts, including variables, methods, and classes.

3. In the area at the bottom are several different windows. The two windows you will be looking at most frequently are the Console and the Markers. Markers contain all of the errors and warnings in your code. Console is the place where Minecraft shows the sysos and other information about your mod.

4. Here is where you can start the game. Generally, you will be using the normal green arrow, which launches the game. The button on the left is a debug mode, which allows you to change some of the code while playing the game. The one on the right builds everything before running.

Creating the Mod File

The final thing you have to do in this hour is actually create the mod file. The easiest way to do that is to copy the `ExampleMod` code and paste it into your mod file. When you do this, you will get two errors. Complete the following steps to fix the errors and then edit a few things:

1. Hover your mouse over the package line error and select the Change Package Declaration option. Alternatively, manually rewrite this line.

2. Next, hover your mouse over the error under `ExampleMod` and select the Rename Type To option. This can also manually be rewritten.

3. Finally, change the `MODID` variable into the modid for your mod. The modid should be something that is different for every single mod. Usually a modid is [yourname]_[modname]. Also make sure that all of the letters are lowercase.

4. Remove the comment from the `init` method. You don't need to do this, but the comment isn't required.

NOTE

Making Your Mod Interesting

This book guides you through the coding aspect of making a mod. However, there is one other thing you might want to take care of, which is making sure people want to play your mod. One of the most important things you can do when creating a mod is making sure that it has a single, distinct idea. If the mod is all over the place and not connected at all, it might not be interesting to have.

An example of a focused mod is one that does nothing but add some recipes to the game, which should have been in vanilla.

The mod file should now look like Listing 2.2. Having a different class name, package name, and modid is normal.

LISTING 2.2   Custom Mod File

```
package com.wuppy.samsmod;

import net.minecraft.init.Blocks;
import cpw.mods.fml.common.Mod;
import cpw.mods.fml.common.Mod.EventHandler;
import cpw.mods.fml.common.event.FMLInitializationEvent;

@Mod(modid = SamsMod.MODID, version = SamsMod.VERSION)
public class SamsMod
```

```
{
    public static final String MODID = "wuppy29_samsmod";
    public static final String VERSION = "1.0";

    @EventHandler
    public void init(FMLInitializationEvent event)
    {
        System.out.println("DIRT BLOCK >> "+Blocks.dirt.getUnlocalizedName());
    }
}
```

This does exactly the same as the ExampleMod, but this brings you a big step closer to creating your own mods. In the next hour, you learn how to create your own recipes as well as make some some other small modifications.

TRY IT YOURSELF ▼

Print Things to the Console

At this point, you might want to print out some custom things to the console.

1. Change `Blocks.dirt` into `Blocks.cobblestone`.

2. Change `"DIRT BLOCK >> "` into `"Cobblestone Block >> "`.

3. Run Minecraft and check if it prints out `"Cobblestone BLOCK >> tile.stonebrick"` in the console.

Summary

In this hour, you learned about the ExampleMod file. All the Java code in here should be clear to you now. Every line, including the package, imports, and so on, has been explained and you should now be able to create your own basic mod class, which you will use throughout this book. You also learned how to create your own package and mod file.

Q&A

Q. Why do you need a custom package for the code?

A. You need it to separate your code from anyone else's code that might be included. For example, if two mods have a class named Mod without a package, Java would only see one of them. It also makes your mod more organized, which makes it easier to work with.

Q. How do I find out the name of, for example, `Blocks.dirt`?

A. If you Ctrl-click Blocks, Eclipse opens up a new tab in the code window with the `Blocks` class. In this class, you can find the variable name of any block in Minecraft.

Q. Where do I find the names of items?

A. You find them in the `Items` class. To print out an item, you, for example, use `Items.apple`. Make sure you import the `Items` class.

Q. Why does the default line print out `tile.dirt`?

A. In Minecraft, `tile.` is added in front of every block name. For items, `item.` is added in front of the actual name.

Workshop

Your mod file is now ready for use. Make sure you understand all of the code by answering the following questions.

Quiz

1. What is wrong with the following modid?

   `"test_ModId"`

2. What does the following code print out?

   `System.out.println("Testing: " + "Answer");`

3. What does `void` in a method mean?

Answers

1. Mod IDs should always be all lowercase.

2. This prints out `"Testing: Answer"`.

3. A `void` method means a method returns nothing.

Exercises

You now have finished the backbone for your mod, which means the mod can quickly grow. Right now, try to print some different names:

1. **Create a** `System.out.println` **that prints out** `"Hello World!"`

2. **Let** `"I am getting an apple with the name"` **followed by the unlocalized name of an apple item show up on the console.**

3. Figure out what the following line of code prints out:

```
System.out.println("Testing Blocks: " + Blocks.bedrock.
➥ getUnlocalizedName() + " And testing Items: "
➥ + Items.book.getUnlocalizedName());
```

Code Answers

1. ```
   System.out.println("Hello World!");
   ```

2. ```
   System.out.println("I am getting an apple with the name" +
   Items.apple);
   ```

3. It prints: `Testing Blocks: tile.bedrock And testing Items: item.book`

HOUR 3

Working with Recipes and Other Small Modifications

What You'll Learn in This Hour:

▶ Learning about recipes in Minecraft

▶ Crafting a recipe

▶ Creating a shapeless recipe

▶ Creating a smelting recipe

▶ Using special `ItemStack`s

▶ Changing the mob spawn in a dungeon

▶ Changing chest items

▶ Examining the results in the mod file

In this hour, you get the opportunity to write your own code to really get started on your own mod. This hour contains some of the most basic Minecraft modifications, including *recipes*, *dungeon* possibilities, and generated *chests*. Thanks to Forge, you can add every kind of recipe in Minecraft. You can also change the mobs, which can be spawned in a dungeon. This can be used to add your own mob, but you can also create, for example, the possibility of a creeper dungeon. Finally, Forge also enables you to change the contents of any *vanilla*-generated chest. Vanilla is the base of Minecraft without any mods installed.

Learning About Recipes in Minecraft

In Minecraft, there are multiple kinds of recipes. There is a difference between smelting iron ore and crafting an iron pickaxe with it. This should be quite logical because you do both in a different block. However, there also is a difference between crafting something like planks and crafting a pickaxe.

There are three types of recipes:

▶ *Crafting* recipes are recipes for which you need certain items or blocks in a specified pattern. Another name for these is *standard* or *shaped* recipes. An example of a crafting recipe is an iron pickaxe.

▶ *Shapeless* recipes are recipes without a defined shape. They also require certain items and blocks, but the pattern doesn't matter. An example of a shapeless recipe is changing the color of wool.

▶ *Smelting* recipes are all used in a furnace. Smelting recipes don't have a shape and never have more than one item or block as an input. An example of a smelting recipe is a gold ingot.

For all of the recipe types, you can only return a single item or block, but you can return several of the same item or block.

Crafting a Recipe

In this section, you finally start actually modding the game. Recipes might not be that big of a change, but several combined recipes can change the way the game is played—especially in combination with custom items, which are explained in Hour 4, "Making Your First Item."

You must add recipe code in the mod file. Listing 3.1 is the mod file from Hour 2, "Creating the Basics for Forge," without the `System.out.println` lines.

LISTING 3.1   Clean Mod File

```
package com.wuppy.samsmod;

import net.minecraft.init.Blocks;
import cpw.mods.fml.common.Mod;
import cpw.mods.fml.common.Mod.EventHandler;
import cpw.mods.fml.common.event.FMLInitializationEvent;

@Mod(modid = SamsMod.MODID, version = SamsMod.VERSION)
public class SamsMod
{
    public static final String MODID = "wuppy29_samsmod";
    public static final String VERSION = "1.0";

    @EventHandler
    public void init(FMLInitializationEvent event)
    {

    }
}
```

The code for recipes can look quite complicated to start with; however, if you begin with a code example, it is easier to understand. The following code snippet shows an example of a recipe. When you add this code, be sure you import the new files.

```
GameRegistry.addRecipe(new ItemStack(Items.apple),
        "XXX",
        "XXX",
        "XXX",
        'X', Blocks.leaves
);
```

Figure 3.1 shows the finished product of this recipe.

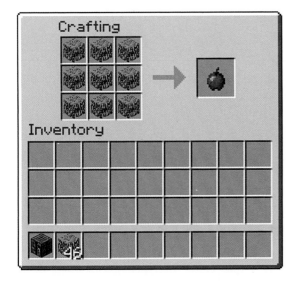

FIGURE 3.1
The Apple recipe in the Minecraft game.

CAUTION

Code Location

This code—as well as any of the other code in this hour—must be placed in the init method or it will not work and will be full of errors.

Using `GameRegistry`

The first part of the first line in the preceding code snippet is GameRegistry. GameRegistry is a file you will frequently use when coding Minecraft Forge mods. This file contains the registry of every recipe as well as items and blocks.

Because you can do so many things with this file, it has many different methods, which all do different things. To create a basic shaped recipe, you need the addRecipe method. This method takes two parameters. The first parameter is an `ItemStack`. An `ItemStack` is another class you will use frequently. When you just use an `Item` or `Block` as a parameter, it creates an `ItemStack` with that object with a stack size of 1 and a metadata of 0. Hour 5, "Creating Multiple Items in a Smart Way," explains exactly what metadata is and how to code it, but examples of metadata are dyes and wool blocks.

The first parameter is the `Item` or `Block` the recipe will return. In this case, it returns a single apple.

Next is what will be used as the input of the recipe.

The Shape of the Recipes

You create these recipes in Minecraft by typing the shape of the crafting table in the recipe using three strings. Each of the three strings contains three spaces, in which you put an item or a block. The following is another example of the crafting table space:

```
"ABC",
"DEF",
"GHI",
```

Each letter in the preceding code snippet represents one of the usable crafting areas in the crafting grid in the game. If you want one of the spots to be empty, you replace one of the spots with a space.

Up to this point in the code, it's just letters. However, those letters must be changed into items and blocks. You do this just below the crafting grid shape. After the last row that ends with a comma, the letter *X* is surrounded by apostrophes, as seen in the full recipe code, which turns it into a Java `character` or `char`—a Java data type like an `int`. After this character, you enter another comma, followed by the block that you want it to represent. For this example, use leaves for the block. The recipe created by the previous code requires each area in the crafting grid to be filled with a leaf and it will then return an apple.

Alternative Shapes

Sometimes, you don't require a 3×3 space to create a crafting recipe. In some cases, you just need a 2×2 area. You do this using the following code:

```
"AB",
"CD",
```

With this code, the 2×2 shape can be placed anywhere in the crafting table. However, some recipes have different shapes. For example, the bread recipe would look something like the following:

```
"AAA",
```

In this recipe, the letter is the same each time because you craft bread using three wheats, but you can simply use different letters.

If you have more than a single item or block used in the shape, you add a comma behind the last item or block, write another pair of apostrophes, and follow that up with the other item or block.

The following code snippet shows an example of using a smaller grid, empty spaces, and multiple components:

```
GameRegistry.addRecipe(new ItemStack(Items.arrow),
        "YZ",
        "X ",
        'X', Items.flint, 'Y', Items.stick, 'Z', Blocks.leaves
);
```

This allows you to craft an arrow in your player inventory using leaves. Figure 3.2 shows the crafting of the recipe.

FIGURE 3.2
A smaller recipe in the player's inventory.

In addition, you might want to have additional options in your recipes. For example, you might want the returned ItemStack to have a size of more than 1. Two other things that you might find interesting for a recipe are metadata for the used and the resulting item or block. You can see all of these things in a single recipe in the following code snippet:

```
GameRegistry.addRecipe(new ItemStack(Items.dye, 2, 1),
      "XY",
      'X', Items.redstone, 'Y', new ItemStack(Items.dye, 1, 1)
);
```

Each of the ItemStacks used in this recipe have three parameters now. The first is still an item or block. The second is the stack size. The resulting item or block can have a stack size of more than 1, but the used items and blocks always need a stack size of 1. The third parameter is the damage or metadata of the item. Metadata starts counting at 0 and goes up to 15. This recipe combines one red stone and one red dye to make two red dyes. Red dye is the second metadata for dyes. Therefore, the damage is 1.

This recipe might seem illogical because this recipe only works when the dye is on the right. For recipes like this, you generally use a shapeless recipe.

Creating a Shapeless Recipe

Shapeless recipes work similar to the way standard recipes work. They are also set in GameRegistry and take the same parameters. The following code is the dye recipe redone in a shapeless recipe:

```
GameRegistry.addShapelessRecipe(new ItemStack(Items.dye, 2, 1)
      Items.redstone, new ItemStack(Items.dye, 1, 1)
);
```

In a shapeless recipe, there is no need for letters or a crafting grid. Simply place up to nine Item, Block, or ItemStack objects after the input ItemStack separated by commas and the recipe will work. Except for that, it works exactly the same.

In the game, you can craft this recipe in the player's inventory and it will look similar to Figure 3.3.

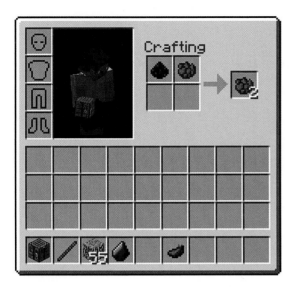

FIGURE 3.3
A shapeless recipe.

Creating a Smelting Recipe

The final type of recipe in Minecraft is a smelting recipe. A smelting recipe only has a single input and a single output slot. The input can, again, only have a stack size of 1, and the output can be more than 1. Another thing to note is that smelting a recipe grants experience. The amount has to be set for the smelting recipe as well. The following code is an example of a smelting recipe:

```
GameRegistry.addSmelting(Blocks.stone, new ItemStack(Blocks.stonebrick), 0.1F);
```

The first parameter can be an `Item`, `Block`, or `ItemStack`, but always with a size of 1. The second parameter has to be an `ItemStack`, and here you can do anything you want with it. The final parameter is a `float` value for the XP you get from smelting this. A `float` in Java is basically a number with decimals. The vanilla smelting recipes have an experience return between 0.1F and 1F, where 0.1F is the recipe for cobblestone into stone and 1F is the recipe for smelting diamond ores.

Figure 3.4 shows this recipe in the game.

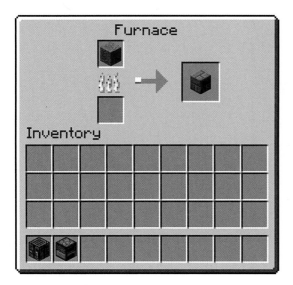

FIGURE 3.4
A smelting recipe.

Using Special `ItemStacks`

It is possible to use a special `ItemStack` in a recipe. To do that, you must first create an `ItemStack` object and then use that in the recipe. The following sample code creates a stone sword with sharpness 1 from a stone sword and a flint. This code uses a new class, so be sure to import it.

```
ItemStack enchantedSwordItemStack = new ItemStack(Items.stone_sword);
enchantedSwordItemStack.addEnchantment(Enchantment.sharpness, 1);

GameRegistry.addShapelessRecipe(enchantedSwordItemStack,
        Items.flint, Items.stone_sword
);
```

This code first creates an object of a normal stone sword. It then adds the sharpness enchantment of level 1 to it. Next, a shapeless recipe is added with the enchanted stone sword as the resulting item. The sword is crafted using a flint and a normal stone sword.

Figure 3.5 displays this recipe in the game.

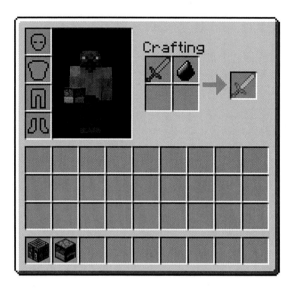

FIGURE 3.5
An enchantment recipe.

TRY IT YOURSELF ▼

Create a Knockback Sword

Try to create a sword with knockback using the previously shown code:

1. Create an ItemStack of any kind of sword.

2. Add the knockback enchantment to it.

3. Create a recipe using an unenchanted version of the sword along with gunpowder, with the returned item being the enchanted sword.

The code answer follows:

```
ItemStack knockbackItemStack = new ItemStack(Items.stone_sword);
knockbackItemStack.addEnchantment(Enchantment.knockback, 1);

GameRegistry.addShapelessRecipe(knockbackItemStack,
        Items.gunpowder, Items.stone_sword
);
```

Changing the Mob Spawn in a Dungeon

One of the more interesting structures in Minecraft is a dungeon where you have to fight mobs from a mob spawner to get loot from chests. For more information about a dungeon check out http://minecraft.gamepedia.com/Dungeon.

Forge is a very good application programming interface (API). It lets you change many small details without directly changing any of the base code. If you do directly change the base code, different mods will not work together.

Removing a Mob

Forge allows you to change the mob spawn in a dungeon using a simple method in your mod file. For example, the following code shows a method that removes spiders from possible spawns in dungeons (again, remember to import the new files):

```
DungeonHooks.removeDungeonMob("Spider");
```

This method removes the spider from the dungeon. It is a method in the DungeonHooks class, which selects the mob that will be spawned in the dungeon. The removeDungeonMob takes a single String parameter, which must be the name of the mob in the code. If you want to know the exact names of all of the mobs in Minecraft, go to the EntityList class in the net.minecraft.entity package of the ForgeSrc library.

Make sure you spell "Spider" correctly or it won't work. You can find the standard mobs spawning in a dungeon in the DungeonHooks file. You can also use this method to remove the spawn of a mob from a different mod, provided you have the name of it.

Adding a Mob

You can also add mobs to the dungeons using the following method:

```
DungeonHooks.addDungeonMob("Creeper", 100);
```

The first parameter is just like the removeDungeonMob method—the code name of the mob. The second parameter is the spawn chance. As is documented in the DungeonHooks file, spiders and skeletons have a 100 chance of spawning. Zombies have a chance of 200.

▼ TRY IT YOURSELF

Add a Mob

Add a different mob using the method shown previously:

1. Find the mob name in the EntityList class, where all the names are listed.

2. Add a method similar to the one shown here to your mod file with a 50 spawn chance.

Changing Chest Items

In Forge, another really useful file can be used to change the contents of basically any vanilla-generated chest.

Removing an Item

The following code snippet shows an example of how to remove an item from a chest (be certain to import new files):

```
ChestGenHooks.removeItem(ChestGenHooks.DUNGEON_CHEST, new
➥ItemStack(Items.saddle));
```

`removeItem` is a method in `ChestGenHooks` that takes two parameters. The first parameter is a `String`. This `String` specifies the chest from which it should remove the item. You can manually type this, but it's suggested to use one of the variables in the `ChestGenHooks` class, because they might change, and using the variable will prevent it from breaking without your noticing.

The second parameter is an `ItemStack` of the item that has to be removed from the chest.

Adding an Item

Just like with the dungeon mobs, you can also add new things to the chest here. The following code shows how to do that:

```
ChestGenHooks.addItem(ChestGenHooks.DUNGEON_CHEST, new
➥WeightedRandomChestContent(new ItemStack(Blocks.cobblestone), 25, 50, 10));
```

This method requires two parameters. The first is just like with `removeItem`, the string that specifies the chest. The second parameter is a `WeightedRandomChestContent`. This is another file that requires four parameters.

The first parameter in the `WeightedRandomChestContent` is an `ItemStack` containing the item or block that should be generated. The second parameter is the minimum stack size in which it will generate. The third parameter is the maximum stack size. The final parameter is the chance of it being chosen. For example, gunpowder has a chance of 10, and a golden apple has a chance of 1.

Examining the Results in the Mod File

After doing all of this, the mod file should look something like the following:

```
package com.wuppy.samsmod;

import net.minecraft.enchantment.Enchantment;
import net.minecraft.init.Blocks;
```

```java
import net.minecraft.init.Items;
import net.minecraft.item.ItemStack;
import net.minecraft.util.WeightedRandomChestContent;
import net.minecraftforge.common.ChestGenHooks;
import net.minecraftforge.common.DungeonHooks;
import cpw.mods.fml.common.Mod;
import cpw.mods.fml.common.Mod.EventHandler;
import cpw.mods.fml.common.event.FMLInitializationEvent;
import cpw.mods.fml.common.registry.GameRegistry;

@Mod(modid = SamsMod.MODID, version = SamsMod.VERSION)
public class SamsMod
{
    public static final String MODID = "wuppy29_samsmod";
    public static final String VERSION = "1.0";

    @EventHandler
    public void init(FMLInitializationEvent event)
    {
        //Recipes
        GameRegistry.addRecipe(new ItemStack(Items.apple),
                "XXX",
                "XXX",
                "XXX",
                'X', Blocks.leaves
        );
        GameRegistry.addRecipe(new ItemStack(Items.arrow),
                "YZ",
                "X ",
                'X', Items.flint, 'Y', Items.stick, 'Z', Blocks.leaves
        );
        GameRegistry.addShapelessRecipe(new ItemStack(Items.dye, 2, 1),
                Items.redstone, new ItemStack(Items.dye, 1, 1)
        );
        GameRegistry.addSmelting(Blocks.stone, new ItemStack(Blocks.stonebrick),
0.1F);

        ItemStack enchantedSwordItemStack = new ItemStack(Items.stone_sword);
        enchantedSwordItemStack.addEnchantment(Enchantment.sharpness, 1);

        GameRegistry.addShapelessRecipe(enchantedSwordItemStack,
                    Items.flint, Items.stone_sword
        );

        //Dungeon changes
        DungeonHooks.removeDungeonMob("Spider");
        DungeonHooks.addDungeonMob("Creeper", 100);
```

```
        ChestGenHooks.removeItem(ChestGenHooks.DUNGEON_CHEST, new
➥ItemStack(Items.saddle));
        ChestGenHooks.addItem(ChestGenHooks.DUNGEON_CHEST, new
➥WeightedRandomChestContent(new ItemStack(Blocks.cobblestone), 25, 50, 10));
    }
}
```

This code adds two standard recipes, a smelting recipe and two shapeless recipes. It also changes up the dungeons a little bit.

Except for this, the code is grouped up a bit and there are a few comments, which quickly tell the reader what the code does. As a best practice, you might want to add comments to your own file as well.

Summary

In this hour, you learned all the important things about recipes. You know what kind of recipes there are in Minecraft, which type is used for each recipe in vanilla, and you also started changing the game by adding some unique recipes to it. After this, you also learned how to edit chests and dungeons without changing any of the vanilla files.

Q&A

Q. Is there a maximum amount of recipes you can add?

A. There is no reachable limit on the amount of recipes. You can add as many as you want.

Q. Is it possible to create recipes that take an item with a stack size of more than 1?

A. Unless you create a custom crafting table, this is impossible.

Q. Are there other files like DungeonHooks **and** ChestGenHooks **in Forge?**

A. There are many files in Forge that change simple, small things. Look around the code a bit if you are looking for something specific. These were just commonly used ones.

Workshop

Finally, you have created something that changes the game. Answer the following questions and do the exercises to make sure you understand it.

Quiz

1. What is the code name of an Ocelot?

2. Does the following smelting recipe give the player a lot of XP?

```
GameRegistry.addSmelting(Items.gold_nugget, new ItemStack(Blocks.
➥obsidian), 3F);
```

3. If you want to create a flint and steel recipe that uses a flint and an iron ingot, which kind of recipe is the best choice?

Answers

1. The name is "Ozelot."

2. Yes, three times as much as smelting diamond ore.

3. The best choice is a shapeless recipe.

Exercises

Create some custom recipes and change up the dungeon spawns:

1. Create a recipe for grass using a dirt block and a vine block.

2. Create a smelting recipe for flint that uses a gravel block.

3. Add Enderman to the possible mob spawns in a dungeon.

4. Add diamond blocks to the possible items in a dungeon.

HOUR 4
Making Your First Item

What You'll Learn in This Hour:

▶ Understanding what an item is
▶ Creating a basic item

This hour contains the basics about items. This hour begins with a short explanation of what items in Minecraft are and uses examples from the game. In this hour, you learn how to write the most basic version of a Minecraft item. Then, you learn how to add a texture to your item. In the other hours of Part II, "Items," you learn more about customizing items.

Understanding What an Item Is

Before creating an item in Minecraft, it's important to know exactly what an item is. It's also useful to know the limitations, requirements, and comparisons of items.

Items are important in Minecraft, but a basic item can't do that much. The player can hold it, it can be dropped on the ground and used in recipes, but, except for that, the most basic kind of item doesn't have much functionality. However, you can *create* incredibly interesting and useful things *with* a basic item. To do that, you first need to know how to make a basic item, which this hour covers. The next three hours cover some special items. Hour 6, "Cooking Up a Food Item," explains how to create food items. Hour 7, "Making Your Own Tools," covers exactly how to make a pickaxe and various other tools, and Hour 8, "Creating Armor," details how to create armor. Although this book focuses on those items, the different kinds of items you can make and what you can do with them are endless.

Now that you know what an item is, you should become familiar with some special cases. For example, mushrooms might seem like items, but they are actually blocks because they can be placed.

A block is a 1 × 1 × 1 meter cube that cannot move. If you want a more detailed explanation of a block, read the start of Hour 9, "Making Your First Block."

NOTE

Blocks and Items

A fun fact about Minecraft is that all blocks are actually items when you have them in your inventory.

An arrow might not seem like an item, but it is. When it's in the inventory, an arrow is an item. However, when the arrow is fired with a bow or a dispenser, it becomes an entity. As mentioned, items can be tools, food, and many other things. Items can also be used to, for example, spawn entities, which is what an entity egg does in Minecraft.

In short, an entity is something that moves around in the Minecraft world. If you want to know more about entities, read the start of Hour 17, "Learning About Entities."

It is important to know what you can and can't do with items. Imagine that you have written a big and complicated item. Then you find out that what you want to do with it is not possible with an item and what you actually require is a block. If you are familiar with what you can and can't do with items, you can plan ahead to create what you require—and avoid frustration later!

Creating a Basic Item

It's time to start creating your own item. To get started, you start in your mod file. Just below the two `String` variables and just above the `init` method, create a new method called `preInit`. The parameter for this method must be `FMLPreInitializationEvent`. Don't forget to add the `@EventHandler` annotation above the method, or your item won't work without showing any errors. Once you have done that, the file should look like Listing 4.1.

LISTING 4.1 Mod File with `preInit` Method

```
package com.wuppy.samsmod;

import net.minecraft.enchantment.Enchantment;
import net.minecraft.init.Blocks;
import net.minecraft.init.Items;
import net.minecraft.item.ItemStack;
import net.minecraft.util.WeightedRandomChestContent;
import net.minecraftforge.common.ChestGenHooks;
import net.minecraftforge.common.DungeonHooks;
import cpw.mods.fml.common.Mod;
import cpw.mods.fml.common.Mod.EventHandler;
import cpw.mods.fml.common.event.FMLInitializationEvent;
import cpw.mods.fml.common.event.FMLPreInitializationEvent;
import cpw.mods.fml.common.registry.GameRegistry;

@Mod(modid = SamsMod.MODID, version = SamsMod.VERSION)
public class SamsMod
```

```
{
    public static final String MODID = "wuppy29_samsmod";
    public static final String VERSION = "1.0";

    @EventHandler
    public void preInit(FMLPreInitializationEvent event)
    {

    }

    @EventHandler
    public void init(FMLInitializationEvent event)
    {
        //Recipes
        GameRegistry.addRecipe(new ItemStack(Items.apple),
                "XXX",
                "XXX",
                "XXX",
                'X', Blocks.leaves
        );
        GameRegistry.addRecipe(new ItemStack(Items.arrow),
                "YZ",
                "X ",
                'X', Items.flint, 'Y', Items.stick, 'Z', Blocks.leaves
        );
        GameRegistry.addShapelessRecipe(new ItemStack(Items.dye, 2, 1),
                Items.redstone, new ItemStack(Items.dye, 1, 1)
        );
        GameRegistry.addSmelting(Blocks.stone, new ItemStack(
➥Blocks.stonebrick), 0.1F);

        ItemStack enchantedSwordItemStack = new ItemStack(
➥Items.stone_sword);
        enchantedSwordItemStack.addEnchantment(Enchantment.sharpness, 1);

        GameRegistry.addShapelessRecipe(enchantedSwordItemStack,
                Items.flint, Items.stone_sword
        );

        //Dungeon changes
        DungeonHooks.removeDungeonMob("Spider");
        DungeonHooks.addDungeonMob("Creeper", 100);
        ChestGenHooks.removeItem(ChestGenHooks.DUNGEON_CHEST, new
➥ItemStack(Items.saddle));
        ChestGenHooks.addItem(ChestGenHooks.DUNGEON_CHEST, new
➥WeightedRandomChestContent(new ItemStack(Blocks.cobblestone), 25, 50, 10));
    }
}
```

There are three initialization phases with Forge: `PreInit`, `Init`, and `PostInit`. `PreInit` is where you register all the basics for your mod. `Init` is where you place mod-specific code that is not directly related to registering. Recipes should also go in `Init`. `PostInit` is where you add code that interacts with other mods.

This forces modders to do all those things at the same time, making it easier for other modders who create mod bridges or other application programming interfaces (APIs) to use a later initialization phase to find out which blocks are added or which mods are installed.

Because of these rules, you need to create the `preInit` method for the registry of items.

To create an item, you first must create a new variable. This is a variable that will likely be used in several files. Therefore, it must be public and static. It must also be placed outside of any methods in the class, just below the two `String` variables used in the `@Mod` line. Because you are going to create an item, the variable should be an item. The name for the variable can be anything you want, but best practice is to give it the name of the item.

In this book, the basic item you create is a key for the dungeon created over the course of this book. The variable line should look like this:

```
public static Item key;
```

If you are getting an error under item, import the `Item` class from the Minecraft package. Be certain to get the one from the Minecraft package, or you will get a lot of errors in the following code.

In the `preInit` method, two lines of code are required to make most items. One line is to let Java know what the `key` object actually is, and the other line is to tell Forge to register it as an item. The following code snippet shows the code for the key. Note that the code contains an error, which you fix shortly.

```
key = new ItemKey();

GameRegistry.registerItem(key, "Key");
```

The top line sets `key` to a class, which you create in a few minutes. It can also be called anything you want, but the general name for it is `Item` followed by the item name. Having an error under the `ItemKey`, or whatever your name for it is, is normal. It's because `ItemKey` is a class that isn't created yet. From now on, this line will be called the *item init line*.

The second line of code registers an item to Forge using the `GameRegistry` file, which makes sure Minecraft knows the item exists and can be used. The method used this time is `registerItem`, which takes two parameters. The first parameter is an `Item` object and the second parameter is a name for it. The name can also be anything you want, but the best way to name it is the name of the item. It's important to make sure that there aren't any duplicate names in the item registry. If there is another item called `Key`, it might not work. However, Forge automatically adds the modid in front of the name you use to register here. This ensures that multiple mods can have an item called `Key` without problems. If *item registry line* is mentioned in this book, it references this line.

The following code shows the `preInit` method and the new variable after adding the item. All the other code in the file is the same, except for a few new imports:

```
public static Item key;

@EventHandler
public void preInit(FMLPreInitializationEvent event)
{
    key = new ItemKey();

    GameRegistry.registerItem(key, "Key");
}
```

Creating an Item File

To fix the error under the class name in the item init line, you create an item file with the name used in the init line. To create a file like that, hover your mouse over the error and click Create Class '...'. This causes the New Java Class window to open. In this window, click Finish. You will now have a file that should look like Listing 4.2.

LISTING 4.2   Empty Item File

```
package com.wuppy.samsmod;

import net.minecraft.item.Item;

public class ItemKey extends Item
{

}
```

To make a fully functional item, you must add a constructor to this file. A constructor is a method without a return type and the method name has to be exactly the same as the class file. A constructor is a special method in Java that is used to create an object for a class. This method will run whenever the `Item` object is created. An empty constructor for `ItemKey` will look as follows:

```
public ItemKey()
{

}
```

There must be two lines of code in this constructor for Minecraft to recognize it as an item and actually use it. The first line makes sure the item has some sort of name:

```
setUnlocalizedName(SamsMod.MODID + "_" + "key");
```

This sets the unlocalized name of the item to something. An item requires an unlocalized name, or it will not show up anywhere. Without a name, it isn't an item. It's important to make sure that the unlocalized name is unique for every item in every mod. To make sure this happens, use the modid of your mod followed by an underscore and then finally the name of the item variable in your mod file. This ensures that there can't possibly be duplicates, because a modid has to be different for every mod installed, and you can't have two variables with the same name.

When you have an item, it doesn't automatically show up in the Creative menu. This is quite useful because not everything should be on one of the Creative tabs. However, in the case of most items, you want it to be visible somewhere. To do that, you will need the following code:

```
setCreativeTab(CreativeTabs.tabMisc);
```

This method requires a single parameter, which is a `CreativeTab`. To get the correct `CreativeTab`, you might want to look through the file in which all of the tabs are listed. `ItemKey` will be added to the Miscellaneous tab.

If you start the game right now, you will see there is an item in the Creative menu with a weird black and purple texture. The name is also strange.

Fixing the Name

To fix the names of an item, you have to add a localization for it. By default, items in Minecraft have the name `item.unlocalizedname.name`. This is not a desirable name and should almost always be changed. You do this by adding localizations. Minecraft has different localizations for every language. If you play Minecraft with a localization different than en_US, which is the default American English, it first tries to look for localizations under that language. If it doesn't find them, it tries to get them from the en_US ones. If it can't find them there either, the default name is used.

Fixing the name of the item is going to be quite a bit of work. First, navigate to the forge folder created in Hour 1, "Setting Up the Minecraft Development Environment." Then enter **src/main/resources**. Figure 4.1 shows the correct folder structure.

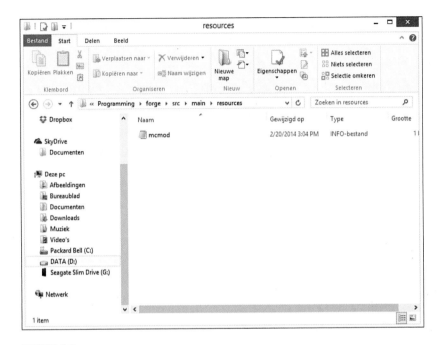

FIGURE 4.1
The folder structure for resources.

In this folder, you need to create a few custom folders. The first folder is called assets. Within the assets folder, you need to make another folder with the name of your modid, which has to be the same as the MODID variable in your mod file. The final folder you need to create is called lang. If you now go into your Eclipse, you should see a white package with the names you just used under the resources folder. In the case of the mod written in this book, the folder structure is assets/wuppy29_samsmod/lang. It should look similar to Figure 4.2.

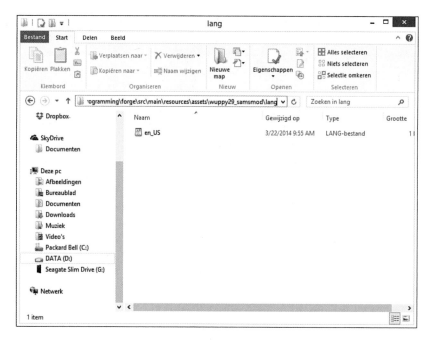

FIGURE 4.2
The folder structure for lang.

CAUTION

The Folder Structure

Be certain that the folder structure follows the exact same structure and has the modid listed correctly. If there is even a minor mistake in one of the folder names, the names and textures will not work.

Once you are certain the folder structure is correct, you need to add a new file. The file should be called en_US.lang.

CAUTION

File Extensions

After creating it, double-check the extension of the file to make sure it's .lang and not something like .lang.txt. If it's .lang.txt, your name localizations will not work.

Open the file using a text editor of your choice. If you look at the name of the item in the game, it's `item.UnlocalizedName.name`. The `.lang` file created is used to add a localized name for the item. To create a localized name for the key, you need the following line in the `.lang` file:

```
item.wuppy29_samsmod_key.name=Key
```

The first part is the name of the item when displayed without localizations. After that, add an equal sign and then add the name on the other side. Ensure there are no spaces between the unlocalized name, the equal sign, and the localized name. If there are, it will either not work or look strange. You can have spaces in the unlocalized and localized names themselves in this file.

NOTE

Translations

If you want your mod to have multiple localizations, you must add an extra `.lang` file. The name of this file is the code of the language, for example `en` or `nl`, followed by the code for the country, for example `US` or `NL`. All the language filenames are available on the Minecraft wiki at http://minecraft.gamepedia.com/Language.

Now when you start the game and take a look at the item you created, the name will be fixed.

Adding a Texture

To fix the strange purple texture on the item, you must do a few things. First, you must actually create the new item texture. It is outside the scope of this book to cover exactly how to create the best textures, but this section does cover the basics. You need the image editor software of your choice, such as GIMP, Photoshop, or Paint. In one of these programs, create a 16×16 pixel image of the item you want. It doesn't really matter what you put in there. However, what does matter is the file format and filename when you save it. The file format has to be `.png`. The filename has to be something you can easily use in code. In this book, it will always be the same name as the variable unless specified differently. The item texture used for the key is called `key.png` and looks like Figure 4.3.

FIGURE 4.3
The key item texture.

Now that you have a texture for the item, you need to place it somewhere where Forge can find it for you. This place is quite similar to the location of the .lang files. In the forge folder, open the following folders: src\main\resources\assets\wuppy29_samsmod, replacing the wuppy29_samsmod part with the modid of your mod. The path should look similar to Figure 4.4.

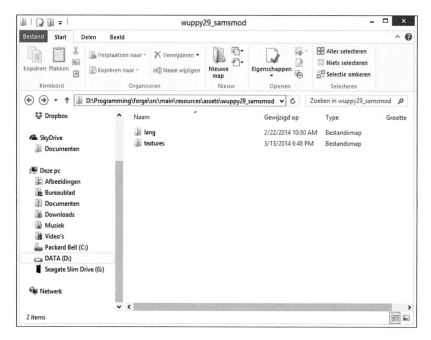

FIGURE 4.4
Modid folder structure.

In this folder should be the lang folder you created earlier. This time, create a folder called textures. In that folder, create a final folder called items. Place the texture file you created earlier in there. In the case of the ItemKey, the texture is Figure 4.3. The folder structure for it should look similar to Figure 4.5.

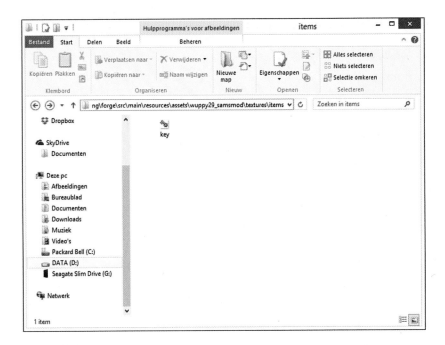

FIGURE 4.5
Item texture folder structure.

Now the texture is ready to be used. Now, you just need to tell Forge to get that texture for the item. To do this, you add a new line of code to the constructor. It should look like the following:

```
setTextureName(SamsMod.MODID + ":" + "key");
```

The texture name has to be first the modid, which should be stored in a variable in your mod file. Then you need a colon and the unlocalized name of the item.

Right now, the constructor looks like this:

```
public ItemKey()
{
        setUnlocalizedName(SamsMod.MODID + "_" + "key");
        setTextureName(SamsMod.MODID + ":" + "key");
        setCreativeTab(CreativeTabs.tabMisc);
}
```

Once you have added this line of code, your item will work. Figure 4.6 shows the key in the game.

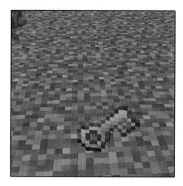

FIGURE 4.6
The `ItemKey` in Minecraft.

This file isn't coded very well because the same `String` is used twice. If you want to change the name of the item, you must change the name in both locations. To make this a little bit easier, create a `private String` that contains key. Then put the `String` variables in these methods.

▼ TRY IT YOURSELF

Rename Your Item

Change the name of your item and change everything accordingly.

1. Change the name `String`.

2. Change the localization and textures.

After completing the Try It Yourself activity and all other tasks in this hour, the whole item file should look like Listing 4.3.

LISTING 4.3   Finished `ItemKey` File

```
package com.wuppy.samsmod;

import net.minecraft.creativetab.CreativeTabs;
import net.minecraft.item.Item;

public class ItemKey extends Item
{
        private String name = "key";

        public ItemKey()
        {
```

```
            setUnlocalizedName(SamsMod.MODID + "_" + name);
            setTextureName(SamsMod.MODID + ":" + name);
            setCreativeTab(CreativeTabs.tabMisc);
        }
}
```

Now when you launch the game, you should see the item with the correct name and the correct texture.

Summary

In this hour, you learned how to create an item. At this point, you should understand what items in Minecraft are and what you can do with them. You should also be able to add a basic item and give it a texture.

Q&A

Q. Is there a maximum number of items you can add to Minecraft?

A. Yes, but it's close to impossible to reach it. However, you should always try to use as few different items as possible. Hour 5, "Creating Multiple Items in a Smart Way," covers how to do that.

Q. How do I add a second item to my mod file?

A. Simply rewrite the code for the first item, but make sure the variables and unlocalized names are all different.

Q. Can you have multiple items using the same file?

A. Yes you can. Just make sure the unlocalized name is different for every item.

Q. Can you add the same item to multiple creative tabs?

A. No, this is not possible.

Workshop

You now know the basics of items. In the next few hours, you will learn more about them. Therefore, it's important to fully understand the basics. To do that, you might want to work through this workshop.

Quiz

1. What would the best unlocalized name be for an item variable called `alarmClock`?

2. What is wrong with the following code?

```
public static Item key;

@EventHandler
public void preInit(FMLPreInitializationEvent event)
{
    GameRegistry.registerItem(key, "Key");
    key = new ItemKey();
}
```

Answers

1. The best unlocalized name is `alarmClock`, because it's generally smartest to use the variable name.

2. The item is registered before initializing it to something. This will crash your mod. Always make sure the `registerItem` method is below the Item init line.

Exercises

Improve the item even more by passing the unlocalized name of the item through the constructor. Some things you will have to do for that:

1. Add a `String` variable to the constructor.

2. Add the unlocalized name in the mod file where you use the constructor, which should be the item init line.

3. Remove the `String` variable in the `ItemKey` class because you don't need it anymore.

The code in the mod file:

```
key = new ItemKey("key");
```

The constructor of `ItemKey`:

```
public ItemKey(String name)
{
        setUnlocalizedName(SamsMod.MODID + "_" + name);
        setTextureName(SamsMod.MODID + ":" + name);
        setCreativeTab(CreativeTabs.tabMisc);
}
```

HOUR 5
Creating Multiple Items in a Smart Way

What You'll Learn in This Hour:

▶ Adding multiple items using the same file

▶ Adding metadata to items

In this hour, you continue with what you learned in Hour 4, "Making Your First Item." You start by learning exactly how to add multiple items using the same file, as in the exercise for Hour 4. After that, you learn how to make items in an even smarter way with metadata. You also learn exactly what metadata is. Using metadata does, however, create a small problem with the textures, which you will then have to code a little differently.

Adding Multiple Items Using the Same File

To add multiple items to the same file, you need to make a small change to the item file you created in Hour 4. Listing 5.1 shows the file from the end of Hour 4.

LISTING 5.1 `ItemKey` File from Hour 4

```
package com.wuppy.samsmod;

import net.minecraft.creativetab.CreativeTabs;
import net.minecraft.item.Item;

public class ItemKey extends Item
{
        private String name = "key";

        public ItemKey()
        {
                setUnlocalizedName(SamsMod.MODID + "_" + name);
                setTextureName(SamsMod.MODID + ":" + name);
                setCreativeTab(CreativeTabs.tabMisc);
        }
}
```

Turning this file into a file that can register multiple items is really easy. You can't have multiple items with the same unlocalized name; the name variable has to be different for every instance of the ItemKey file. The following steps enable this:

1. Remove the String name variable.

2. Add a String to the constructor parameters called itemName.

3. Use itemName in the places where you used name.

After doing that, the item file should look like Listing 5.2.

LISTING 5.2 ItemKey File for Multiple Items

```
package com.wuppy.samsmod;

import net.minecraft.creativetab.CreativeTabs;
import net.minecraft.item.Item;

public class ItemKey extends Item
{
        public ItemKey(String itemName)
        {
                setUnlocalizedName(SamsMod.MODID + "_" + itemName);
                setTextureName(SamsMod.MODID + ":" + itemName);
                setCreativeTab(CreativeTabs.tabMisc);
        }
}
```

When you have the file like this, an error appears in the mod file under the ItemKey() part. The error is because you do not have a String in the constructor call. To fix this, add a String in the brackets. For the item up to this point, the itemName will be greyKey. This also means the texture and localization names have to change from key to greyKey. For clarity, the item key variable will also be renamed to greyKey. The preInit and variable line should, after changing this, look as follows:

```
public static Item greyKey;

@EventHandler
public void preInit(FMLPreInitializationEvent event)
{
    greyKey = new ItemKey("greyKey");

    GameRegistry.registerItem(greyKey, "GreyKey");
}
```

To add a second key to this, simply copy all of the item code and change the names everywhere. The following code contains a second item called redKey. Localization and textures have been added following the same name.

```
public static Item greyKey;
public static Item redKey;

@EventHandler
public void preInit(FMLPreInitializationEvent event)
{
    greyKey = new ItemKey("greyKey");
    redKey = new ItemKey("redKey");

    GameRegistry.registerItem(greyKey, "GreyKey");
    GameRegistry.registerItem(redKey, "RedKey");
}
```

The en_US.lang file looks like this:

```
item.wuppy29_samsmod_greyKey.name=Grey Key
item.wuppy29_samsmod_redKey.name=Red Key
```

And, finally, redKey.png has been added to the items folder in the same location as the already existing texture. It looks like Figure 5.1.

FIGURE 5.1
The red key.

The folder path should be added in and should look like Figure 5.2.

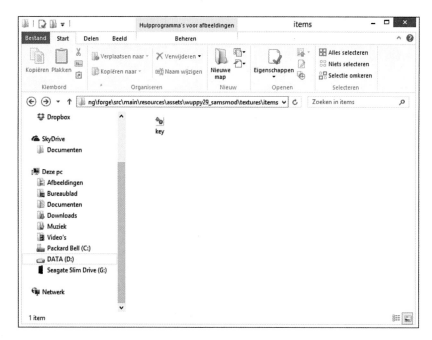

FIGURE 5.2
The item texture folder path.

▼ TRY IT YOURSELF

Create Some Useful Items

You will use several items throughout this book that will, for example, be dropped from a block or entity. Create an item called samdust and another called samingot. Create both of them using a single item file called ItemSamGeneric using what you learned with ItemKey.

The items will look like the following in the mod file:

```
public static Item samdust;
public static Item samingot;
```

And the following code needs to be added to the preInit method:

```
samdust = new ItemSamGeneric("samdust");
samingot = new ItemSamGeneric("samingot");
GameRegistry.registerItem(samdust, "SamDust");
GameRegistry.registerItem(samingot, "SamIngot");
```

Finally, ItemSamGeneric will look like Listing 5.3.

LISTING 5.3 `ItemSamGeneric`

```
package com.wuppy.samsmod.items;

import com.wuppy.samsmod.SamsMod;

import net.minecraft.creativetab.CreativeTabs;
import net.minecraft.item.Item;

public class ItemSamGeneric extends Item
{
        public ItemSamGeneric(String name)
        {
                setUnlocalizedName(SamsMod.MODID + "_" + name);
                setTextureName(SamsMod.MODID + ":" + name);
                setCreativeTab(CreativeTabs.tabMisc);
        }
}
```

The textures for these items are shown in Figures 5.3 and 5.4. Figures 5.5 and 5.6 show the items in the game.

FIGURE 5.3
Sam's dust texture.

FIGURE 5.4
Sam's ingot texture.

FIGURE 5.5
Sam's dust in the game.

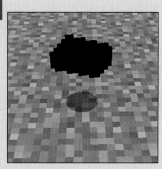

FIGURE 5.6
Sam's ingot in the game.

Right now, there are two items in the SamsMod mod—not counting the ones you just created in the Try It Yourself activity. The two items are almost exactly the same. It's a waste of item IDs to use two different items. The limit of items in a single game is very high and you won't reach it with a single mod, but there are many people playing with over 100 mods at the same time. In that case, the total amount of items may come close to the limit, which is around 30,000. Therefore, it's always smart to use as few different items as possible. The easiest way to do this is by using metadata.

Adding Metadata to Items

Metadata is used in both items and blocks. It can be used to have multiple items without actually using multiple item IDs. An example of item metadata is dyes. They are all basically the same item. Instead of using up 16 different IDs, all of them are saved in a single one using metadata.

Now that you know what metadata is, you should add it to the two key items. To get metadata in the item, you must change a few things. First, you have to make a few changes to the constructor. Second, you must create a way to make every item have a different name, which is a bit more work than it is now. Third, you must add multiple images. Finally, you are required to tell Minecraft how many metadatas there are and how many should be added to the Creative menu.

Changing the Constructor

In the constructor, remove the `setTextureName` line. The parameter from the constructor should also be removed. After doing these things, the constructor should look similar to the following:

```
public ItemKey()
{
        setUnlocalizedName(SamsMod.MODID + "_" + "key");
        setCreativeTab(CreativeTabs.tabMisc);
}
```

Removing the Name

Don't forget to change any references to a changed constructor. In this case, change the item init lines.

There is one method you need to add to the constructor, which is called setHasSubTypes. This method takes one parameter, which is a boolean. A boolean can be either true or false. In this method, it has to be true.

You have to change the code within the setUnlocalizedName method back to what it used to be, which is using MODID + "_" and ending it with the name of the item. This means ItemKey can only be used for one specific item with metadata. Making ItemKey work with multiple items with metadata would be a lot of work, and it would be much easier to write multiple files in that case. The unlocalized name for the ItemKey with metadata will be key.

After doing these things, the constructor should look like the following code. This code will give you an error in the SamsMod, which you fix shortly.

```
public ItemKey()
{
        setUnlocalizedName(SamsMod.MODID + "_" + "key");
        setHasSubtypes(true);
        setCreativeTab(CreativeTabs.tabMisc);
}
```

setHasSubTypes makes sure the item can have metadata. You also must ensure every metadata has a different name.

Fixing the Name

Now you have to add a new variable to the ItemKey file. When using metadata, you need a variable that can hold the names of every subitem. To do this, a String array can be used. First, create a basic String variable like you did for the String name. Now you have to change this variable into a String array. To do that, add [] behind String. Now, after the comma, add an equal sign and then two curly braces. In those braces, add the metadata names. Because they are Strings, surround the metadata names with quotation marks, and separate the different values with commas. For a grey and a red key, the name variable looks like the following code snippet:

```
private String[] name = {"grey", "red"};
```

Next, add a replacement for the setUnlocalizedName method you removed from the constructor. The method you have to replace it with is called getUnlocalizedName. The difference between the setUnlocalizedName used with normal items is that the setUnlocalizedName was used and the getUnlocalizedName here is overwritten into something else. The code for a getUnlocalizedName for an item with metadata should look like this:

```
public String getUnlocalizedName(ItemStack par1ItemStack)
{
    int metadata = MathHelper.clamp_int(par1ItemStack.getItemDamage(), 0, 15);
    return super.getUnlocalizedName() + "." + name[metadata];
}
```

getUnlocalizedName is a method that returns a String. The method is quite frequently used in Minecraft. The method takes one parameter, which is an ItemStack. Because you are writing a method, you don't have to worry about where it will come from. Minecraft will call getUnlocalizedName somewhere with an ItemStack in there. Normally, it would use the method in Item, but if it is an ItemKey, it will use the one in ItemKey.

In this method are two lines. The first basically gets the metadata of the ItemStack in the parameter and stores it in a variable. The second line is a bit more complicated. It starts with super.getUnlocalizedName. This makes the getUnlocalizedName in Item run. Like a normal item, this returns the standard unlocalized name of the item. However, this is the same for every metadata item, which would create problems, because Minecraft wouldn't be able to keep them apart. To fix this, it's followed by a dot and finally by the name set in the name variable.

As mentioned before, this method is overwritten from a different method in the Item class. If Minecraft ever updates and the name of the method in the Item class changes, this method will stop working. However, it will not tell you that it isn't working. To make sure you will notice the change, an @Override annotation should be added above the method. This makes sure that, if the method has changed, it gives an error. That may sound bad, but it makes tracking changes in the Minecraft code and then changing them accordingly in your code much easier. Therefore, an @Override annotation should be added to any method that is overwritten from a different method that is not in your code.

When you add this method, you might have quite a few errors under it. This can be fixed by importing all of the classes.

Fixing the Textures

To fix the textures, you need one new variable and two new methods. The variable is easy. It should be a private `IIcon[]`. The name doesn't really matter, but icons will be the name used in this book. One problem with `IIcon` is that the file only exists on the Minecraft client. If you try to create this variable on the server, it will crash telling you the file can't be found. To fix this, you have to add an annotation above it that specifies it can only be used on the client. The variable along with the annotation looks like the following:

```
@SideOnly(Side.CLIENT)
private IIcon[] icons;
```

If this code contains errors, import all of the files used here, which should fix that.

Registering the Images

Now you have an empty `IIcon` array. It has to be filled by a method that can be used to register all the icons. Minecraft has a method for that called `registerIcons`. This method is the same for any metadata item in the same mod. For `ItemKey`, it looks like this:

```
@SideOnly(Side.CLIENT)
@Override
public void registerIcons(IIconRegister par1IconRegister)
{
        icons = new IIcon[name.length];

        for(int i = 0; i < icons.length; i++)
        {
                icons[i] = par1IconRegister.registerIcon(SamsMod.MODID +
➡":" + "key" + " " + name[i]);
        }
}
```

It might seem like a complicated method, but it is actually quite easy. The first thing you should notice is that this method has two annotations above it: the `@SideOnly` and the `@Override`. You can always have multiple annotations on a single method, variable, or class. In this case, it makes sure that this method is only run on the client and that it gives an error when the method no longer exists in a later version of Minecraft.

The first thing this method does is create the `IIcon` array equal to the size of the `name` array. This means there are as many icons as there are item names. Because every item requires a different name, there are also as many icons as there are items. After creating the array of `IIcons` with the right size, it loops through all of them, using a simple `for` loop, which starts at zero and ends at the length of the array.

In the `for` loop, it assigns an icon for every index of the `icons` array. First, it gets the index of the loop by using `icons[i]`. It then gets the icon by using the `IIconRegistry` parameter and accessing the `registerIcon` method in there. This method takes a `String` and returns an `Icon`. The `String` has to be quite specific. The first part of the `String` has to be the mod ID. It then needs a colon. After the colon, you need the name of the texture file. This can be anything you want, but in this case it is the name of the item, `key`, followed by a space and the name of the metadata-specific item.

In this code, a different `String` is made for the colon, the name of the item, and the space. This is done to make it more readable, but you could do them all in a single pair of quotation marks.

The texture for the grey key will now be called: `key grey.png`.

The texture for the red key will be called: `key red.png`.

Using the Images

Now the file has multiple icons registered, but the item doesn't know how to use the array without telling it to. To tell it to use the icon array and also give a different texture for each metadata, you need the following method:

```
@Override
public IIcon getIconFromDamage(int par1)
{
    return icons[par1];
}
```

This is a very easy method, and it does exactly what the name suggests. It gets the icon based on the damage value. The `par1` parameter in this method is the metadata, and it returns the index in the `icons` array based on that number.

This method will crash if you try to use an item that doesn't have a name and, therefore, texture assigned to it, so make sure that never happens.

Finally, you must add one more method to make sure every metadata of the item will be displayed in the Creative menu. The method looks like this:

```
@SuppressWarnings({ "unchecked", "rawtypes" })
@SideOnly(Side.CLIENT)
@Override
public void getSubItems(Item par1, CreativeTabs par2CreativeTabs, List par3List)
{
    for (int x = 0; x < name.length; x++)
    {
        par3List.add(new ItemStack(this, 1, x));
    }
}
```

This method has one new annotation that you haven't seen yet called @SuppressWarnings. Minecraft has been coded in a way where Java has quite a few warnings. Most of these warnings are not at all a problem, but for many people having yellow lines everywhere can be quite annoying. The @SuppressWarnings annotation makes sure there won't be several of those lines in the getSubItems method.

This method contains a for loop. The second number makes sure it doesn't loop more than the maximum metadata of the item. In the for loop, it adds an ItemKey ItemStack with a size of one and a metadata from within the for loop to par3List. This makes sure it's in the Creative menu.

The Code After Adding Metadata

The whole ItemKey file should look like Listing 5.4.

LISTING 5.4 `ItemKey` with Metadata

```java
package com.wuppy.samsmod;

import java.util.List;

import net.minecraft.client.renderer.texture.IIconRegister;
import net.minecraft.creativetab.CreativeTabs;
import net.minecraft.item.Item;
import net.minecraft.item.ItemStack;
import net.minecraft.util.IIcon;
import net.minecraft.util.MathHelper;
import cpw.mods.fml.relauncher.Side;
import cpw.mods.fml.relauncher.SideOnly;

public class ItemKey extends Item
{
    private String[] name = {"grey", "red"};

    @SideOnly(Side.CLIENT)
    private IIcon[] icons;

    public ItemKey()
    {
        setUnlocalizedName(SamsMod.MODID + "_" + "key");
        setHasSubtypes(true);
        setCreativeTab(CreativeTabs.tabMisc);
    }

    @Override
    public String getUnlocalizedName(ItemStack par1ItemStack)
    {
```

```
        int metadata = MathHelper.clamp_int(par1ItemStack.getItemDamage(),
➥0, 15);
        return super.getUnlocalizedName() + "." + name[metadata];
    }


    @SideOnly(Side.CLIENT)
    @Override
    public void registerIcons(IIconRegister par1IconRegister)
    {
            icons = new IIcon[name.length];

            for(int i = 0; i < icons.length; i++)
            {
                    icons[i] = par1IconRegister.registerIcon(SamsMod.MODID +
➥":" + "key" + " " + name[i]);
            }
    }


    @Override
    public IIcon getIconFromDamage(int par1)
    {
        return icons[par1];
    }


    @SuppressWarnings({ "unchecked", "rawtypes" })
    @SideOnly(Side.CLIENT)
    @Override
    public void getSubItems(Item par1, CreativeTabs par2CreativeTabs,
➥List par3List)
    {
        for (int x = 0; x < name.length; x++)
        {
            par3List.add(new ItemStack(this, 1, x));
        }
    }
}
```

You also need to make a few small changes to the mod file. When you added multiple items to the mod file, you used the ItemKey twice, which is no longer possible because both items were combined using metadata. Any code related to the redKey will be removed and greyKey will be changed into key. The registerItem name for GreyKey will also change into Key. The mod file should look like Listing 5.5.

LISTING 5.5   Mod File with Metadata Keys

```java
package com.wuppy.samsmod;

import net.minecraft.enchantment.Enchantment;
import net.minecraft.init.Blocks;
import net.minecraft.init.Items;
import net.minecraft.item.Item;
import net.minecraft.item.ItemStack;
import net.minecraft.util.WeightedRandomChestContent;
import net.minecraftforge.common.ChestGenHooks;
import net.minecraftforge.common.DungeonHooks;
import cpw.mods.fml.common.Mod;
import cpw.mods.fml.common.Mod.EventHandler;
import cpw.mods.fml.common.event.FMLInitializationEvent;
import cpw.mods.fml.common.event.FMLPreInitializationEvent;
import cpw.mods.fml.common.registry.GameRegistry;

@Mod(modid = SamsMod.MODID, version = SamsMod.VERSION)
public class SamsMod
{
    public static final String MODID = "wuppy29_samsmod";
    public static final String VERSION = "1.0";

    public static Item key;

    @EventHandler
    public void preInit(FMLPreInitializationEvent event)
    {
        key = new ItemKey();

        GameRegistry.registerItem(key, "Key");
    }

    @EventHandler
    public void init(FMLInitializationEvent event)
    {
        //Recipes
        GameRegistry.addRecipe(new ItemStack(Items.apple),
                "XXX",
                "XXX",
                "XXX",
                'X', Blocks.leaves
        );
        GameRegistry.addRecipe(new ItemStack(Items.arrow),
                "YZ",
                "X ",
                'X', Items.flint, 'Y', Items.stick, 'Z', Blocks.leaves
```

```
        );
        GameRegistry.addShapelessRecipe(new ItemStack(Items.dye, 2, 1),
                Items.redstone, new ItemStack(Items.dye, 1, 1)
        );
        GameRegistry.addSmelting(Blocks.stone, new ItemStack(Blocks.stonebrick),
➡0.1F);

        ItemStack enchantedSwordItemStack = new ItemStack(Items.stone_sword);
        enchantedSwordItemStack.addEnchantment(Enchantment.sharpness, 1);

        GameRegistry.addShapelessRecipe(enchantedSwordItemStack,
                    Items.flint, Items.stone_sword
        );

        //Dungeon changes
        DungeonHooks.removeDungeonMob("Spider");
        DungeonHooks.addDungeonMob("Creeper", 100);
        ChestGenHooks.removeItem(ChestGenHooks.DUNGEON_CHEST, new
➡ItemStack(Items.saddle));
        ChestGenHooks.addItem(ChestGenHooks.DUNGEON_CHEST, new
➡WeightedRandomChestContent(new ItemStack(Blocks.cobblestone), 25, 50, 10));
    }
}
```

If you launched the game now, you would notice that both of the items are displayed in the
Creative menu and that they look the way they should. However, the names don't work just yet.
To fix this, you must change the .lang file to use the new names. The .lang file looks like this
for the ItemKeys:

```
item.wuppy29_samsmod_key.grey.name=Grey Key
item.wuppy29_samsmod_key.red.name=Red Key
```

Now when you launch the game, the items have the right texture and name. They also only use
a single ID, which improves the chance of your mod working with other mods, which is always
something you should try to increase.

Figure 5.7 shows the red key working in the game.

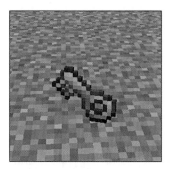

FIGURE 5.7
Red key in the game.

Summary

In this hour, you learned how to add items in a smart way. Even though the code for using multiple items in the same file isn't used anymore in this mod, it is code you will likely use when you are coding. You also learned what metadata is and how to use it. It's very important to keep working with metadata for as many different items as you can to keep the mod working well with others.

Q&A

Q. **What is the maximum number of items that can be added to Minecraft?**

A. The total amount of items can't go over 32,000 and about 200 are taken up by Minecraft.

Q. **What is the maximum number for the metadata of an item?**

A. The maximum metadata of an item is around 32,000 as well. However, you will have to change the metadata variable in the `getUnlocalizedName` method to not be maxed at 15.

Q. **Is there metadata for things like blocks?**

A. Yes there is. This is covered in Hour 10, "Creating Multiple Blocks in a Smart Way."

Workshop

Now you know how to add multiple items to Minecraft in a smart way. Most mods contain a lot of items, so it's important to master these techniques.

Quiz

1. What will happen if you don't use different names for each metadata of an item?

2. What is wrong with your item if you have a black and purple texture?

3. How would you figure out if the texture name is wrong?

Answers

1. To Minecraft, they will all be the same and because of that, some very weird things can happen.

2. The textures for the item either don't have the right name or they are not in the right folder. Make sure you check that the folder structure follows the right rules. Alternatively, make sure the texture names are the same as the unlocalized names for the items

3. Print out the part after the colon in the `registerIcons` method using a `System.out.println`.

Exercises

Add a third metadata to the item created in this hour. *Hint:* You only have to edit the item file for it. Also don't forget to edit the `.lang` file and add a new texture.

Cooking Up a Food Item

What You'll Learn in This Hour:

▶ Understanding food in Minecraft

▶ Creating a food item

▶ Adding a potion effect

In this hour, you learn how to make your first special item: You create a food item—a berry. You use this item in Hour 11, "Making Your Blocks Unique," when you create a bush for it. Then, in Hour 14, "Generating Plants," you learn how to make the bush show up in the world so it can finally be used. However, before you make a food item, you should know a few things about food in Minecraft.

Understanding Food in Minecraft

When you play Minecraft, you see one food bar in the graphical user interface (GUI). However, there are actually two of them in the game. The visible food bar is called the foodLevel in code. The other invisible bar is called foodSaturationLevel. The way these levels work is that, as long as the saturation is above zero, the foodLevel stays the same and the foodSaturationLevel goes down instead. When the foodLevel goes below a certain level, it either stops going down or it starves you, depending on the difficulty level you are playing on. When the foodSaturationLevel becomes zero, nothing happens other than the foodLevel starts going down.

When you eat a food item, both the saturation and food level go up. Some food items make the saturation go up much higher but make the food level go up only a little bit. Other food items make the saturation go up a little and make the food level go up a lot. When the foodLevel is 1 and the saturation goes up, the foodLevel stays the same; even if you should be hurt by starvation because of the foodLevel, you shouldn't be hurt. Making sure your item is well balanced with both the food and saturation level is important when making a proper food item.

You should know one other important detail about food: You can tame wolves in Minecraft using a bone. When you have a wolf as your pet, you can heal it using certain types of food.

When creating a food item, you can set whether you can use this food item to heal wolves. Thus, when creating food items, it is important to determine if a wolf should be able to eat it.

Creating a Food Item

Now that you know how food works in Minecraft, it is time to create your own food item. To do this, you add a new item to the mod file.

The Mod File Code

First, add the basic item code to the file, which is as follows in the mod file:

```
public static Item berry;
```

Then, add the following to the `preInit` method:

```
berry = new ItemBerry();
GameRegistry.registerItem(berry, "Berry");
```

With this code, you have an error under `ItemBerry`. That is because you haven't yet created that class.

Creating the `ItemBerry` Class

To create the `ItemBerry` class, hover your mouse over the error and click Create Class. You will get a file that looks like Listing 6.1.

LISTING 6.1 Empty `ItemBerry` File

```
package com.wuppy.samsmod;

import net.minecraft.item.Item;

public class ItemBerry extends Item {

}
```

In this file, change the extended type from `Item` into `ItemFood`, which results in an error under `ItemFood`. Fix it by importing the file. After that, another error appears under `ItemBerry`. To fix that, hover your mouse over the error. Click Create Constructor `ItemBerry(int, float, boolean)` in the menu that appears. Make sure you get the constructor with the `float` value.

The values you get in the constructor are likely very unclear. In Listing 6.2, the variables in the listing don't have the same names as they have when you add the constructor. They have been changed into the variables they represent instead of unclear names. You don't have to do this in your own file, but it's smart nonetheless.

LISTING 6.2 Clear Constructor

```
package com.wuppy.samsmod;

import net.minecraft.item.ItemFood;

public class ItemBerry extends ItemFood
{
    public ItemBerry(int food, float saturation, boolean wolfFood)
    {
        super(food, saturation, wolfFood);
    }
}
```

When you add this constructor to the file, you get a different error in the item init line under new `ItemBerry()` because you are not passing the required parameters.

The first parameter is the called food. This is the number by which the `foodLevel` increases in Minecraft. Even though the food bar in the game has 10 food bits, the maximum `foodLevel` can be 20. An item like a porkchop has a heal of 8. If you make it higher, the food is considered better. The berries are going to be easy to obtain. Because of that, the food level is 3, which is 1.5 food bits in the game.

The second parameter is saturation. This bar starts out at 5F, which could be considered the maximum value, although it is able to go higher. If you make this value higher, it takes longer for the player's `foodLevel` to start going down. The highest saturation level of a food item in the game is 1.2F, which is for a golden carrot. For the berries, the saturation level is 0.3F, which is the same as a melon.

The final parameter is if wolves should be eating it. Because wolves normally eat berries, they will in the game as well. To make your food edible for wolves, return `true`. Otherwise, you return `false`.

The item init line now looks like this:

```
berry = new ItemBerry(3, 0.3F, true);
```

Now you must do a few things that are required for every item. You must add an extra `String` variable to the end of the constructor called name. Don't add this to the super constructor though. After adding the name variable, use it in `setUnlocalizedName` and `setTextureName`.

CAUTION

Super

Never add code before the `super` line in your constructor or you will get errors.

You must also add the name to the item init line in the mod file. For the berry item, the name will be berry. Don't forget to add localization and a texture for the item, just like you did for the basic item. Figure 6.1 shows the berry texture.

FIGURE 6.1
The berry texture.

And the localization for the berry looks like this:

```
item.wuppy29_samsmod_berry.name=Berry
```

When you launch the game now, you should be able to eat the item and it should have the correct texture as well as the correct name.

▼ TRY IT YOURSELF

Display Line Numbers

You might have already noticed that large files can sometimes look quite complicated. However, if you do make a mistake, an error log generally returns a code line where the problem is.

Your Eclipse screen should look similar to Figure 6.2.

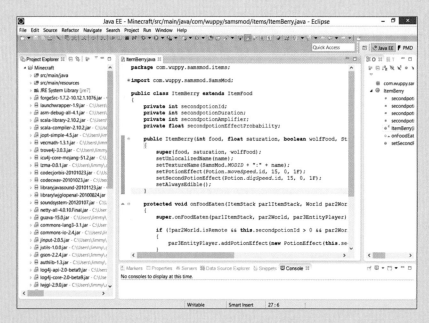

FIGURE 6.2
The Eclipse screen.

It would be useful for reading code, writing code, and fixing crashes to have line numbers show up on this screen. Complete the following steps for that.

1. Click the Window menu at the top of the Eclipse screen.

2. Select the Preferences option, as shown in Figure 6.3. In this window you need to find the option for line numbers.

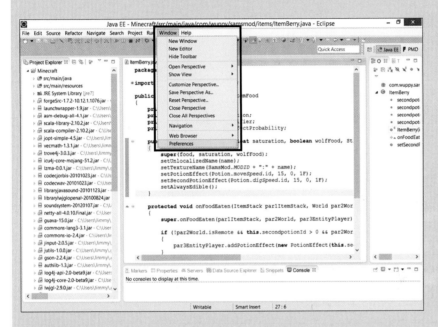

FIGURE 6.3
The Preferences command on the Window menu.

The Preferences window opens, as shown in Figure 6.4.

FIGURE 6.4
The Preferences window.

3. Expand the General option, the Editors option, and then click Text Editors. Don't expand Text Editors, just click the word. The Text Editors options appear in the right pane, as shown in Figure 6.5.

FIGURE 6.5
The Text Editors options.

4. Click the Show Line Numbers check box, highlighted in Figure 6.5.

5. Finally, click Apply and then click OK to save these settings and display the line numbers.

The same class as shown in Figure 6.2 should now look like Figure 6.6. You should see that the line numbers are now displayed to the left of the code.

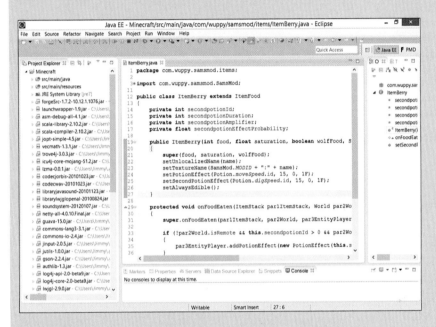

FIGURE 6.6
The Eclipse screen with line numbers.

Adding a Potion Effect

Items such as the spider eye and rotten flesh give the player a potion effect when the item is eaten. You can do this using the `setPotionEffect` method. For example, the `setPotionEffect` method could look like the following:

```
setPotionEffect(Potion.moveSpeed.id, 15, 0, 1F);
```

This method has four parameters.

The first parameter is a number. This number is used to select which kind of potion effect will be used. The best way to do this is not to directly put in a number, but, instead, to select a potion in the `Potion` class and add `.id` on the end. This turns the potion into the ID of the potion and, thus, makes it usable in this method.

The second parameter is the length of the potion in seconds. In this case, the potion affects the player for 15 seconds.

The third parameter is the level of the potion. These levels start at 0 and the highest level depends on the potion type. Although potions you create in the game typically don't go above level 1, which is II in the game, several potions can get a higher level and are, thus, also more effective.

The last parameter is the chance that the effect will take place. This number can range from 0F to 1F, where a higher value is a higher chance. 1F gives the effect to the player 100 percent of the time.

▼ TRY IT YOURSELF

Play with Potions

Play around with potions for a bit by using different potion types, durations, and levels. There are a few hidden potions, which you can't normally use in Minecraft. One example of this is a potion for jump height.

If you try to use multiple potion effects on the same item, you will run into some problems. The standard maximum amount of potions an item can have is one. It is possible to add a second potion effect to this item by following the instructions in the Exercise at the end of this hour.

If you have a food item that is mainly available for the potion effect, you might want to make it edible when the food bar is full. You can do this using a simple method in the constructor, which is called `setAlwaysEdible`.

After adding all of this code, the `ItemBerry` file should look similar to Listing 6.3.

LISTING 6.3 Finished `ItemBerry` File

```
package com.wuppy.samsmod;

import net.minecraft.item.ItemFood;
import net.minecraft.potion.Potion;

public class ItemBerry extends ItemFood
{
    public ItemBerry(int food, float saturation, boolean wolfFood, String name)
    {
        super(food, saturation, wolfFood);
        setUnlocalizedName(SamsMod.MODID + "_" + name);
        setTextureName(SamsMod.MODID + ":" + name);
        setPotionEffect(Potion.moveSpeed.id, 15, 0, 1F);
```

```
        setAlwaysEdible();
    }
}
```

Figure 6.7 shows the `ItemBerry` in the game.

FIGURE 6.7
`ItemBerry` in the game.

NOTE

No Limit

Due to space constraints, this book only teaches you how to create a limited amount of item types. However, the possible amount of things an item can do is endless. Therefore, it's important for you to explore further than just reading this book. If you want to make unique items, learn some Java and play around with the code in Minecraft. By exploring and experimenting, you will learn to make a really interesting mod.

Summary

In this hour, you learned about food and food items in Minecraft. First, you learned how food in Minecraft works, which includes saturation and hunger. These numbers handle the food for the player. After this, you created your own food item, which uses these values. Finally, you learned some basic food customization by adding a potion effect to the food.

Q&A

Q. How does the food item created in this hour end up in the Creative menu? There isn't a `setCreativeTab` method in there.

A. The `setCreativeTab` is in the `ItemFood` file. Because that file is extended, it is also in the custom item file, although you don't see it.

Q. Is there a limit to the amount of food items you can add?

A. Yes, but it's the same as with normal items, and it's, therefore, almost unreachable.

Q. Can you add multiple potion effects to an item?

A. Yes, you can. In the Exercise at the end of this hour, you learn how to add a method for a second potion effect, but you can always add more.

Workshop

Now that you understand how to make food items, complete the following quiz to ensure you have mastered the information.

Quiz

1. What would happen if you change the extended type from `ItemBerry` **back to** `Item`?

2. What decreases first?

   A. Saturation

   B. Hunger

Answers

1. `ItemBerry` would no longer work as a food item. It would also create errors under the `ItemFood`-specific methods used.

2. The answer is A. Hunger will only decrease once saturation is zero.

Exercises

Add a second potion effect to the food item created in this hour. To do that, you copy and change the name of the `setPotionEffect` method, change the names of the variables and add them to the file, and overwrite the `onFoodEaten` method to also use the secondary potion effect. Finally, don't forget to use the new potion effect method in the constructor.

The new `ItemBerry` file should look similar to Listing 6.4.

LISTING 6.4   `ItemBerry` with a Second Potion Effect

```
package com.wuppy.samsmod;

import net.minecraft.entity.player.EntityPlayer;
import net.minecraft.item.ItemFood;
import net.minecraft.item.ItemStack;
import net.minecraft.potion.Potion;
```

```
import net.minecraft.potion.PotionEffect;
import net.minecraft.world.World;

public class ItemBerry extends ItemFood
{
    private int secondpotionId;
    private int secondpotionDuration;
    private int secondpotionAmplifier;
    private float secondpotionEffectProbability;

    public ItemBerry(int food, float saturation, boolean wolfFood, String name)
    {
        super(food, saturation, wolfFood);
        setUnlocalizedName(SamsMod.MODID + "_" + name);
        setTextureName(SamsMod.MODID + ":" + name);
        setPotionEffect(Potion.moveSpeed.id, 15, 0, 1F);
        setSecondPotionEffect(Potion.digSpeed.id, 15, 0, 1F);
        setAlwaysEdible();
    }

    protected void onFoodEaten(ItemStack par1ItemStack, World par2World,
➥EntityPlayer par3EntityPlayer)
    {
        super.onFoodEaten(par1ItemStack, par2World, par3EntityPlayer);

        if (!par2World.isRemote && this.secondpotionId > 0 &&
➥par2World.rand.nextFloat() < this.secondpotionEffectProbability)
        {
            par3EntityPlayer.addPotionEffect(new PotionEffect(
➥this.secondpotionId, this.secondpotionDuration * 20,
➥this.secondpotionAmplifier));
        }
    }

    public ItemFood setSecondPotionEffect(int par1, int par2, int par3,
➥float par4)
    {
        this.secondpotionId = par1;
        this.secondpotionDuration = par2;
        this.secondpotionAmplifier = par3;
        this.secondpotionEffectProbability = par4;
        return this;
    }
}
```

Making Your Own Tools

What You'll Learn in This Hour:

▶ Creating a `ToolMaterial`

▶ Creating a pickaxe

▶ Creating special tools for harvesting different blocks

This hour covers another special item type called tools. Tools are commonly used in Minecraft because they are almost the only things that you can use to remove blocks outside of Creative mode. In addition, swords are considered tools in Minecraft and are also used in fighting. Without tools, you can't do that much in Minecraft. Therefore, it's useful to know how to make them. You can find more information about tools at http://minecraft.gamepedia.com/Tools.

Creating a `ToolMaterial`

Before you can create a custom tool, you must create a custom `ToolMaterial`. A `ToolMaterial` is, as the name suggests, the material the tool is made up of. This material is very important for the tool. It tells Minecraft which blocks it can mine, how much damage it will do, how fast it mines, how long it can be used, and several other things. To create your own `ToolMaterial`, add the following code to the mod file just below the `Item` variables:

```
ToolMaterial samium = EnumHelper.addToolMaterial("samium", 3, 1000, 9.5F, 3.5F, 10);
```

With this code, you create a `ToolMaterial` called samium. You create it using a file called `EnumHelper`. In that file is a method called `addToolMaterial`, which takes six parameters.

The first parameter is the name of the material. The name for this isn't very important. The only thing that you should keep in mind is that it should be a unique name and that you can easily recognize it as the `ToolMaterial` you want it to be.

The second parameter is the harvest level of the tool. The harvest level decides which kind of blocks you can properly mine. If you go to the `ToolMaterial` class, which is inside `Item`, you will be able to see which material has which harvest level. If the material has a higher harvest level, it is able to mine more blocks. Harvest level 3 means you can mine as much as the diamond pickaxe. This means you can mine basically everything except for bedrock, which is impossible to break.

The third parameter is the amount of times the tool can be used. Certain types of actions performed with certain tools decrease this number by more than one; however, generally, mining a block decreases it by one. A pickaxe with this `ToolMaterial` should be able to dig a thousand blocks.

The fourth parameter is the tool speed. This is a number only used for tools like a pickaxe and an axe. This doesn't affect swords or hoes. A higher tool speed mines things faster. You can easily compare the tool speed with vanilla tools in the `ToolMaterial` class.

The fifth parameter is the damage the tool will do. Even though the sword is the only tool to effectively damage entities, this value affects every tool. Tools made with the `samium` `ToolMaterial` do 3.5 points of damage. Swords using the `samium` `ToolMaterial` use 3.5 with the extra amount set in `ItemSword`.

The final parameter is the enchantability. This is a bit of a weird number, but if this is higher, the chance of getting more or better enchantments is higher. However, even with a high enchantability, great enchantments are not guaranteed.

Creating a Pickaxe

Now that you have a `ToolMaterial`, it is time to use it in a tool.

The Mod File Code

To add a tool to the mod file, add the following code to the mod file:

```
public static Item sampickaxe;
ToolMaterial samium = EnumHelper.addToolMaterial("samium", 3, 1000, 9.5F, 3.5F,
➥10);
```

Additionally, add the following code to the `preInit` method:

```
sampickaxe = new ItemSamPickaxe(samium, "sampickaxe");

GameRegistry.registerItem(sampickaxe, "SamPickaxe");
```

All of this code should be familiar to you at this point. The only thing that stands out is that the `ItemSamPickaxe` has the `ToolMaterial` as its first parameter. This is required for creating tools because of the file that will be extended in the `ItemSamPickaxe` class.

Creating the `ItemSamPickaxe` **Class**

Just like with the other items created in earlier hours, hover your mouse over `ItemSamPickaxe` and select Create Class. Then change the extended type from `ItemTool` into `ItemPickaxe`. This gives you an error under `ItemSamPickaxe` telling you it should have a constructor with a single parameter: `ToolMaterial`. Don't do this. Instead, add the code shown in Listing 7.1.

LISTING 7.1 `ItemSamPickaxe` **Constructor**

```
package com.wuppy.samsmod;

import net.minecraft.item.ItemPickaxe;

public class ItemSamPickaxe extends ItemPickaxe
{
        public ItemSamPickaxe(ToolMaterial material, String name)
        {
                super(material);
        }
}
```

This code makes sure that the `name` parameter used in the mod file can still be used. It also makes sure that the constructor in `ItemPickaxe` with just the `ToolMaterial` is also called, which is required.

Now, just like any other item file, add the following two lines of code to the constructor:

```
setUnlocalizedName(SamsMod.MODID + "_" + name);
setTextureName(SamsMod.MODID + ":" + name);
```

Also, just like the other items, don't forget to add a localization, which looks like the following code snippet for the pickaxe. Add the following code to the en_US.lang file:

```
item.wuppy29_samsmod_sampickaxe.name=Sam's Pickaxe
```

And don't forget to add a texture. The Sam's Pickaxe uses the texture shown in Figure 7.1.

FIGURE 7.1
The Sam's Pickaxe texture.

Figure 7.1 will be saved as `sampickaxe.png` in the items folder.

Now you have a fully functional pickaxe in Minecraft. The full `SamsPickaxe` class is displayed in Listing 7.2.

LISTING 7.2 `SamsPickaxe` Completed

```
package com.wuppy.samsmod;

import net.minecraft.item.Item.ToolMaterial;
import net.minecraft.item.ItemPickaxe;

public class ItemSamPickaxe extends ItemPickaxe
{
        public ItemSamPickaxe(ToolMaterial material, String name)
        {
                super(material);
                setUnlocalizedName(SamsMod.MODID + "_" + name);
                setTextureName(SamsMod.MODID + ":" + name);
        }
}
```

▼ TRY IT YOURSELF

Create the Other Tools

Try creating all of the other tools in Minecraft. If you are stuck somewhere, you can look at the code in the mod class and `Item` classes in Listings 7.3 to 7.8.

The code to add other tools to the mod file is shown in Listings 7.3 and 7.4.

LISTING 7.3   Mod File with All Tool Code Outside of the `preInit` Method

```
public static Item sampickaxe;
public static Item samaxe;
public static Item samhoe;
public static Item samshovel;
public static Item samsword;

ToolMaterial samium = EnumHelper.addToolMaterial("samium", 3, 1000, 9.5F, 3.5F,
➡10);
```

LISTING 7.4   All of the New Code in `preInit`

```
sampickaxe = new ItemSamPickaxe(samium, "sampickaxe");
samaxe = new ItemSamAxe(samium, "samaxe");
samhoe = new ItemSamHoe(samium, "samhoe");
```

```
samshovel = new ItemSamShovel(samium, "samshovel");
samsword = new ItemSamSword(samium, "samsword");

GameRegistry.registerItem(sampickaxe, "SamPickaxe");
GameRegistry.registerItem(samaxe, "SamsAxe");
GameRegistry.registerItem(samhoe, "SamsHoe");
GameRegistry.registerItem(samshovel, "SamsShovel");
GameRegistry.registerItem(samsword, "SamsSword");
```

Listings 7.5 to 7.8 contain the code for the four new tools.

LISTING 7.5 The `ItemSamAxe` Class

```
package com.wuppy.samsmod;

import net.minecraft.item.Item.ToolMaterial;
import net.minecraft.item.ItemAxe;

public class ItemSamAxe extends ItemAxe
{
        public ItemSamAxe(ToolMaterial material, String name)
        {
                super(material);
                setUnlocalizedName(SamsMod.MODID + "_" + name);
                setTextureName(SamsMod.MODID + ":" + name);
        }
}
```

LISTING 7.6 The `ItemSamHoe` Class

```
package com.wuppy.samsmod;

import net.minecraft.item.Item.ToolMaterial;
import net.minecraft.item.ItemHoe;

public class ItemSamHoe extends ItemHoe
{
        public ItemSamHoe(ToolMaterial material, String name)
        {
                super(material);
                setUnlocalizedName(SamsMod.MODID + "_" + name);
                setTextureName(SamsMod.MODID + ":" + name);
        }
}
```

LISTING 7.7   The `ItemSamShovel` Class

```
package com.wuppy.samsmod;

import net.minecraft.item.Item.ToolMaterial;
import net.minecraft.item.ItemSpade;

public class ItemSamShovel extends ItemSpade
{
        public ItemSamShovel(ToolMaterial material, String name)
        {
                super(material);
                setUnlocalizedName(SamsMod.MODID + "_" + name);
                setTextureName(SamsMod.MODID + ":" + name);
        }
}
```

LISTING 7.8   The `ItemSamSword` Class

```
package com.wuppy.samsmod;

import net.minecraft.item.Item.ToolMaterial;
import net.minecraft.item.ItemSword;

public class ItemSamSword extends ItemSword
{
        public ItemSamSword(ToolMaterial material, String name)
        {
                super(material);
                setUnlocalizedName(SamsMod.MODID + "_" + name);
                setTextureName(SamsMod.MODID + ":" + name);
        }
}
```

All the code in the tools should look similar to the code in the pickaxe. The only small exception is that the item file for a shovel is called `ItemSpade`.

The following are the localizations in the `en_US.lang` file:

```
item.wuppy29_samsmod_samaxe.name=Sam's Axe
item.wuppy29_samsmod_samhoe.name=Sam's Hoe
item.wuppy29_samsmod_samshovel.name=Sam's Shovel
item.wuppy29_samsmod_samsword.name=Sam's Sword
```

Figures 7.2 to 7.5 contain the textures for the tools.

FIGURE 7.2
ItemSamAxe.

FIGURE 7.3
ItemSamHoe.

FIGURE 7.4
ItemSamShovel.

FIGURE 7.5
ItemSamSword.

Figures 7.6 to 7.10 show the tools in the game.

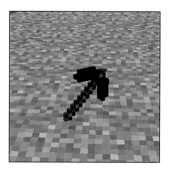

FIGURE 7.6
The pickaxe in the game.

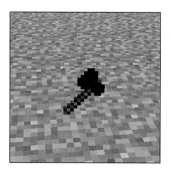

FIGURE 7.7
The axe in the game.

FIGURE 7.8
The hoe in the game.

FIGURE 7.9
The shovel in the game.

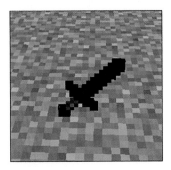

FIGURE 7.10
The sword in the game.

Creating Special Tools for Harvesting Different Blocks

Because there are only five vanilla tools, the selection is quite limited. Sometimes a mod should contain a custom tool. This book can't cover every type of custom tool. Instead, you learn how to create your own custom tools by creating a paxel. A *paxel* is a pickaxe and axe in one.

The Mod File Code

The code in the mod file for a paxel is exactly the same as for any other tool. This has to be added to the class itself:

```
public static Item sampaxel;
```

And these two lines have to be added to the preInit method:

```
sampaxel = new ItemSamPaxel(sampaxel, "sampaxel");
GameRegistry.registerItem(sampaxel, "SamsPaxel");
```

Creating the `ItemSamPaxel` Class

Create `ItemSamPaxel` and make it extend `ItemTool`. When you add this, it creates an error under `ItemSamPaxel` telling you to add a constructor. Don't do this. Instead, create a constructor similar to the other tools. It should have the same parameters, and except for the line starting with `super`, the code will be exactly the same. When you are finished, the file should look like this:

```
package com.wuppy.samsmod;

import net.minecraft.item.ItemTool;

public class ItemSamPaxel extends ItemTool
{
        public ItemSamPaxel(ToolMaterial material, String name)
        {
                setUnlocalizedName(SamsMod.MODID + "_" + name);
                setTextureName(SamsMod.MODID + ":" + name);
        }
}
```

You will have an error under `ItemSamPaxel` telling you it must invoke a `super` constructor. To do that, you need a new variable. The code required for this variable is quite complicated, and looks like this:

```
private static Set blocks = Sets.newHashSet(new Block[] { });
```

This line creates a variable called `blocks`. It is a `Set`, which is a certain type of data structure in programming. However, the only thing you should worry about is the `Block` array. Place the blocks this tool will be effective against inside the curly braces separated by a comma.

NOTE

Getting the Blocks

You can easily find the blocks you want to add by going to other tool files and copying what those have in the `Block` array.

Once you have added all of the blocks you want this tool to be able to mine, it's time to create the `super` constructor. This constructor requires three parameters.

The first is a `float` value for the damage on the player. If you want to create a tool that is also a weapon, having a high value here makes that possible.

The second parameter is the `ToolMaterial` that is the first parameter of the constructor used in the current file.

The final parameter is the `Set` of blocks you just created.

Listing 7.9 shows the completed set for a paxel, where the `blocks` variable contains all of the blocks mineable by a pickaxe and an axe.

LISTING 7.9   `ItemSamPaxel`

```
package com.wuppy.samsmod;

import java.util.Set;

import com.google.common.collect.Sets;

import net.minecraft.block.Block;
import net.minecraft.init.Blocks;
import net.minecraft.item.ItemTool;

public class ItemSamPaxel extends ItemTool
{
        private static Set blocks = Sets.newHashSet(new Block[]
➥{Blocks.cobblestone, Blocks.double_stone_slab, Blocks.stone_slab,
➥Blocks.stone, Blocks.sandstone, Blocks.mossy_cobblestone, Blocks.iron_ore,
➥Blocks.iron_block, Blocks.coal_ore, Blocks.gold_block, Blocks.gold_ore,
➥Blocks.diamond_ore, Blocks.diamond_block, Blocks.ice, Blocks.netherrack,
➥Blocks.lapis_ore, Blocks.lapis_block, Blocks.redstone_ore, Blocks.lit_
➥redstone_ore, Blocks.rail, Blocks.detector_rail, Blocks.golden_rail,
➥Blocks.activator_rail, Blocks.planks, Blocks.bookshelf, Blocks.log,
➥Blocks.log2, Blocks.chest, Blocks.pumpkin, Blocks.lit_pumpkin});

        public ItemSamPaxel(ToolMaterial material, String name)
        {
                super(3, material, blocks);
                setUnlocalizedName(SamsMod.MODID + "_" + name);
                setTextureName(SamsMod.MODID + ":" + name);
        }
}
```

In addition to having the `Set` variable, you also require two methods from the `ItemPickaxe` and one from the `ItemAxe`. One of the methods is present in both files, which specifies which block materials the tool is able to break at the fast speed and which at the slow speed. For example, shovels have the fast speed on dirt and the slow speed on stone. The method specific to the pickaxe makes sure it can mine some of the harder blocks based on the harvest level for the `ToolMaterial` used with the pickaxe. The two methods copied and combined should look as follows:

```
public boolean func_150897_b(Block block)
{
    return block == Blocks.obsidian ? this.toolMaterial.getHarvestLevel() == 3 :
➡(block != Blocks.diamond_block && block != Blocks.diamond_ore ? (block !=
➡Blocks.emerald_ore && block != Blocks.emerald_block ? (block !=
➡Blocks.gold_block && block != Blocks.gold_ore ? (block != Blocks.iron_
➡block && block != Blocks.iron_ore ? (block != Blocks.lapis_block && block
➡!= Blocks.lapis_ore ? (block != Blocks.redstone_ore && block != Blocks.lit_
➡redstone_ore ? (block.getMaterial() == Material.rock ? true :
➡(block.getMaterial() == Material.iron ? true : block.getMaterial()
➡== Material.anvil)) : this.toolMaterial.getHarvestLevel() >= 2) :
➡this.toolMaterial.getHarvestLevel() >= 1) : this.toolMaterial.getHarvestLevel()
➡>= 1) : this.toolMaterial.getHarvestLevel() >= 2) :
➡this.toolMaterial.getHarvestLevel() >= 2) : this.toolMaterial.getHarvestLevel()
➡>= 2);
}

public float func_150893_a(ItemStack itemStack, Block block)
{
    return block.getMaterial() != Material.iron && block.getMaterial() !=
➡Material.wood && block.getMaterial() != Material.plants && block.getMaterial()
➡!= Material.vine && block.getMaterial() != Material.anvil && block.getMaterial()
➡!= Material.rock ? super.func_150893_a(itemStack, block) :
➡this.efficiencyOnProperMaterial;
}
```

If you want to add an extra material that this tool should be able to break, go into
func_150893_a and add another block.getMaterial() != and then the material that
should be supported.

NOTE

Tool Variety

This code teaches you how to create a paxel, but there are many different tools that you can
make—not just combinations of already existing ones, but also completely unique ones. This is just
an example, and you can use it to learn how to create custom tools in general.

It is easy to change some more details about your tool by going into ItemTool and selecting the
method that decides what a certain action does and then overwriting it. Normally, tools take two
damage when they are used as weapons. This is done in the hitEntity method. If you want to
overwrite and make it only take one damage like a normal sword, you would have to add the
following method to the custom tool:

```
public boolean hitEntity(ItemStack par1ItemStack, EntityLivingBase
➥par2EntityLivingBase, EntityLivingBase par3EntityLivingBase)
{
    par1ItemStack.damageItem(1, par3EntityLivingBase);
    return true;
}
```

Another possibility of making it a custom tool is to overwrite the onBlockDestroyed method. You could make a certain block drop something extra or others not at all. Alternatively, you could make it place a different block. With a few simple and smart changes to existing code, your basic and possibly boring or useless tools can become something unique and interesting to use.

The localization for the paxel looks like the following:

```
item.wuppy29_samsmod_sampaxel.name=Sam's Paxel
```

Figure 7.11 shows the texture for the paxel, and Figure 7.12 shows it in the game.

FIGURE 7.11
Paxel texture.

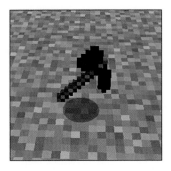

FIGURE 7.12
The Paxel in the game.

Summary

In this hour, you learned how to use and create your own `ToolMaterial`. You explored the available parameters as well. You learned how to create your own basic tools and how to use this knowledge to create custom tools, such as a paxel. Finally, you also learned how to make your tools truly unique by overwriting certain methods.

Q&A

Q. Can you have multiple tools under the same metadata?

A. Yes. Tool damage is not stored as metadata and because of that, it is possible.

Q. Can you create a tool that is able to mine everything?

A. Of course. Simply add all of the blocks and materials in the right places. The only problem might be bedrock.

Q. Is there a maximum amount of `ToolMaterial`s there can be?

A. There is a limit, but it's unreachable.

Workshop

You now know how to create the basic tools and also how to write custom ones. Complete the following quiz to ensure you understand the covered topics.

Quiz

1. What would happen if you don't include `func_150897_b` in a pickaxe type tool?
2. What is the third parameter in a `ToolMaterial`?
3. What is diamond `ToolMaterial` called in code?

Answers

1. The pickaxe won't be able to mine some of the harder blocks like obsidian.
2. The third parameter is the amount of times the tool can be used.
3. It's called `EMERALD`.

Exercises

Create a spax, which is a spade and an axe in one, by using the same technique used to create the paxel.

A spax should look similar to Listing 7.10.

LISTING 7.10   ItemSamSpax

```
package com.wuppy.samsmod;

import java.util.Set;

import net.minecraft.block.Block;
import net.minecraft.block.material.Material;
import net.minecraft.init.Blocks;
import net.minecraft.item.ItemStack;
import net.minecraft.item.ItemTool;

import com.google.common.collect.Sets;

public class ItemSpax extends ItemTool
{
    private static Set blocks = Sets.newHashSet(new Block[] {Blocks.grass,
➡Blocks.dirt, Blocks.sand, Blocks.gravel, Blocks.snow_layer, Blocks.snow,
➡Blocks.clay, Blocks.farmland, Blocks.soul_sand, Blocks.mycelium, Blocks.planks,
➡Blocks.bookshelf, Blocks.log, Blocks.log2, Blocks.chest, Blocks.pumpkin,
➡Blocks.lit_pumpkin});

    protected ItemSpax(ToolMaterial material, String name)
    {
        super(3, material, blocks);
        setUnlocalizedName(SamsMod.MODID + "_" + name);
        setTextureName(SamsMod.MODID + ":" + name);
    }

    public boolean func_150897_b(Block p_150897_1_)
    {
        return p_150897_1_ == Blocks.snow_layer ? true : p_150897_1_ == Blocks.snow;
    }

    public float func_150893_a(ItemStack p_150893_1_, Block p_150893_2_)
    {
        return p_150893_2_.getMaterial() != Material.wood && p_150893_2_
➡.getMaterial() != Material.plants && p_150893_2_.getMaterial() != Material.vine ?
➡super.func_150893_a(p_150893_1_, p_150893_2_) : this.efficiencyOnProperMaterial;
    }
}
```

The texture of the tool is shown in Figure 7.13, and you can see it in the game in Figure 7.14.

FIGURE 7.13
Spax texture.

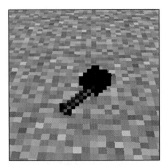

FIGURE 7.14
The spax in the game.

Creating Armor

What You'll Learn in This Hour:

▶ Creating your `ArmorMaterial`

▶ Creating the armor

▶ Customizing armor

In the last few hours, you learned about most of the special items used in many mods. Truly unique items are something you will have to create yourself, but with this and the last few hours, you should be able to get quite far without much help. In this hour, you learn how to create armor. First, you learn about `ArmorMaterial`, which is similar to `ToolMaterial`. You then learn how to make all the armor pieces, and, finally, you learn how to customize those.

Creating Your `ArmorMaterial`

Just like when creating tools, it's important to create a material the armor will be made from first. The code for an `ArmorMaterial` should look like this:

```
ArmorMaterial samarmor = EnumHelper.addArmorMaterial("samarmor", 20,
➥new int[] { 3, 7, 6, 3 }, 10);
```

The code for tools and armor has quite a lot of things in common because they are closely related in Minecraft. However, there are some small changes here and there. The first part of this line, up to the parameters, is very similar to the `ToolMaterial` code. The parameters are a little different, though.

The first parameter is the name of the material. It's important that there aren't any other mods with the same `ArmorMaterial` name, but it's unlikely for that to happen.

The second parameter is the maximum amount of damage the armor can absorb. This code seems like it can only take 20 hits. However, the actual maximum damage is a bit weird. In `ItemArmor`, you will find a variable called `maxDamageArray`. When you do the second parameter times the right index of the `maxDamageArray`, you will find the actual max damage. The array used has four variables, just like the third parameter in the `ArmorMaterial` line. Armor also has four parts. This means that each index specifies settings for one part of the armor.

The first number in the array is the helmet. The second is for the chestplate, the third is for the leggings, and the final one is for the boots.

The third parameter is the damage reduction amount in an array following the same structure as the `maxDamageArray`. This amount is directly visible to the player by way of shields. The total of all the four armor parts for diamond is 20, which is exactly the same as the amount of half shields there are in the graphical user interface (GUI).

The final parameter is the same as with the `ToolMaterial` and is the enchantability. This number specifies how many chances for enchantment there are on the tool. A higher number makes sure there is a higher chance for enchantments.

Creating the Armor

Now it's time to create the armor items.

The Mod File Code

Just like with any other item, you need to create the object, initialize it, and finally register it. Listing 8.1 shows all of the armor code required in the mod file. The `Item` objects are also ordered like the arrays used for the `ArmorMaterial`.

LISTING 8.1 Armor Code

```
//armor
public static Item samhelmet;
public static Item samchest;
public static Item samleggings;
public static Item samboots;

ArmorMaterial samarmor = EnumHelper.addArmorMaterial("samarmor", 20,
➥new int[] { 3, 7, 6, 3 }, 10);
```

Listing 8.2 shows the code that is required to be added in the `preInit` method.

LISTING 8.2   preInit Armor Code

```
//armor
samhelmet = new ItemSamArmor(samarmor, 0, "samhelmet");
samchest = new ItemSamArmor(samarmor, 1, "samchestplate");
samleggings = new ItemSamArmor(samarmor, 2, "samleggings");
samboots = new ItemSamArmor(samarmor, 3, "samboots");

//armor
GameRegistry.registerItem(samhelmet, "SamsHelmet");
GameRegistry.registerItem(samchest, "SamsChest");
GameRegistry.registerItem(samleggings, "SamsLeggings");
GameRegistry.registerItem(samboots, "SamsBoots");
```

The `ItemSamArmor` used in Listing 8.2 has three parameters. First is the `ArmorMaterial`. The second parameter is the index of the armor piece. The final parameter is the unlocalized name, which is also used in the texture, just like with any other item.

The following are the localizations for the armor items, which you must add to `en_US.lang`:

```
item.wuppy29_samsmod_samhelmet.name=Sam's Helmet
item.wuppy29_samsmod_samchestplate.name=Sam's Chestplate
item.wuppy29_samsmod_samleggings.name=Sam's Leggings
item.wuppy29_samsmod_samboots.name=Sam's Boots
```

Creating the `ItemSamArmor` Class

With this code, you have errors under `ItemSamArmor` because the class doesn't exist just yet. To create it, hover your mouse over the error and click Create Class.

The `ItemSamArmor` class should extend `ItemArmor`. When you do this and import the file, you get an error under `ItemSamArmor` telling you it needs a certain type of constructor. Instead of doing that, you create your own constructor with the same parameters as used in the mod file. The constructor should look like the following:

```
public ItemSamArmor(ArmorMaterial material, int armorType, String name)
{
        super(material, 0, armorType);
        setUnlocalizedName(SamsMod.MODID + "_" + name);
        setTextureName(SamsMod.MODID + ":" + name);
}
```

Most of this code should be easy to understand by now because it's mostly the same as with any other item. The only surprising piece of code is the second parameter in the `super` constructor. This second number is the render index for the armor. The number is only used for the vanilla armor textures, so it's not really required with custom armor. Because of this, the easiest thing to do is to set it to zero.

The textures for the armor pieces look like Figures 8.1 to 8.4.

FIGURE 8.1
Helmet texture.

FIGURE 8.2
Chestplate texture.

FIGURE 8.3
Leggings texture.

FIGURE 8.4
Boot texture.

All of these textures will obviously be saved in the textures/items folder like any other item texture. Additionally, the filename will be the same as the name in code, which is the third parameter of the constructor.

Figures 8.5 to 8.8 display the items within the game.

FIGURE 8.5
The helmet in the game.

FIGURE 8.6
The chestplate in the game.

FIGURE 8.7
The leggings in the game.

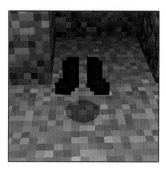

FIGURE 8.8
The boots in the game.

Creating the Worn Armor Texture

If you launch the game right now and try to put on your armor, you will see that it works. However, it will not have the textures similar to the item icons. Instead, it looks like white-colored cloth armor. To get your custom texture on the armor, you first have to make it. Figures 8.9 and 8.10 are the two armor textures required for this.

FIGURE 8.9
Armor texture 1.

FIGURE 8.10
Armor texture 2.

These textures might look very unclear, but they are easy to understand if you know what you are looking at. These textures are a 2D representation of a 3D texture, where the 2D texture gets folded around the player model in the game.

In armor texture 1, the upper-left part is the helmet. The lower-left part is the texture for the boots and, finally, everything to the right is for the chestplate. Armor texture 2 contains the leggings of the armor.

Both of the images contain a lot of empty space. However, most of the empty pixels can actually be used on the armor. For example, in the second texture, the area to the right of the little box at the top will contain the texture for the bottom of the arm. However, because the hands would go there, this part is empty. It is also possible to add a second layer to the helmet, giving the illusion of something like hair. You could play around with this a little to find out what goes where.

Next, you need to place the textures somewhere so Forge can use them. The folder structure is assets/[modid]/models/armor. This should look like Figure 8.11.

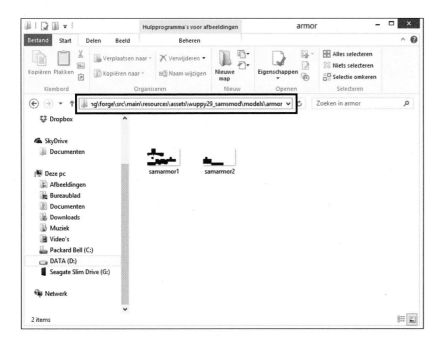

FIGURE 8.11
Armor folder structure.

For the armor set you are creating now, the textures will be saved as `samarmor1` and `samarmor2`. It is suggested, but not required, to follow both the folder structure and naming conventions of the files.

The final thing required for the textures is to tell the code where to find the texture files. To do that, you need a method called `getArmorTexture`. In this method, you must decide which piece of the armor requires which texture. You will have to write the method in such a way that it checks if the item is the helmet, the boots, or the chestplate, and assign texture one to it. If it's not any of those, it should check if the item is the leggings for armor texture two. If it's neither of those, something must have gone wrong and both of the textures are wrong. In this case, the best thing to do is print out something is wrong and return null. Doing all of this in code should look like this:

```
public String getArmorTexture(ItemStack stack, Entity entity, int slot,
➥String type)
{
        if (stack.getItem() == SamsMod.samhelmet || stack.getItem() ==
➥SamsMod.samchest || stack.getItem() == SamsMod.samboots)
        {
                return SamsMod.MODID + ":models/armor/samarmor1.png";
        }
        else if(stack.getItem() == SamsMod.samleggings)
        {
                return SamsMod.MODID + ":models/armor/samarmor2.png";
        }
        else
        {
                System.out.println("Invalid Item");
                return null;
        }
}
```

Figure 8.12 shows the armor worn by the player in the game.

FIGURE 8.12
The armor in the game.

NOTE

Armor Pieces

Creating all the armor pieces is not required. If you only want a helmet, you don't have to code the other three items, and it will work just fine.

Customizing Armor

Armor is less customizable than something like tools or food. There is only one thing that can be added to the armor to edit it. However, this one thing is also incredibly powerful and you can do a lot with it.

The one thing you can edit is a method, which looks like the following code snippet. Add the following method to the `ItemSamArmor` class:

```
public void onArmorTick(World world, EntityPlayer player, ItemStack itemStack)
{

}
```

This method contains an object of the world, the player, as well as the armor item stack. Some examples of what you could do with this are as follows:

1. Check to see if the player is in water and then replace the water with air.

2. Make the player not have to breathe for a really long time.

3. Repair the armor whenever the player is in lava.

4. Make a player immune to lava damage.

Basically, there is an endless list of things you could do with this. You can check any amount of blocks near the player using both the world and the player objects. It is also possible to interact with the armor item using the `itemStack` variable.

Throughout this book, you might find methods in either the `World` or `EntityPlayer`, which could be used to customize your armor. It would, however, be impossible to explain every single customization there is, because, as mentioned before, the list is endless and it's also far too specific to be taught. Instead, you must experiment and learn these things yourself, which you can easily do when you finish Hour 24, "What's Next." The armor, which will be in the mod created over the course of this book, will not contain the `onArmorTick` method.

Summary

In this hour, you learned how to create a custom `ArmorMaterial`. With this, you are now also able to create your custom armor. Additionally, you learned how to apply a texture to worn armor as well as how to customize your armor into something unique.

In all the hours in Part II, "Items," you learned something about items. At this point, you should know how to create a basic item. You have also learned about metadata items. Hours 6, 7, and 8 covered the most commonly used special items in Minecraft. With the knowledge gained in these hours, you should be able to come up with some truly original and interesting items, making your mod the one everyone wants to have installed when playing Minecraft.

Q&A

Q. **Is there a maximum amount of armor items you can have?**

A. Not really. The maximum amount of items is the upper limit for this, which is basically unreachable.

Q. **Can you have a total defense of more than 20?**

A. Yes, you can. It will not show it on the graphical user interface, but it will work.

Q. **Do I have to have two armor textures?**

A. If you have all four armor pieces, yes. If you don't have the leggings, you don't need the second armor texture.

Workshop

Complete the following workshop to make sure you understand everything up to this point.

Quiz

1. What is the second parameter of the `addToolMaterial` method used earlier, and how does it work?

2. What is the `ArmorMaterial` for diamond called?

3. What would happen if you don't have the `getArmorTexture` method?

Answers

1. The second parameter is the amount of damage an armor piece is able to take. It is multiplied by a value in the `ItemArmor` file.

2. `DIAMOND`. Even though it's called `EMERALD` for tools, it has the normal name for armor.

3. Your armor would look like the standard armor on the player. The standard armor is white leather.

Exercises

Make armor that allows the player to breathe under water. *Hint:* To do this, you must look in `EntityPlayer` and find a method containing the word *Air*.

The code answer should look similar to the following:

```java
public void onArmorTick(World world, EntityPlayer player, ItemStack itemStack)
{
        if(itemStack.getItem().getUnlocalizedName() == "samhelmet")
        {
                if(player.isInWater())
                {
                        player.setAir(20);
                }
        }
}
```

First, you check if the ticking armor is a helmet. Then, you check to make sure the player is actually under water to make sure it doesn't slow down the server or client too much. If the player is in water, the air is set to something higher than zero to make sure the player doesn't drown.

HOUR 9
Making Your First Block

What You'll Learn in This Hour:

▶ Understanding what a block is

▶ Creating a basic block

▶ Adding a block texture

In this hour, you learn exactly what a block is and what it isn't in Minecraft. Then, you create a block and add a texture to it. You also learn how to make some basic customizations to the block. Further changes and more interesting blocks are covered in the next few hours.

Understanding What a Block Is

It's important to know the limitations as well as features of something you will be creating. A block in Minecraft is a 1×1×1 area. A block is often thought of as a square, and in Minecraft, it is. However, it doesn't have to be filled completely. If you have a block like stairs, you can't add anything in the open space it leaves. This is because, even though it doesn't seem like it, the area that is left open is filled with the stairs. The same thing can be seen with a mushroom. It's not a full block, but it fills up the entire square.

One block that might be confusing after this explanation is a stone slab. If you place a stone slab somewhere, the entire block should be filled up. However, when you place a second slab in the same place, it works. It might seem like there are now two blocks in the same space, which is impossible. The way this is done is through a smart trick. When you place a stone slab on a block that is already filled with a slab, it actually removes the first slab and puts a double slab in its place, which is a different block.

An important, and obvious, feature of a block is that it can't move. Generally, if you see a block move, it's not actually a block. It might seem like water flows around, and therefore moves, but it's actually placing, changing, and removing blocks all of the time.

One final thing to note about a block is that it doesn't open up a window when it's clicked. If a block has a graphical user interface (GUI), it's not exactly a block, but a tile entity. A *tile entity* is a block and an entity in one. Examples of tile entities are chests and furnaces. Tile entities are covered in Hour 12, "Creating a Tile Entity."

Creating a Basic Block

Now that you know what you will be making, it's time to actually make it.

The Mod File Code

Adding a block to Minecraft is quite similar to adding an item. You start with creating a `Block` object. The name you choose should be something recognizable and should represent the block it will be. The block that you create in this hour is an ore. This ore will drop dust that can be smelted into ingots and those ingots will be used to create Sam's armor pieces. The name of the block will be `samStone`. You will add two more lines of code to the mod file. Both of them are very similar to the item lines.

You must add a line to initialize the block. The class that it will initialize with will be called `BlockSamStone`. `BlockSamStone` will not contain any parameters, but you could follow the smart naming system used for the items, which requires you to add a `String` parameter. The code for that would be exactly the same.

Another thing you must take care of is block registry. For blocks, this is also done in `GameRegistry`, but with the method `registerBlock` instead of `registerItem`. The parameters are the same, though. The first parameter is the block and the second parameter is the name for it.

Add the following code to the mod file:

```
public static Block samStone;
```

Then add the following code into the `preInit` method:

```
samStone = new BlockSamStone();

GameRegistry.registerBlock(samStone, "SamStone");
```

Creating the `BlockSamStone` Class

The error under `BlockSamStone` is normal, and you can easily fix it by creating the class. To do this, hover your mouse over the error, click Create Class, and then click Finish. This gives you a `Block` class similar to Listing 9.1, which also contains errors.

LISTING 9.1 Standard Block Code

```
package com.wuppy.samsmod;

import net.minecraft.block.Block;

public class BlockSamStone extends Block
{

}
```

Now the error in the mod class is gone, but a new one has appeared in the `Block` class. To fix this, you must add a constructor. Because the constructor used in the mod class is empty, this must be empty as well. However, the `Block` class, which is extended, requires you to add a constructor containing a material. To get both the mod class and the `Block` class to work properly, you need to add a constructor without parameters. Then within the constructor, add a `super` with a single parameter. This parameter must be a `Material`. For the stone, the `Material` will be rock, but you can look in the `Material` class for other possible materials. The code should look like the following code snippet:

```
public BlockSamStone()
{
        super(Material.rock);
}
```

In addition to the `super` constructor, you also need to add an unlocalized name as well as the texture name for the block. With these lines, the class should look like Listing 9.2.

LISTING 9.2 BlockSamStone with the Texture and Name Code

```
package com.wuppy.samsmod;

import net.minecraft.block.Block;
import net.minecraft.block.material.Material;

public class BlockSamStone extends Block
{
        String name = "samstone";

        public BlockSamStone()
        {
                super(Material.rock);
                setBlockName(SamsMod.MODID + "_" + name);
                setBlockTextureName(SamsMod.MODID + ":" + name);
        }
}
```

Several things might look surprising in this code. First, a `String` variable is created containing the name. This is created because the same name is used several times. When you want to—or have to change it sometime in the future—you will only have to change what the `name` variable contains instead of replacing it wherever it's used.

The other two potentially confusing things are the method names for the texture and unlocalized name. Unlike with items where it's `setUnlocalizedName`, it is `setBlockName`. For the texture name, you use `setBlockTextureName` instead of simply `setTextureName` like you use for items.

Do not forget to add this block to the right Creative menu using the `setCreativeTab` method, which takes a single parameter. This parameter is the same as for items, where it requires a single `CreativeTab` object. If you go to the `CreativeTab` class, you will be able to see how the in-game Creative tabs are called in code.

Customizing Your Block

You also need to set a few block-specific things. Every block has a hardness, a blast resistance, and a step sound. Finally, a harvest level is also something you might want to add for certain blocks.

The hardness of a block decides how long it takes for it to be broken by whatever tool it should be broken by. The type of tool it's most easily broken by is decided by the material, but you can edit the length of the break time with the hardness. The method you use to set this is called `setHardness`. This method takes one parameter, which is a `float`. A `float` is similar to an `int` in Java, which means it's also a number. However, the difference is that `float`s can have decimals. Often, a `float` is followed by an F in Java to make it obvious to the reader as well as to Java that it is a `float` and not another number type. The higher the number, the longer it takes for the block to be broken. The hardness levels of vanilla blocks can be found in the `Blocks` class. Because the `SamStone` will be an ore, the hardness should be similar to other ore blocks. Stone has a hardness of 1.5F and most ores are slightly higher than that. For the `SamStone`, the hardness will be 2.0F.

If you want your block to be unbreakable like bedrock, the hardness should be –1.0F.

Blast resistance is very similar to hardness. However, instead of it being the breakability for tools, it's the breakability for explosions. These explosions include creepers as well as TNT. The method name used for this is `setResistance`. Just like `setHardness`, it requires a single `float` value, which decides how hard it is to be exploded. You don't have to have this method, but it is used for many blocks. Normal stone has a resistance of 10F, whereas ores have a resistance of 5F. Because `SamStone` is also going to be an ore, the value used for it will also be 5F.

If you want your block to be unbreakable, the resistance could be set to 6,000,000, which is the same as bedrock. There are no explosives in the game that could ever break a block with a resistance that high.

A third thing you might want to add to your block is a step sound. This is the sound that will be played when a player or mob walks over it. Generally, when you walk over a block, it has multiple different sounds it is able to play and it picks randomly from those. When you select a single `StepSound`, it usually takes all of those sounds for that specific type. Additionally, the step sound also decides which break sound it will have. The method you need to add a step sound is `setStepSound`. This method takes a single parameter. This parameter is a `Block.StepSound` object. When you add this method in the constructor of your block, you don't have to worry about creating a custom step sound. Instead, you can look in the `Block` class and select the variable name for the step sound you want and use that. For `BlockSamStone`, the step sound is called `soundTypeStone`.

The final method you might want to add to your basic block is the harvest level. The harvest level is quite important for a block, although it is not required. It manages two important things for your block. First, the harvest level manages which tools can properly break it. If you don't have a harvest level, the block will be properly breakable by every tool in the game. Properly breakable means that the block drops what it should. For example, when you mine stone with your hands, it won't drop anything at all.

Second, the harvest level also manages which level of the appropriate tool is able to mine it. Each material has a different harvest level, as you likely noticed in Hour 7, "Making Your Own Tools." The vanilla harvest levels are 0 for wood and gold, 1 for stone, 2 for iron, and 3 for diamond. If you mine the block with the right tool, but of a not-high-enough level, it won't work. For example, if you try to mine diamonds with a stone pickaxe, you won't get any.

TRY IT YOURSELF ▼

Create an Unbreakable Block

Create your own unbreakable block. A block is unbreakable when:

- ▶ The hardness is –1.
- ▶ The resistance is 6,000,000.

Adding the following code to the constructor makes the block unbreakable:

```
setHardness(-1.0F);
setResistance(6000000.0F);
```

The method you use to set the harvest level is called `setHarvestLevel`. This method can have either two or three parameters. The first one is always a `String` with the name of the tool where the choice is "pickaxe," "shovel," and "axe." The second one is the tool level you want it to have. The third parameter, if you want to use it, is the metadata of the block. Because of this, you can make metadata blocks breakable by different levels of tools. For `SamStone`, the harvest tool will be a pickaxe and the level will be 2, making it only minable by iron or better.

After adding all of these methods, the `BlockSamStone` file looks like Listing 9.3.

LISTING 9.3   BlockSamStone with the New Methods

```
package com.wuppy.samsmod;

import net.minecraft.block.Block;
import net.minecraft.block.material.Material;
import net.minecraft.creativetab.CreativeTabs;

public class BlockSamStone extends Block
{
        String name = "samstone";

        public BlockSamStone()
        {
                super(Material.rock);
                setBlockName(SamsMod.MODID + "_" + name);
                setBlockTextureName(SamsMod.MODID + ":" + name);
                setCreativeTab(CreativeTabs.tabBlock);
                setHardness(2F);
                setResistance(5F);
                setStepSound(soundTypeStone);
                setHarvestLevel("pickaxe", 2);
        }
}
```

Next, you add the localization for the block in the `lang` file. To add localizations for a block, you can simply use the already existing `lang` files you used for the items. The localization needed for the `samStone` should look like the following:

```
tile.wuppy29_samsmod_samstone.name=Sam's Stone
```

To localize blocks, always use `tile.[unlocalizedname].name`. Make sure the unlocalized name in the `lang` file is exactly the same as in the code, or Minecraft will not be able to find it. Furthermore, don't put spaces around the equal sign. If you put a space before the equal sign,

Minecraft won't be able to find it, because the name would be different. If you have a space after the equal sign, the block name will start with a space.

NOTE

Further Customization

Of course there is much more customization possible for blocks. However, due to space constraints, it isn't possible to show you how to do every possible customization—and then it wouldn't be a custom block anyway! An easy way to find out about more customization is by looking at the vanilla code.

There are two very important classes when it comes to customization. The first is `Blocks`, where you can find methods used to set some things for certain types of blocks. The second is the `Block` class. In this class, you will find all the methods you could use in a block. There is certainly something in there that you can use to customize yours the way you want.

Adding a Block Texture

To add a texture to the block, you first have to create the texture. Just like with items, it has to be 16×16 pixels and has to be saved as a `.png` file. The name of the image must be the same as the unlocalized name used for the block. In the case of the Sam's Stone created up to this point, the texture will be called `samstone.png`. This image will look like Figure 9.1.

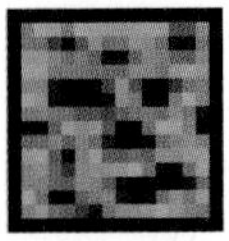

FIGURE 9.1
The Sam's Stone texture.

In addition to giving it a name, it's also important to add this image in the correct location. Go to the resources folder that you use for the lang and item texture files and then enter assets/[your modid]/textures, as shown in Figure 9.2.

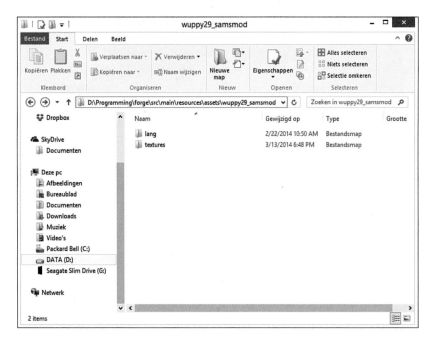

FIGURE 9.2
Textures folder path.

In here, you add a new folder called blocks. This folder will contain all of the block textures you will be using when modding. The path for this should look like Figure 9.3.

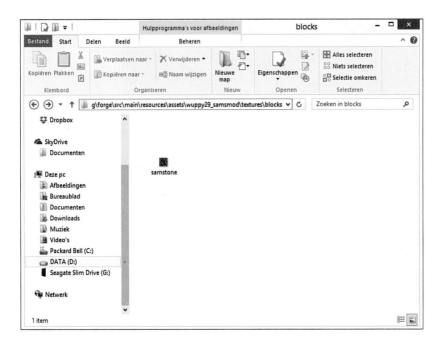

FIGURE 9.3
Block textures folder path.

Once you have created this folder, add the texture you made for the block, which is Figure 9.1 for Sam's Stone. This adds the texture to the block without any extra code. The single `setBlockTextureName` method is enough. You may, however, have to refresh Eclipse using F5 for the texture to show up properly.

If you have done everything correctly up to this point, you should be able to see the block, as shown in Figure 9.4.

FIGURE 9.4
The block in the game.

Summary

In this hour, you learned that a block is not able to move. As soon as it moves, something special is going on. Another important thing to keep in mind about blocks is that they always fill a 1×1×1 area and there can't ever be two blocks in the same area.

In addition to learning about what blocks are, you also learned how to add them to your mod file as well as how to create your custom block file with some basic settings, such as hardness and resistance. Finally, you also added a texture to your block.

Q&A

Q. Is there a maximum number of blocks you can add to Minecraft?

A. Yes. There is a maximum of 4,096 blocks in Minecraft. About 150 are taken up by Minecraft itself, so make sure you don't use too many. In Hour 10, "Creating Multiple Blocks in a Smart Way," you learn how to use metadata for blocks, which should help.

Q. How do I add a second block to my mod file?

A. Simply rewrite the code for the first block, but make sure the variables and unlocalized names are all different.

Q. Can you have multiple blocks using the same file?

A. Yes, you can. Just make sure the unlocalized name is different for every block.

Q. Can you add the same block to multiple Creative tabs?

A. No, this is not possible.

Workshop

You have learned the basics of blocks. In the next few hours, you learn more about them. Therefore, it's important to fully understand the basics. To ensure you understand the basics of blocks, complete the following quiz.

Quiz

1. What would be the best unlocalized name for a block variable called `computerScreen`?

2. What is wrong with the following code?

    ```
    public static Block samStone;

    @EventHandler
    public void preInit(FMLPreInitializationEvent event)
    {
        //Block init
        GameRegistry.registerBlock(samStone, "SamStone");

        samStone = new BlockSamStone();
    }
    ```

Answers

1. The best unlocalized name for `computerScreen` is `computerScreen` because it's smart to keep the variable name and unlocalized name the same.

2. The block is registered before initializing it to something. This will crash your mod. Always make sure the `registerBlock` method is below the block init line.

Exercises

To make the Sam's Stone block actually useful, it will drop dust, which can be smelted into an ingot. You should already have the dust and ingot item in your mod class from the Try This Yourself element in Hour 5, "Creating Multiple Items in a Smart Way." If you don't, go back and do it. Next, make the block drop the dust using the `getItemDropped` method. This code should look similar to the following:

```
public Item getItemDropped(int meta, Random rand, int fortune)
{
        return SamsMod.samdust;
}
```

Creating Multiple Blocks in a Smart Way

What You'll Learn in This Hour:

▶ Adding metadata to blocks
▶ Adding block textures

In this hour, you build upon what you learned in Hour 5, "Creating Multiple Items in a Smart Way," as well as Hour 9, "Making Your First Block." Hour 5 covered metadata for items, which is quite similar to metadata for blocks. For an explanation of what metadata is, read through the information given in Hour 5. In Hour 9, you learned how to create a basic block. In this hour, you learn how to add multiple blocks using metadata.

Adding Metadata to Blocks

The basic structure of a metadata block is very similar to that of a normal block. Because of this, the Sam's Stone created in Hour 9 will be changed in such a way that the first metadata is an ore and the second is a decorative block. The ore will be added to the world generation in Hour 13, "Generating Ores."

One very important thing to note when working with metadata is that every metadata of the same block will have the same material. Therefore, it could be important to plan which blocks will be grouped up in metadata. Thankfully, the decorative metadata block also has to be stone, so both can be in the same metadata block.

When you add metadata to an already existing block, you must add quite a bit of code. However, before you start adding code, you must remove an important line of code. That line is the setBlockTextureName. You will replace this with a different code.

Improving the Creative Menu and Registry

In addition to the new texture code, which you add in a short while, you need to add only one new method to your block class. The method looks like Listing 10.1.

LISTING 10.1 The New Method

```
@SuppressWarnings({ "unchecked", "rawtypes" })
@SideOnly(Side.CLIENT)
@Override
public void getSubBlocks(Item par1, CreativeTabs par2CreativeTabs, List par3List)
{
        for (int var4 = 0; var4 < 2; ++var4)
        {
                par3List.add(new ItemStack(par1, 1, var4));
        }
}
```

This code loops through each metadata of the block and adds it to the Creative menu. The most important part of the code in here is var4 < 2. This makes sure that the first two metadatas, which are 0 and 1, are added to the Creative menu. If you add a third metadata, you must change the 2 to 3 to make sure the third metadata will be shown on the menu as well.

NOTE

Metadata in the Creative Menu

getSubBlocks is the method that adds your metadata to the menu, but this method isn't required. If you don't have this method, it only displays the block with metadata 0, which is preferable in certain cases.

Next, you edit the GameRegistry line in the SamsMod class for the block. A normal block registry looks like the following:

```
GameRegistry.registerBlock(samStone, "SamStone");
```

For metadata blocks, it should look like this:

```
GameRegistry.registerBlock(samStone, ItemSamStone.class, "SamStone");
```

Between the first and the second parameter of the original GameRegistry line, a new parameter must be added. This parameter is a new Item class, which you create next. This file holds the unlocalized names of the blocks as well as makes sure Minecraft handles them as metadata blocks.

Creating the ItemBlock Class

To create the new file, simply hover your mouse over the error under it and select Create Class. Once the class is created, make it extend the ItemBlock class. Don't forget to import it or it gives you an error. When it is imported, you get an error telling you it requires a constructor with a `Block` parameter, which you should then add. At this point, you should have a file that looks like Listing 10.2.

LISTING 10.2   The `ItemSamStone` Class

```
package com.wuppy.samsmod;

import net.minecraft.block.Block;
import net.minecraft.item.ItemBlock;

public class ItemSamStone extends ItemBlock
{
        public ItemSamStone(Block block)
        {
                super(block);
        }
}
```

As mentioned, this class takes care of the metadata as well as the names for the block. This means you must add code to actually make that happen. The first piece of code required makes sure Minecraft knows it is working with metadata. The code for that is `setHasSubTypes`. This method takes a single parameter which is a `boolean`. A `boolean` can be either `true` or `false`. Because the block will have subtypes, this parameter must be the word `true`.

Now, add two methods to this class. The first method makes sure that when you break the block, it drops the correct metadata. That method looks like the following:

```
@Override
public int getMetadata(int par1)
{
    return par1;
}
```

This method might seem strange. It returns what it gets without changing it. However, if you don't have this method, it always returns zero, which messes up the drops of the metadata blocks.

The second method makes sure the unlocalized names are different for each block. The method that you must overwrite for this is called `getUnlocalizedName`. For the `SamStone`, it should look like the following:

```
@Override
public String getUnlocalizedName(ItemStack itemstack)
{
        String name = "";
        switch(itemstack.getItemDamage())
        {
```

```
case 0:
        name = "ore";
        break;
case 1:
        name = "wall";
        break;
default:
        System.out.println("Invalid metadata for Block SamStone");
        name = "broken";
        break;
}
return getUnlocalizedName() + "." + name;
}
```

Because this method overwrites another method, the @Override annotation is useful to add because it tells you when your method isn't overwriting it anymore when the name changes. This method has a single ItemStack parameter, which contains the block that needs to be named. In the method, a switch is made for all of the metadatas in the block. Metadata 0 is an ore and metadata 1 is a wall block. If, for whatever reason, a block with a higher metadata exists, something is wrong, in which case it tells the programmer by writing a line to the console.

Once it has the name of the specific block, it gets the standard name, using getUnlocalizedName, then a dot, and, finally, the metadata-specific name.

The whole ItemSamStone class should now look like Listing 10.3.

LISTING 10.3   The Finished ItemSamStone Class

```
package com.wuppy.samsmod;

import net.minecraft.block.Block;
import net.minecraft.item.ItemBlock;
import net.minecraft.item.ItemStack;

public class ItemSamStone extends ItemBlock
{
        public ItemSamStone(Block block)
        {
                super(block);
                setHasSubtypes(true);
        }

        @Override
        public String getUnlocalizedName(ItemStack itemstack)
        {
                String name = "";
                switch(itemstack.getItemDamage())
```

```
          {
          case 0:
                  name = "ore";
                  break;
          case 1:
                  name = "wall";
                  break;
          default:
                  System.out.println("Invalid metadata for Block SamStone");
                  name = "broken";
                  break;
          }
          return getUnlocalizedName() + "." + name;
     }


     @Override
     public int getMetadata(int par1)
     {
          return par1;
     }
}
```

Because the getUnlocalizedName method has changed, the localizations in the .lang files should be changed as well. For the first metadata block, you should add .ore between samstone and .name. Follow the same naming rules for the second metadata block, making both lines look like the following code snippet:

```
tile.wuppy29_samsmod_samstone.ore.name=Sam's Stone
tile.wuppy29_samsmod_samstone.wall.name=Sam's Wall
```

If you launch the game now, you will notice that there are two blocks in the Block menu. They do have the correct names, but the textures are black and purple squares. To fix this, you must add a few lines of code to the BlockSamStone class. Additionally, you need to create a second texture and change the names of the textures.

Adding Block Textures

As mentioned, you must do quite a few things to make multiple textures work. First, you must add new code for the removed setBlockTextureName line. To do this, you need an IIcon array, which stores the images of the blocks. One problem with IIcon is that it only exists on the client because the server doesn't work with rendering things and, therefore, doesn't require the image of a block. To make sure the variable is only created when the class is read in client mode, you must add the `@SideOnly(Side.CLIENT)` piece of code from the `getSubBlocks` method as well. With the annotation, the variable should look like the following:

```
@SideOnly(Side.CLIENT)
private IIcon[] icons;
```

This `IIcon` array has to be filled with icons during initialization. To do this, you can use a method called `registerBlockIcons`. For the `SamStone` block, it will look like the following code. One important thing to note is that if the textures don't exist, this code will likely crash.

```
@Override
@SideOnly(Side.CLIENT)
public void registerBlockIcons(IIconRegister par1IconRegister)
{
        icons = new IIcon[2];

        for (int i = 0; i < icons.length; i++)
        {
                icons[i] = par1IconRegister.registerIcon(SamsMod.MODID + ":" +
➥"samstone" + i);
        }
}
```

This is again a method that only exists on the client, so it's important to have the `@SideOnly` line above it. Additionally, this overwrites a method in `Block`, so an `@Override` annotation is also suggested, although not required.

The code in this method starts by initializing the `IIcon` array to a size of 2. If you want to add an extra texture to a new metadata block, this number should be increased. Once it has made the array, it loops through each value in it and registers an icon to it. The `String` that has to be added in `registerIcon` is the `MODID` followed by a colon. This ensures the texture is taken from the correct folder. The second part of the `String` is the name of the texture. Usually, the texture for a metadata block is the name of the block followed by the texture index for the block. In this case, the first block, Sam's Ore, tries to get the texture `samstone0`, where *samstone* is the name. The second block gets the texture `samstone1`.

In addition to registering the icons, it's also important to use them. The method for this is called `getIcons` and is really simple for basic metadata blocks. The method is shown in the following code snippet:

```
@Override
@SideOnly(Side.CLIENT)
public IIcon getIcon(int par1, int par2)
{
        return icons[par2];
}
```

If the textures are not present or if you add a metadata without increasing the icon's size, this code will crash.

The second parameter is the metadata. Because of the way the icon's array is set up, this number can directly be used to return the correct IIcon.

The whole BlockSamStone class should look like Listing 10.4.

LISTING 10.4   The Finished BlockSamStone

```java
package com.wuppy.samsmod;

import java.util.List;

import net.minecraft.block.Block;
import net.minecraft.block.material.Material;
import net.minecraft.client.renderer.texture.IIconRegister;
import net.minecraft.creativetab.CreativeTabs;
import net.minecraft.item.Item;
import net.minecraft.item.ItemStack;
import net.minecraft.util.IIcon;
import cpw.mods.fml.relauncher.Side;
import cpw.mods.fml.relauncher.SideOnly;

public class BlockSamStone extends Block
{
        String name = "samstone";

        @SideOnly(Side.CLIENT)
        private IIcon[] icons;

        public BlockSamStone()
        {
                super(Material.rock);
                setBlockName(SamsMod.MODID + "_" + name);
                setCreativeTab(CreativeTabs.tabBlock);
                setHardness(2F);
                setResistance(5F);
                setStepSound(soundTypeStone);
                setHarvestLevel("pickaxe", 2);
        }

        @Override
        @SideOnly(Side.CLIENT)
        public void registerBlockIcons(IIconRegister par1IconRegister)
        {
                icons = new IIcon[2];
```

```
            for (int i = 0; i < icons.length; i++)
            {
                    icons[i] = par1IconRegister.registerIcon(SamsMod.MODID +
➡":" + "samstone" + i);
            }
    }

    @Override
    @SideOnly(Side.CLIENT)
    public IIcon getIcon(int par1, int par2)
    {
            return icons[par2];
    }

    @SuppressWarnings({ "unchecked", "rawtypes" })
    @SideOnly(Side.CLIENT)
    @Override
    public void getSubBlocks(Item par1, CreativeTabs par2CreativeTabs,
➡List par3List)
    {
            for (int var4 = 0; var4 < 2; ++var4)
            {
                    par3List.add(new ItemStack(par1, 1, var4));
            }
    }
}
```

Finally, you must add the actual textures. The first texture is already there and is currently named samstone. This is the texture of metadata 0 and, therefore, it has to be renamed to samstone0 when using metadata blocks. Figure 10.1 shows the texture for metadata 1, which is Sam's Wall.

FIGURE 10.1
The Sam's Wall texture.

Figure 10.1 will be stored as samstone1 in the blocks folder. When you have added these files and followed the code correctly, you will see two blocks with the correct names and textures in the block's Creative tab.

Add a Third Metadata Block

Add a third metadata to `SamStone`. To do this, update the `ItemBlock` file to contain a third unlocalized name and extend the `IIcon` array in the block. Don't forget to add it to the Creative menu by increasing the number in `getSubBlocks`.

The Sam's Wall block looks like Figure 10.2 in the game.

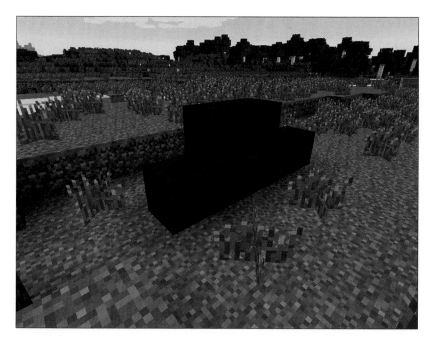

FIGURE 10.2
The new block in the game.

You might notice that the top of the block has a different texture than the sides. You learn how to do this in Hour 11, "Making Your Blocks Unique."

Summary

In this hour, you learned about metadata blocks. You learned that for a metadata block, an `ItemBlock` class is required. This `ItemBlock` class handles most of the metadata work for the block because it contains the unlocalized names as well as enables subtypes, which is required for metadata. Additionally, you learned how to add multiple textures to a single block. Each metadata gets a single texture. In Hour 11, you learn how to use this code to give different textures to sides of the block.

Q&A

Q. Is there a maximum amount of metadata a single block can have?

A. Yes, for blocks you can't have more than 16 metadatas.

Q. Is there a way to add more blocks under the same block?

A. Yes. You can add a close-to-infinite amount of blocks using Named Binary Tag (NBT), which is slightly more complicated and is not extensively covered in this book. For information about NBT, read the following website: http://minecraft.gamepedia.com/NBT_format

Q. Can different metadatas be on different Creative tabs?

A. No, just like the material, this is the same for all of the subblocks.

Workshop

Metadata is something you will use frequently when working with blocks because the amount of blocks in Minecraft is limited. Therefore, it's important to fully understand them.

Quiz

1. What would happen without the `ItemBlock` file?

2. Why would you add a crashable option in your code?

Answers

1. The block would work the same, but if you tried placing the block, it wouldn't work. There are some other issues that could appear, such as placement with the wrong metadata.

2. Sometimes it's better for a program to crash than to work with something that is actually broken.

Exercises

Edit the `BlockSamStone` class in such a way it can be used for multiple different blocks with metadata. You can do this by adding the unlocalized name as well as the metadata number in the constructor.

HOUR 11
Making Your Blocks Unique

What You'll Learn in This Hour:

▶ Adding sided textures

▶ Making half blocks

▶ Creating a plant

In this hour, you use what you learned in the two previous hours about blocks to create some interesting blocks. It's nice to know how to make blocks, but without custom ones, the mod wouldn't be very interesting to use. This hour covers a few reasonably commonly used block types and settings, with which you can do a lot of interesting things. These include plants, sided textures, and not completely solid blocks.

Adding Sided Textures

To add different textures to different sides of a block, you need texture code very similar to metadata blocks. You won't use setBlockTextureName, but an IIcon array along with the registerBlockIcons and getIcon methods to provide the textures for your block. This book shows you how to change the metadata texture code from BlockSamStone to let one of the metadatas have a second texture. The important texture-related code should look similar to Listing 11.1.

LISTING 11.1 Texture Code in `BlockSamStone`

```
@SideOnly(Side.CLIENT)
private IIcon[] icons;

@Override
@SideOnly(Side.CLIENT)
public void registerBlockIcons(IIconRegister par1IconRegister)
{
        icons = new IIcon[2];
```

```
        for (int i = 0; i < icons.length; i++)
        {
                icons[i] = par1IconRegister.registerIcon(SamsMod.MODID + ":" +
➥"samstone" + i);
        }
}

@Override
@SideOnly(Side.CLIENT)
public IIcon getIcon(int par1, int par2)
{
        return icons[par2];
}
```

If any of this code isn't clear to you, reread Hour 10, "Creating Multiple Blocks in a Smart Way," which explains all of the code in here.

The texture that is added looks like Figure 11.1. It is placed on the top and bottom of Sam's Wall, which is the second block.

FIGURE 11.1
Sam's Wall secondary texture.

Figure 11.1 displays samstone2.png because it is the third texture used in BlockSamStone. If you want to add a third metadata with a custom texture, the image for that should be called samstone3.png.

Because an extra image is now added, it also has to be registered in the BlockSamStone class. Doing this is really simple. In the registerIcons method, the size of the IIcon array has to be increased from 2 into 3, which automatically loads the samstone2.png image, which has just been added.

Next, the getIcon method has to be edited in such a way that it first checks the metadata and then for each metadata selects the right texture based on the side. As mentioned in Hour 10, the second parameter of getIcon is the metadata. The first is the side of the block. The new code for getIcon should look like Listing 11.2.

LISTING 11.2   `getIcon` with the New Texture

```
@Override
@SideOnly(Side.CLIENT)
public IIcon getIcon(int par1, int par2)
{
        switch(par2)
        {
        case 0:
                return icons[0];
        case 1:
                if(ForgeDirection.getOrientation(par1) == ForgeDirection.UP ||
ForgeDirection.getOrientation(par1) == ForgeDirection.DOWN)
                        return icons[2];
                else
                        return icons[1];
        default:
                System.out.println("Problems with getting the icon for
BlockSamStone");
                return null;
        }
}
```

First, a switch is made for the metadata, par2. If it is metadata 0, meaning the ore, texture zero will be selected. Otherwise, it's likely metadata 1. In this case, an `if` and `else` statement are required to check for the sides.

`ForgeDirection` is a class made by Forge to easily get the sides of a block. The method `getOrientation` takes an integer and turns it into `ForgeDirection`, which is much easier to read. Top and bottom textures in Minecraft are 0 and 1, but with `ForgeDirection` you don't have to remember those numbers. Instead, you can easily turn them into sides.

If the side is either the top or the bottom, the third texture is applied to the block. If it's neither of those, the second texture is used.

When the metadata isn't 0 or 1, something is wrong and it should be fixed. Therefore, a message is printed out for the programmer, you, to read, and null is returned, which will likely cause crashes.

Right now, the block should look like Figure 11.2.

FIGURE 11.2
The block in the game.

Making Half Blocks

You now learn how to make a half block. These blocks are not in the final version of Sam's Mod, but they are commonly used in mods, so it is important to know.

To make sure a block isn't a 1×1×1 square, you need a single line of code in the constructor along with one method to make sure the blocks around it look good as well.

The line of code you have to add to the constructor is as follows:

```
this.setBlockBounds(0.0F, 0.0F, 0.0F, 1.0F, 0.5F, 1.0F);
```

This method contains six float values. The first three are the x, y, and z values of the starting position and the last three are the x, y, and z of the ending position. The starting position is the bottom corner with the lowest x and z value, and the ending position is at the top with the highest x and z value of the block.

In this case, the width and depth are the complete block, but the height is only half. These numbers can obviously change to make blocks of different shapes.

Create Different Shapes

Try to create a few differently shaped blocks, such as the following:

▶ A block that's only half the size of a normal block in width, height, and depth

▶ A quarter block

▶ A half block suspended in the air

If you start the game and place this block next to any other block, you will notice that the block becomes blue and that you can look through it into the world. This is obviously not something you want, so you add a method to prevent this from happening. The method for that is as follows:

```
@Override
public boolean isOpaqueCube()
{
    return false;
}
```

When you restart the game and place this block against another block, you will notice that it looks normal again.

NOTE

Other Shapes

As you might have noticed already, you can only have square-shaped blocks using `setBlockBounds`. However, there are blocks in the game that aren't squares. These blocks aren't made using `setBlockBounds`, but with an `ISimpleBlockRenderingHandler`, which is a class in Forge made for custom rendering. An example of an `ISimpleBlockRenderingHandler` can be found in Appendix A, "Additional Code Fragments."

With this new code, `BlockSamStone` should look similar to Listing 11.3.

LISTING 11.3 `BlockSamStone` as Half Blocks

```
package com.wuppy.samsmod;

import java.util.List;

import net.minecraft.block.Block;
import net.minecraft.block.material.Material;
```

```
import net.minecraft.client.renderer.texture.IIconRegister;
import net.minecraft.creativetab.CreativeTabs;
import net.minecraft.item.Item;
import net.minecraft.item.ItemStack;
import net.minecraft.util.Facing;
import net.minecraft.util.IIcon;
import net.minecraft.world.IBlockAccess;
import net.minecraftforge.common.util.ForgeDirection;
import cpw.mods.fml.relauncher.Side;
import cpw.mods.fml.relauncher.SideOnly;

public class BlockSamStone extends Block
{
        String name = "samstone";

        @SideOnly(Side.CLIENT)
        private IIcon[] icons;

        public BlockSamStone()
        {
                super(Material.rock);
                setBlockName(SamsMod.MODID + "_" + name);
                setCreativeTab(CreativeTabs.tabBlock);
                setHardness(2F);
                setResistance(5F);
                setStepSound(soundTypeStone);
                setHarvestLevel("pickaxe", 2);

                this.setBlockBounds(0.0F, 0.0F, 0.0F, 1.0F, 0.5F, 1.0F);
        }

        @Override
        public boolean isOpaqueCube()
        {
            return false;
        }

        @Override
        @SideOnly(Side.CLIENT)
        public void registerBlockIcons(IIconRegister par1IconRegister)
        {
                icons = new IIcon[3];
```

```
                for (int i = 0; i < icons.length; i++)
                {
                        icons[i] = par1IconRegister.registerIcon(SamsMod.MODID +
➥":" + "samstone" + i);
                }
        }


        @Override
        @SideOnly(Side.CLIENT)
        public IIcon getIcon(int par1, int par2)
        {
                switch(par2)
                {
                case 0:
                        return icons[0];
                case 1:
                        if(ForgeDirection.getOrientation(par1) ==
➥ForgeDirection.UP || ForgeDirection.getOrientation(par1) == ForgeDirection.DOWN)
                                return icons[2];
                        else
                                return icons[1];
                default:
                        System.out.println("Problems with getting the icon
➥for BlockSamStone");
                        return null;
                }
        }


        @SuppressWarnings({ "unchecked", "rawtypes" })
        @SideOnly(Side.CLIENT)
        @Override
        public void getSubBlocks(Item par1, CreativeTabs par2CreativeTabs,
➥List par3List)
        {
                for (int var4 = 0; var4 < 2; ++var4)
                {
                        par3List.add(new ItemStack(par1, 1, var4));
                }
        }
}
```

▼ TRY IT YOURSELF

Block Bounds Based on Metadata

Use the method `setBlockBoundsBasedOnState` to make sure only the second metadata block has the half block shape. To do this, you don't need the line of code in the constructor. Instead, you combine it with the `IBlockAccess` variable to find the metadata and use the `setBlockBounds` in there.

An example of the code where only the second metadata is a half block is as follows:

```
public void setBlockBoundsBasedOnState(IBlockAccess world, int x, int y, int z)
{
        if(world.getBlockMetadata(x, y, z) == 1)
        {
                setBlockBounds(0F, 0F, 0F, 1F, 0.5F, 1F);
        }
}
```

The `setBlockBounds` line in the constructor has to be removed.

Creating a Plant

The next unique kind of block you might want to add to your mod is a plant. Plants are metadata blocks, but they require quite a lot of special code.

Coding the Basics

To add a plant, you need to combine most of the information you know up to this point. However, just like any other block, you add it to your mod class with code similar to this:

```
public static Block samPlant;
```

Add the following code in the `preInit` method:

```
samPlant = new BlockSamPlant();

GameRegistry.registerBlock(samPlant, "SamPlant");
```

Additionally, the start of the `BlockSamPlant` class is similar to the standard blocks as well. You need to add a constructor, add a `super` with the `Material`, set the unlocalized name, and so forth. After adding this basic code, the `BlockSamPlant` class should look like Listing 11.4.

LISTING 11.4 The Basics in `BlockSamPlant`

```
package com.wuppy.samsmod;

import net.minecraft.block.Block;
import net.minecraft.block.material.Material;
import net.minecraft.creativetab.CreativeTabs;

public class BlockSamPlant extends Block
{
        public BlockSamPlant()
        {
                super(Material.plants);
                setBlockName(SamsMod.MODID + "_" + "samplant");
                setCreativeTab((CreativeTabs)null);
                setHardness(0.0F);
                setBlockBounds(0F, 0.0F, 0F, 1F, 0.25F, 1F);
                setStepSound(soundTypeGrass);
        }
}
```

Note that `BlockSamPlant` doesn't have a `setBlockTextureName` line. That is because a plant generally has multiple different textures, which means you have to use the alternative way of registering the texture.

Another interesting line of code in this file is the `setCreativeTab` method. This line simply makes sure the `BlockSamPlant` doesn't show up in the Creative menu at all.

Two lines of code are aimed to make it more plantlike—the hardness, which makes this plant instantly breakable, and the shape, which is the same as vanilla wheat.

Additionally, a localization has been added to the `lang` file as follows:

```
tile.wuppy29_samsmod_samplant.name=Sam's Plant
```

Now, add the multiple-icon-related code, which should look like Listing 11.5.

LISTING 11.5 Icon Code for `BlockSamPlant`

```
@SideOnly(Side.CLIENT)
private IIcon[] icons;

@Override
@SideOnly(Side.CLIENT)
public void registerBlockIcons(IIconRegister par1IconRegister)
{
        icons = new IIcon[3];
```

```
        for (int i = 0; i < icons.length; i++)
        {
                icons[i] = par1IconRegister.registerIcon(SamsMod.MODID + ":" +
➥"samplant" + i);
        }
}


@Override
@SideOnly(Side.CLIENT)
public IIcon getIcon(int par1, int par2)
{
        if(par2 < 0 || par2 >= 3)
        {
                System.out.println("Something is wrong with the metadata
➥for BlockSamPlant!");
                return icons[0];
        }
        else
                return icons[par2];
}
```

BlockSamPlant has three stages, which means the IIcon array has three images at the indexes 0, 1, and 2. Textures for this also have to be made. For BlockSamPlant, they look like Figures 11.3, 11.4, and 11.5.

FIGURE 11.3
First growth stage of BlockSamPlant.

FIGURE 11.4
Second growth stage of BlockSamPlant.

FIGURE 11.5
Third growth stage of `BlockSamPlant`.

In the `getIcon` method, the metadata of the block is checked. If it is for some reason below zero or above or equal to three, it is set to the first image, because either number is illegal. If it isn't an unusual number, it simply returns the image based on the metadata.

Even though a crop has metadata, it is generally not required to make an `ItemBlock` class for it because you won't be working with picking up and placing the different metadatas. Instead, most plants work with a seed.

Making It a Crop

There are several methods that you need to add to the `BlockSamPlant` class before it is fully functional as a crop.

Making It Look Like a Crop

The following method makes sure that the new block looks like a crop:

```
@Override
public int getRenderType()
{
    return 6;
}
```

There are other render types, which can be found by looking through custom-rendered blocks.

Making Sure the Game Knows It's a Plant

Now it's time to actually make sure `BlockSamPlant` is recognized and works as a crop. To do that, change the extended class from `Block` into `BlockBush`. The class also has to implement `IGrowable`, making the class line look like this:

```
public class BlockSamPlant extends BlockBush implements IGrowable
```

When you add this code, you will likely get some errors. First, you have to import the `BlockBush` and `IGrowable` classes. Once you have done that, it asks you to add a few methods, which look like this:

```
@Override
public boolean func_149851_a(World var1, int var2, int var3, int var4,
➡boolean var5) {
    // TODO Auto-generated method stub
    return false;
}


@Override
public boolean func_149852_a(World var1, Random var2, int var3, int var4,
➡int var5) {
    // TODO Auto-generated method stub
    return false;
}


@Override
public void func_149853_b(World var1, Random var2, int var3, int var4,
➡int var5) {
    // TODO Auto-generated method stub

}
```

Unfortunately, these methods aren't localized yet and, therefore, they have the unclear `func` names.

First, `func_149851_a` has to be coded. This is a method that checks if it is possible for bonemeal to be applied. In the case of the crop, bonemeal is allowed to be used as long as the metadata isn't at the top level or higher, which is 2. The method should look like this:

```
@Override
public boolean func_149851_a(World world, int x, int y, int z, boolean var5)
{
    return world.getBlockMetadata(x, y, z) != 2;
}
```

If this function is passed when applying bonemeal, the next function is checked, which is `func_149852_a`. This method should contain a random chance for the bonemeal to succeed. If you want the bonemeal to always work, simply return `true` always. Otherwise, a simple random number can be created using the `rand` variable in the method. For this plant, it looks like the following:

```
@Override
public boolean func_149852_a(World world, Random rand, int x, int y, int z)
{
    return true;
}
```

After running both of these checks, it is time to actually code what should happen when the bonemeal is applied. You do this in the `func_149853_b` method. For `BlockSamPlant` bonemeal, simply increase the growth stage by one. In that case, the method is as follows:

```
@Override
public void func_149853_b(World world, Random rand, int x, int y, int z)
{
        int next = world.getBlockMetadata(x, y, z) + 1;


        if(next > 2)
                next = 2;


        world.setBlockMetadataWithNotify(x, y, z, next, 2);
}
```

In the `func_149853_b` method, the metadata is retrieved and increased. Even though you checked for the metadata in an earlier method, it's wise to do it again here in case some other mod uses the same methods to make a different plant-growing material, which can happen, and doesn't use the metadata check method correctly. Then, the metadata is set using `setBlockMetadataWithNotify`. This method makes sure the metadata of an existing block is changed. In the `setBlockMetadataWithNotify` line, the location as well as the new metadata is used. However, there is an extra number, which is 2. This number should basically always be 2 to make sure the client knows the block is actually there.

TRY IT YOURSELF ▼

Make a Random Plant

Make a more random plant for bonemeal. Make bonemeal only work once every three times. However, when it does, make it add between 0 and 2 to the metadata.

The code for that should look like this:

```
@Override
public boolean func_149852_a(World world, Random rand, int x, int y, int z)
{
        if(rand.nextInt(3) == 0)
                return true;
        else
                return false;
}
```

```
@Override
public void func_149853_b(World world, Random rand, int x, int y, int z)
{
        int next = world.getBlockMetadata(x, y, z) + rand.nextInt(3);

        if(next > 2)
                next = 2;


        world.setBlockMetadataWithNotify(x, y, z, next, 2);
}
```

Natural Growing

Next is a very important method. This method makes sure that the plant grows without bonemeal. The method is called `updateTick` and handles the growing of the block. For BlockSamPlant, the code should look as follows:

```
public void updateTick(World world, int x, int y, int z, Random rand)
{
    super.updateTick(world, x, y, z, rand);

    if (world.getBlockLightValue(x, y + 1, z) >= 9)
    {
        int l = world.getBlockMetadata(x, y, z);

        if (l < 2)
        {
            if (rand.nextInt(5) == 0)
            {
                ++l;
                world.setBlockMetadataWithNotify(x, y, z, l, 2);
            }
        }
    }
}
```

Simply put, this code makes sure the metadata is only improved when it is in the right situation.

First, you have to call the `super` to make sure the normal tick code in Minecraft is run. If you skip this line, you will likely encounter an error.

Once the normal code is run, check the light value. Most plants only grow in the daylight and so does this one. Minecraft has light values ranging from 0 to 14, where 0 is completely dark and 14 is the brightest light. A value of 9 ensures that it's day.

Now you know that the block is in the right light, but before increasing the metadata, it's important that the metadata doesn't go higher than the registered icons. If that happens, Minecraft will likely crash.

There is one check left, which is a random check. In this case, it makes sure it only grows once every five updates.

All the checks are done and the metadata is increased. Then `setBlockMetadataWithNotify` is called. This changes the metadata and synchronizes the server with the client to make sure both of them know it has changed. The last number in here should always be 2.

Adding a Seed

Now that you have a working plant, it would be nice to have a way to actually get them. For the `BlockSamPlant`, this is done in two ways: first, with a seed, and second, with world generation of the plants themselves. Hour 14, "Generating Plants," explains how to do the generation.

To add a seed item, you add the basic code you need for every item to the mod file. However, the constructor of the seed item does have to be different. Also note that the following code has an error.

Add the following code to the class:

```
public static Item samseed;
```

This is the required code for the `preInit` method:

```
samseed = new ItemSamSeed(samPlant);

GameRegistry.registerItem(samseed, "SamSeed");
```

You should be familiar with all of the code in here. An `Item` object is created, after which it is set to `ItemSamSeed`, which will be created shortly, and then the item is registered. The only extra piece of code is that the parameter of the `ItemSamSeed` is `samPlant`. This parameter should always be the plant, which should be planted by the seed.

Now to fix the error under the `ItemSamPlant`, the class must be created, which you can easily do by hovering your mouse over the error and clicking Create Class. The standard class should look like Listing 11.6.

LISTING 11.6   The Standard `ItemSamPlant` Class

```
package com.wuppy.samsmod;

import net.minecraft.item.Item;

public class ItemSamSeed extends Item {

}
```

In this class, you add several methods. Just like any other item or block, you start with a constructor. This constructor has a single parameter, which is a `Block`. It looks like this at this point:

```
public ItemSamSeed(Block plant)
{
}
```

Next, you create two private variables. One is a `Block`, called `plant`. The other has to be a `String`, which contains the name of the seed. Only the `String` has to be initialized there. The name is "samseed". Next, both of the variables have to be used. For the `Block` variable, this means setting it equal to the `plant` parameter of the constructor. For the name, this means setting the unlocalized and texture names. The constructor with the variables should look like Listing 11.7.

LISTING 11.7   `ItemSamPlant`'s Constructor

```
private Block plant;

private String name = "samseed";

public ItemSamSeed(Block plant)
{
        this.plant = plant;
        setUnlocalizedName(SamsMod.MODID + "_" + name);
        setTextureName(SamsMod.MODID + ":" + name);
        setCreativeTab(CreativeTabs.tabMaterials);
}
```

The code related to the name is very similar to any other item. It simply sets the unlocalized and texture names like any other item. The only possibly weird line of code is `this.plant = plant`. It might seem like the variable is being set to itself, but it's actually setting the plant in the class to the plant in the parameter. Whenever you preface a piece of code, whether that is a variable or a method, it tries to find it in the class and not in the method itself. In this case, it finds the plant variable of the class.

One extra line of code is the `setCreativeTab` line, although you should understand that by now. Because the unlocalized name and texture name have been set now, a localization and a texture are needed. The localization for the `ItemSamSeed` looks like this:

```
item.wuppy29_samsmod_samseed.name=Sam's Seed
```

The texture looks like Figure 11.6 and is saved as `samseed.png`.

FIGURE 11.6
The Sam's Seed texture.

Now the basic code for the Sam's Seed item is done. Next, it's important to make sure it's actually a seed. You do this by making it implement `IPlantable`. When you add the `extends IPlantable` code to the class line, it first gives you an error under it telling you it should be imported. Import this file and you get an error under the class name. To fix this one, add the unimplemented methods. When you do that, code is added that should look similar to this:

```java
@Override
public EnumPlantType getPlantType(IBlockAccess world, int x, int y, int z) {
    // TODO Auto-generated method stub
    return null;
}

@Override
public Block getPlant(IBlockAccess world, int x, int y, int z) {
    // TODO Auto-generated method stub
    return null;
}

@Override
public int getPlantMetadata(IBlockAccess world, int x, int y, int z) {
    // TODO Auto-generated method stub
    return 0;
}
```

All of these methods are really easy to fill in. The first method, `getPlantType`, requires you to return an `EnumPlantType` to make sure Java knows which kind of plant is being added. In the case of Sam's Seed, this method looks like this:

```
@Override
public EnumPlantType getPlantType(IBlockAccess world, int x, int y, int z)
{
        return EnumPlantType.Crop;
}
```

To find other plant types, go to the `EnumPlantType` class and select the one that best fits the plant you are creating.

The `getPlant` method decides which plant will be placed when the seed is used and `getPlantMetadata` sets the metadata of the plant on placement. Both of the methods should look like this for Sam's Seed:

```
@Override
public Block getPlant(IBlockAccess world, int x, int y, int z)
{
        return plant;
}
```

```
@Override
public int getPlantMetadata(IBlockAccess world, int x, int y, int z)
{
        return 0;
}
```

None of these methods is directly used for the plant, but it's likely that certain mods use it for seed planters, so, therefore, it's important to add this code.

Now it's time to make the seed actually plant something when it is right-clicked. The method for that looks like this:

```
public boolean onItemUse(ItemStack par1ItemStack, EntityPlayer
➥par2EntityPlayer, World par3World, int par4, int par5, int par6, int par7, float
➥par8, float par9, float par10)
{
    if (par7 != 1)
    {
        return false;
    }
    else if (par2EntityPlayer.canPlayerEdit(par4, par5, par6, par7,
➥par1ItemStack) && par2EntityPlayer.canPlayerEdit(par4, par5 +
➥1, par6, par7, par1ItemStack))
    {
        if(par3World.getBlock(par4, par5, par6) == Blocks.dirt ||
➥par3World.getBlock(par4, par5, par6) == Blocks.grass)
        {
            if (par3World.isAirBlock(par4, par5 + 1, par6))
            {
```

```
                    par3World.setBlock(par4, par5 + 1, par6, this.plant);
                    --par1ItemStack.stackSize;
                    return true;
            }
            else
            {
                    return false;
            }
        }
        else
        {
            return false;
        }
    }
    else
    {
        return false;
    }
}
```

First, a check is made to make sure the player is clicking the top of the block. Because most plants can only be placed on top of a block, this is very important. If it is on any other side, nothing else is done.

Next, a check is made to make sure the block and the one above are allowed to be changed by the player. If so, it is checked if the block the plant will be placed on is allowed for the plant, which means it has to be dirt or grass. One more required check is if the location where the plant will be placed is air.

If all of these things are correct, the plant is placed and the seed stack decreased by one. Every other option returns `false` and doesn't do anything.

`ItemSamSeed` should look like Listing 11.8.

LISTING 11.8   Finished `ItemSamSeed`

```
package com.wuppy.samsmod;

import net.minecraft.block.Block;
import net.minecraft.creativetab.CreativeTabs;
import net.minecraft.entity.player.EntityPlayer;
import net.minecraft.init.Blocks;
import net.minecraft.item.Item;
import net.minecraft.item.ItemStack;
import net.minecraft.world.IBlockAccess;
import net.minecraft.world.World;
```

```
import net.minecraftforge.common.EnumPlantType;
import net.minecraftforge.common.IPlantable;

public class ItemSamSeed extends Item implements IPlantable
{
        private Block plant;

        private String name = "samseed";

        public ItemSamSeed(Block plant)
        {
                this.plant = plant;
                setUnlocalizedName(SamsMod.MODID + "_" + name);
                setTextureName(SamsMod.MODID + ":" + name);
                setCreativeTab(CreativeTabs.tabMaterials);
        }

        public boolean onItemUse(ItemStack par1ItemStack, EntityPlayer
➥par2EntityPlayer, World par3World, int par4, int par5, int par6,
➥int par7, float par8, float par9, float par10)
        {
                if (par7 != 1)
                {
                    return false;
                }
                else if (par2EntityPlayer.canPlayerEdit(par4, par5, par6, par7,
➥par1ItemStack) && par2EntityPlayer.canPlayerEdit(par4, par5 + 1, par6,
➥par7, par1ItemStack))
                {
                        if(par3World.getBlock(par4, par5, par6) == Blocks.dirt ||
➥par3World.getBlock(par4, par5, par6) == Blocks.grass)
                        {
                            if (par3World.isAirBlock(par4, par5 + 1, par6))
                            {
                                    par3World.setBlock(par4, par5 + 1, par6,
➥this.plant);

                                    --par1ItemStack.stackSize;
                                    return true;
                            }
                            else
                            {
                                    return false;
                            }
                        }
                        else
                        {
```

```
                return false;
            }
        }
        else
        {
            return false;
        }
    }

    @Override
    public EnumPlantType getPlantType(IBlockAccess world, int x, int y, int z)
    {
        return EnumPlantType.Crop;
    }

    @Override
    public Block getPlant(IBlockAccess world, int x, int y, int z)
    {
        return plant;
    }

    @Override
    public int getPlantMetadata(IBlockAccess world, int x, int y, int z)
    {
        return 0;
    }
}
```

Customizing the Plant

Next, it would be nice to give the plant some customization to make it different from all the other existing plants. One of the methods you can add for that is canPlaceBlockOn. This method decides on which blocks this plant can grow. BlockSamPlant is able to grow on dirt and grass, so it would look like this:

```
protected boolean canPlaceBlockOn(Block block)
{
    if(block == Blocks.dirt || block == Blocks.grass)
        return true;
    else
        return false;
}
```

In this code, the Block parameter is the block the plant is placed on. This simply checks if it is dirt or grass and returns true, allowing the plant to be placed. Any other block returns false.

One other customization you might want to add to the plant is the dropping of items. You can add drops to a block in several ways. If there is only a single drop, do this by using `getItemDropped` and `getQuantity` dropped, which, respectively, require you to return an `Item` and an `int` to set the drops.

If you want to drop more than one thing, you do something a little different. First, you add this method:

```
public void dropBlockAsItemWithChance(World world, int par1, int par2,
➥int par3, int par4, float par5, int par6)
{
    super.dropBlockAsItemWithChance(world, par1, par2, par3, par4, par5, 0);
}
```

This makes sure a different method is called. That method is `getDrops`, which allows you to add multiple drops to a broken block.

For Sam's Plant, this looks like the following:

```
@Override
public ArrayList<ItemStack> getDrops(World world, int x, int y,
➥int z, int metadata, int fortune)
{
    ArrayList<ItemStack> ret = new ArrayList<ItemStack>();
    if (metadata >= 2)
    {
        for (int i = 0; i < 3 + fortune; ++i)
        {
            if (world.rand.nextInt(15) <= 7)
            {
                ret.add(new ItemStack(SamsMod.berry, 1, 0));
            }
        }
    }


    for(int i = 0; i < 1+ fortune; i++)
    {
        ret.add(new ItemStack(SamsMod.samseed, 1 + world.rand.nextInt(1
➥+ fortune), 0));
    }


    return ret;
}
```

This method checks if the plant is fully grown; if so, it goes through a `for` loop, which randomly adds a berry to the items that are being dropped. If the player is using an item with fortune to harvest, the drop chance is higher. The same thing happens for the seeds. However, there is no random. A seed always drops 1 plus the level of fortune.

The whole `BlockSamPlant` class should look like Listing 11.9.

LISTING 11.9   The Completed `BlockSamPlant`

```
package com.wuppy.samsmod;

import java.util.ArrayList;
import java.util.Random;

import net.minecraft.block.Block;
import net.minecraft.block.BlockBush;
import net.minecraft.block.IGrowable;
import net.minecraft.block.material.Material;
import net.minecraft.client.renderer.texture.IIconRegister;
import net.minecraft.creativetab.CreativeTabs;
import net.minecraft.init.Blocks;
import net.minecraft.init.Items;
import net.minecraft.item.Item;
import net.minecraft.item.ItemStack;
import net.minecraft.util.IIcon;
import net.minecraft.world.World;
import cpw.mods.fml.relauncher.Side;
import cpw.mods.fml.relauncher.SideOnly;

public class BlockSamPlant extends BlockBush implements IGrowable
{
        @SideOnly(Side.CLIENT)
        private IIcon[] icons;

        public BlockSamPlant()
        {
                super(Material.plants);
                setBlockName(SamsMod.MODID + "_" + "samplant");
                setCreativeTab((CreativeTabs)null);
                setHardness(0.0F);
                setBlockBounds(0F, 0.0F, 0F, 1F, 0.25F, 1F);
                setStepSound(soundTypeGrass);
        }

        @Override
        @SideOnly(Side.CLIENT)
        public void registerBlockIcons(IIconRegister par1IconRegister)
        {
                icons = new IIcon[3];
```

```
            for (int i = 0; i < icons.length; i++)
            {
                    icons[i] = par1IconRegister.registerIcon(SamsMod.MODID +
➡":" + "samplant" + i);
            }
    }

    @Override
    @SideOnly(Side.CLIENT)
    public IIcon getIcon(int par1, int par2)
    {
            if(par2 < 0 || par2 >= 3)
            {
                    System.out.println("Something is wrong with the metadata
➡for BlockSamPlant!");
                    return icons[0];
            }
            else
                    return icons[par2];
    }

    @Override
    public int getRenderType()
    {
            return 6;
    }

    public void updateTick(World world, int x, int y, int z, Random rand)
    {
            super.updateTick(world, x, y, z, rand);

            if (world.getBlockLightValue(x, y + 1, z) >= 9)
            {
                    int l = world.getBlockMetadata(x, y, z);

                    if (l < 2)
                    {
                            if (rand.nextInt(5) == 0)
                            {
                                    ++l;
                                    world.setBlockMetadataWithNotify(x, y, z, l, 2);
                            }
                    }
            }
    }

    protected boolean canPlaceBlockOn(Block block)
    {
```

```
            if(block == Blocks.dirt || block == Blocks.grass)
                    return true;
            else
                    return false;
    }


    public void dropBlockAsItemWithChance(World world, int par1,
➥int par2, int par3, int par4, float par5, int par6)
    {
            super.dropBlockAsItemWithChance(world, par1, par2, par3, par4,
➥par5, 0);
    }

    @Override
    public ArrayList<ItemStack> getDrops(World world, int x, int y,
➥int z, int metadata, int fortune)
    {
            ArrayList<ItemStack> ret = new ArrayList<ItemStack>();

            if (metadata >= 2)
            {
                for (int i = 0; i < 3 + fortune; ++i)
                {
                    if (world.rand.nextInt(15) <= 7)
                    {
                            ret.add(new ItemStack(SamsMod.berry, 1, 0));
                    }
                }
            }


            for(int i = 0; i < 1+ fortune; i++)
            {
            ret.add(new ItemStack(SamsMod.samseed, 1 +
➥world.rand.nextInt(1 + fortune), 0));
            }


            return ret;
    }

    @Override
    public boolean func_149851_a(World world, int x, int y, int z, boolean var5)
    {
            return world.getBlockMetadata(x, y, z) != 2;
    }
```

```
@Override
public boolean func_149852_a(World world, Random rand, int x, int y, int z)
{
        return true;
}


@Override
public void func_149853_b(World world, Random rand, int x, int y, int z)
{
        int next = world.getBlockMetadata(x, y, z) + 1;

        if(next > 2)
                next = 2;


        world.setBlockMetadataWithNotify(x, y, z, next, 2);
}
}
```

Figure 11.7 shows the plants in the game.

FIGURE 11.7
The plants in the game.

Figure 11.8 shows the seed item used to plant this plant in the game.

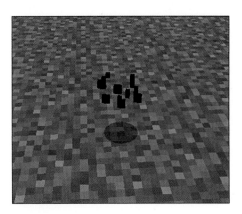

FIGURE 11.8
The seed in the game.

Summary

In this hour, you learned a lot about customizing blocks. First, you learned how to have different textures based on the sides of the block. After this, you made half blocks and otherwise-shaped blocks. Finally, you created your most difficult block yet, which is a plant. This plant only grows in the light and can only be placed on dirt or grass. It drops berries and seeds when it's broken.

Q&A

Q. **Is there a maximum amount of plants that can be added to the game?**

A. Plants are considered normal blocks, so the same maximum amount applies here.

Q. **Are there other customizations possible?**

A. Of course there are. Two ways to get to know how to customize your blocks are, first, to look in the `Block` class, in which interesting customization methods can be found. Alternatively, take a look at the code of an already existing vanilla block and see how it is coded there.

Workshop

In this hour, you learned how to create a lot of specific things for your blocks. It's important to know how to customize them because that is what makes your mod unique and interesting to use. Make sure you understand the customization by going through the following workshop.

Quiz

1. Why is an `ItemBlock` file not required for a crop?

2. How would you increase the growth speed of your crop?

Answers

1. Because the crop is always placed with a metadata of zero, the `ItemBlock` file isn't really required.

2. You can do this by editing the `updateTick` method.

Exercises

Edit the drops of the plant in such a way that it always drops a golden apple as well as all of the already existing items.

Listing 11.10 shows the code required to do that.

LISTING 11.10   Drops with a Golden Apple

```
@Override
public ArrayList<ItemStack> getDrops(World world, int x, int y, int z,
➥int metadata, int fortune)
{
    ArrayList<ItemStack> ret = new ArrayList<ItemStack>();

    if (metadata >= 2)
    {
        for (int i = 0; i < 3 + fortune; ++i)
        {
            if (world.rand.nextInt(15) <= 7)
            {
                ret.add(new ItemStack(SamsMod.berry, 1, 0));
            }
        }
    }
```

```
    for(int i = 0; i < 1+ fortune; i++)
    {
        ret.add(new ItemStack(SamsMod.samseed, 1 +
➥world.rand.nextInt(1 + fortune), 0));
    }


    ret.add(new ItemStack(Items.golden_apple, 1, 0));

    return ret;
}
```

Creating a Tile Entity

What You'll Learn in This Hour:

▶ Understanding what a tile entity is
▶ Creating a tile entity block
▶ Creating a tile entity
▶ Server synchronization

In this hour, you learn how to make a tile entity. Even though the name contains "Entity," a tile entity can be considered a block. First, you need to know exactly what a tile entity is because it is quite complex. Then after you know what a tile entity is, it's time to use one and create a basic one.

Understanding What a Tile Entity Is

A tile entity in Minecraft could be considered an entity, which has the same place as the block it is on. Tile entities can be used to store extra information about a block as well as open up interfaces, hold items, and many other things.

Tile entities can be considered one of the most difficult parts of Minecraft. If you don't count the generation of the world or the way everything is shown onto the screen, tile entities are the most complicated. Because they are complicated, they are also extremely customizable. You can do basically everything with a tile entity. Some examples of a tile entity are chests, dispensers, furnaces, and crafting tables. However, you can create endless other things with them as well. A lot of more complicated mods use them for some more interesting behaviors. An example could be a multiblock structure, where several blocks work together to do a single thing. Another example could be making pipes that transport liquids or energy.

One problem with all of these examples, as well as tile entities in general, is that they are far too complex and too specific to be properly explained. Because tile entities are so important and common, it's important to have a basic understanding. Although the complexity of a tile entity is beyond the scope of this book, this hour covers how to create the basic code for a tile entity.

The tile entity you create in this hour is a very simple one. The block has 10 textures. All of those textures are black with a white number from 0 to 9 on them. The tile entity updates the texture every second. Even though this might sound really simple, this task takes quite a lot of work.

Creating a Tile Entity Block

To create a block that is a tile entity, you first need a basic block. The code for the tile entity you create in this hour is as follows:

```
public static Block samTE;
```

In addition, add this code to the preInit method:

```
samTE = new BlockSamTE();
GameRegistry.registerBlock(samTE, "SamTE");
```

When you add this, an error should appear under BlockSamTE, which you can fix by creating the file. After adding the BlockSamTE class, cleaning it up a bit, and adding the most basic constructor to remove all of the errors, the class should look like Listing 12.1.

LISTING 12.1   The Basic `BlockSamTE` Class

```
package com.wuppy.samsmod;

import net.minecraft.block.Block;
import net.minecraft.block.material.Material;

public class BlockSamTE extends Block
{
        public BlockSamTE()
        {
                super(Material.rock);
        }
}
```

You must now add two required variables to this block:

```
private String name = "samte";
```

```
private IIcon[] icons;
```

The first one, as the name suggests, holds the name of the block. This is used the same as with any other block. The same goes for the IIcon array, which is used to store the textures for this block.

To make sure the block will work properly and is reasonably customized, the constructor should look like the following:

```java
public BlockSamTE()
{
        super(Material.rock);
        setBlockName(SamsMod.MODID + "_" + name);
        setCreativeTab(CreativeTabs.tabBlock);
        setHardness(2F);
        setResistance(5F);
        setStepSound(soundTypeStone);
        setHarvestLevel("pickaxe", 2);
}
```

All of this code has been explained in the previous hours about blocks, so nothing in this code should be surprising. The following code handles the 10 different textures for the block. This code is also covered in the previous hours. If you need to refresh your memory, read Hour 10, "Creating Multiple Blocks in a Smart Way," again.

```java
@Override
@SideOnly(Side.CLIENT)
public void registerBlockIcons(IIconRegister par1IconRegister)
{
        icons = new IIcon[10];

        for (int i = 0; i < icons.length; i++)
        {
                icons[i] = par1IconRegister.registerIcon(SamsMod.MODID + ":" +
➥"samte" + i);
        }
}

@Override
@SideOnly(Side.CLIENT)
public IIcon getIcon(int par1, int par2)
{
        return icons[par2];
}
```

Even though this block has 10 different metadatas, it always drops as metadata 0 and is not placed as anything different than metadata 0. Therefore, an ItemBlock is not required.

Additionally, only the block with metadata 0 is displayed in the Creative menu, so the `getSubBlocks` method is not required here.

The Block textures look like Figure 12.1.

FIGURE 12.1
The tile entity textures.

These textures are saved as individual 16×16 pixel textures.

This block also needs a localization in the `en_US.lang` file, which should look like this:

```
tile.wuppy29_samsmod_samte.name=Sam's TileEntity
```

Adding a Tile Entity to the Block

Now that the basic code for the block has been added, it's time to turn it into a block that also has a tile entity. To do this, the class should extend `BlockContainer` instead of `Block`. Once you change the extended type, an error appears under the `BlockSamTE` part, which you can fix by adding the unimplemented methods. This method is a single one and should look like the following:

```
@Override
public TileEntity createNewTileEntity(World var1, int var2)
{
        // TODO Auto-generated method stub
        return null;
}
```

What you should write in this method is very simple. It should simply return the `TileEntity` class you are creating. In the case of the `BlockSamTE`, this is called `TileEntitySam`. Because the class hasn't been made yet, the following code contains an error:

```
@Override
public TileEntity createNewTileEntity(World var1, int var2)
{
        return new TileEntitySam();
}
```

At this point, the `BlockSamTE` is done and should look like Listing 12.2.

LISTING 12.2   The Completed `BlockSamTE`

```java
package com.wuppy.samsmod;

import net.minecraft.block.BlockContainer;
import net.minecraft.block.material.Material;
import net.minecraft.client.renderer.texture.IIconRegister;
import net.minecraft.creativetab.CreativeTabs;
import net.minecraft.tileentity.TileEntity;
import net.minecraft.util.IIcon;
import net.minecraft.world.World;
import cpw.mods.fml.relauncher.Side;
import cpw.mods.fml.relauncher.SideOnly;

public class BlockSamTE extends BlockContainer
{
        private String name = "samte";

        private IIcon[] icons;

        public BlockSamTE()
        {
                super(Material.rock);
                setBlockName(SamsMod.MODID + "_" + name);
                setCreativeTab(CreativeTabs.tabBlock);
                setHardness(2F);
                setResistance(5F);
                setStepSound(soundTypeStone);
                setHarvestLevel("pickaxe", 2);
        }

        @Override
        @SideOnly(Side.CLIENT)
        public void registerBlockIcons(IIconRegister par1IconRegister)
        {
                icons = new IIcon[10];

                for (int i = 0; i < icons.length; i++)
                {
                        icons[i] = par1IconRegister.registerIcon(SamsMod.MODID +
➥":" + "samte" + i);
                }
        }

        @Override
        @SideOnly(Side.CLIENT)
```

```
public IIcon getIcon(int par1, int par2)
{
        return icons[par2];
}


@Override
public TileEntity createNewTileEntity(World var1, int var2)
{
        return new TileEntitySam();
}
}
```

Creating a Tile Entity

Before actually creating the `TileEntity` class, it is a good idea to register it in the mod file first. Just like most other things you have to register for your mod, you can do this using the `GameRegistry` class. You use a method called `registerTileEntity`, which looks like the following for `TileEntitySam`:

`GameRegistry.`*`registerTileEntity`*`(TileEntitySam.`**`class`**`, "TE_samTE");`

The first parameter in this method is the tile entity you want to register, followed by `.class`. The second parameter is the unlocalized name of the tile entity. However, because the tile entity will never show its name, it's not required to add a localization for it in the `en_US.lang` file.

Now it's time to actually create the `TileEntitySam` class. You can do this by hovering your mouse over the error under `TileEntitySam` and clicking Create Class.

After creating the class, make sure it extends `TileEntity`, making the class look like Listing 12.3.

LISTING 12.3   Initial `TileEntitySam` Class

```
package com.wuppy.samsmod;

import net.minecraft.tileentity.TileEntity;

public class TileEntitySam extends TileEntity {

}
```

One of the most important methods for a `TileEntity` is called `updateEntity`. In here, you should put all of the code related to updating based on time.

An important thing to note about Minecraft is that it works with ticks. Ticks are the name Minecraft uses for updates. There should always be 20 ticks in a second, but this can vary a little bit based on many things, such as the computer or the amount of things on the screen.

`TileEntitySam` should update the texture of the block it's on every second. This means that `updateEntity`, which runs every tick, should have a counter that counts up to 20 and then updates the texture. Because the texture has to change, the metadata will have to change as well. When looping through the metadata, it should never go above the highest index in the `IIcon` array of the block or it will crash because there is no texture. Therefore, there should also be a check based on the metadata. To get the metadata, a `World` object is needed to use the `getBlockMetadata` method. Additionally, the x, y, and z position have to be known and used in the method. However, `updateEntity` doesn't contain any of these variables.

Thankfully, every tile entity in the game has a `World` object called `worldObj` and an x, y, and z coordinate with the variable names xCoord, yCoord, and zCoord. Because of these variables, it's possible to get the metadata of the block.

So what is required is some way of counting to 20 as well as getting the metadata of the block to check if it doesn't go too high. To make sure the game slows down as minimally as possible with a lot of these tile entities, the time check should be made first. It would not be useful to calculate the metadata every time, even though it will only be used once every 20 updates.

The code for the counter should look like this:

```
private int counter = 0;

@Override
public void updateEntity()
{
        counter++;

        if(counter == 20)
        {
                counter = 0;
        }
}
```

Next, another private `int` must be made that will store the metadata. It should also be used inside of the counter check to get the metadata.

```
private int metadata;

@Override
public void updateEntity()
{
        counter++;
```

```
    if(counter == 20)
    {
        counter = 0;

        metadata = worldObj.getBlockMetadata(xCoord, yCoord, zCoord);
    }
}
```

Note the difference between the initialization of the counter and metadata variables. The counter is initialized to 0 at creation because that will always start at zero regardless of the starting state of the tile entity. The metadata does not get initialized at creation, but instead gets initialized when the counter reaches 20. This is because the metadata is not always 0 when the first update is run. Even though the block is always placed with metadata 0, when the game is stopped and restarted, it's likely that it won't be 0. Therefore, it is not wise to initialize this at the start, but only once the value is retrieved using the getBlockMetadata method.

Now that the metadata is there, it should be increased by one. Do this simply by adding +1 to the metadata line, which should then look like the following:

```
metadata = worldObj.getBlockMetadata(xCoord, yCoord, zCoord) + 1;
```

However, because the metadata is increased now, there needs to be a check to make sure it doesn't go above 9 and if so, set to 0. With this check added, the updateEntity method should look like this:

```
@Override
public void updateEntity()
{
        counter++;

        if(counter == 20)
        {
                counter = 0;

                metadata = worldObj.getBlockMetadata(xCoord, yCoord, zCoord) + 1;

                if(metadata > 9)
                    metadata = 0;
        }
}
```

There is just one more line of code, which is relatively easy. This line actually changes the metadata of the block. For that, the setBlockMetadataWithNotify method in World can be used. setBlockMetadataWithNotify has the same parameters as setBlock, except for the Block parameter, which doesn't exist. The updateEntity method looks like this:

```
@Override
public void updateEntity()
{
        counter++;

        if(counter == 20)
        {
                counter = 0;

                metadata = worldObj.getBlockMetadata(xCoord, yCoord, zCoord) + 1;

                if(metadata > 9)
                        metadata = 0;

                if(!worldObj.isRemote)
                        worldObj.setBlockMetadataWithNotify(xCoord, yCoord, zCoord,
➥metadata, 2);
        }
        super.updateEntity();
}
```

At the end of the method, `super.updateEntity();` is used to make sure that any code in any of the extended classes in the `updateEntity` method is run as well.

Additionally, a check is added just above `setBlockMetadataWithNotify`. In Minecraft, there is a client and a server, even when you are just playing on your own. The client does basically nothing other than rendering. Most logic, especially logic that can cause things to become asynchronized, should be handled on the server. Therefore, the metadata change code should only run on the server, which you can do by adding `!worldObj.isRemote` in an `if` statement above.

Server Synchronization

Another important thing a tile entity can do is synchronize with the server and, therefore, interact with the player. The player interaction and server synchronization for this tile entity is simple. When the block is right-clicked, the counter that switches the metadata stops until it's right-clicked again. Because this changes how the block works, this has to be synchronized between the server and the client.

The first thing required for this is a Boolean that is checked to see if the counter should change. The variable should look like this:

```
private boolean counterEnabled = true;
```

This variable should also be used in the `updateEntity` method to make sure the counter is only enabled when this is `true`. With a check for that in there, it should be as follows:

```
@Override
public void updateEntity()
{
        if(counterEnabled)
        {
                counter++;

                if(counter == 20)
                {
                        counter = 0;

                        metadata = worldObj.getBlockMetadata(xCoord, yCoord, zCoord) +
1;

                        if(metadata > 9)
                                metadata = 0;

                        if(!worldObj.isRemote)
                                worldObj.setBlockMetadataWithNotify(xCoord,
yCoord, zCoord, metadata, 2);
                }
        }

        super.updateEntity();
}
```

So `counterEnabled` is based on right-clicking a block. To make sure this works, two things are required: first, a method in the `Block` class that runs when the block is right-clicked and second, a method in the tile entity that responds to that.

NOTE

Eclipse Autocompletion

At this point, you should already know that when you enter `syso` and press Ctrl+Space, it automatically replaces it with `System.out.println`, which saves time. However, the Ctrl+Space key combination can also be used on almost everything else in Eclipse. Figure 12.2 shows an example of this.

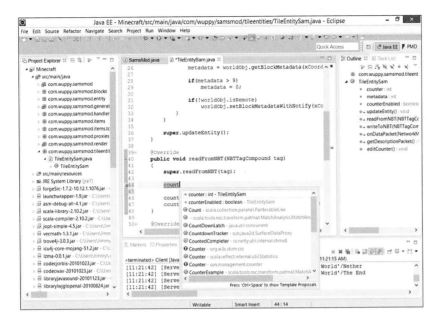

FIGURE 12.2
Autocompletion in Eclipse.

When you are halfway through a class or variable name, you can press Ctrl+Space, which makes Eclipse try to autocomplete it. If there is only a single option, it instantly puts it down like with `syso`. If there are multiple options, such as with the word count in the tile entity, it pops up a window, which you can navigate by mouse or arrow keys. Then once you find your desired entry, either click it or press Enter to automatically place the entry for you.

Adding Right-Clicking to Your Block

The method required in `BlockSamTE` is called `onBlockActivated`. Here, you should check to see if the tile entity on the block is actually `TileEntitySam`. Even though it should always be there and no other tile entity can take its place, there should be checks for it, in case something goes wrong somewhere. For example, suppose a different mod changes your tile entity accidentally or on purpose. The method should look like the following. It has an error under `editCounter`, which is a method you add in just a bit.

```
@Override
public boolean onBlockActivated(World world, int x, int y, int z,
➥EntityPlayer player, int side, float hitX, float hitY, float hitZ)
{
        TileEntity entity = world.getTileEntity(x, y, z);
```

```
    if(entity != null)
    {
            if(entity instanceof TileEntitySam)
            {
                    TileEntitySam samEntity = (TileEntitySam) entity;

                    if(!world.isRemote)
                            samEntity.editCounter();

                    return true;
            }
    }
    return false;
}
```

All the variables in this method should be clear by their name. The last four parameters are the only ones that might need a bit more explaining. The `side` parameter is the side of the block that is hit. The sides work exactly the same as with the sided textures. The last three parameters are the exact coordinates of where the block was right-clicked.

When the block is right-clicked, the tile entity on its place is retrieved using `getTileEntity`. After this, a check is made if the entity isn't null and is a `TileEntitySam`. If so, a variable for that is made storing the `TileEntitySam`. Then a check is made to make sure the code runs on the server side and a new method in the tile entity is called, which is `editCounter`. `editCounter` contains the logic on changing the variable. `BlockSamTE` should now look like Listing 12.4.

LISTING 12.4   Right-Clicking in `BlockSamTE`

```
package com.wuppy.samsmod;

import net.minecraft.block.BlockContainer;
import net.minecraft.block.material.Material;
import net.minecraft.client.renderer.texture.IIconRegister;
import net.minecraft.creativetab.CreativeTabs;
import net.minecraft.entity.player.EntityPlayer;
import net.minecraft.tileentity.TileEntity;
import net.minecraft.util.IIcon;
import net.minecraft.world.World;
import cpw.mods.fml.relauncher.Side;
import cpw.mods.fml.relauncher.SideOnly;
```

```java
public class BlockSamTE extends BlockContainer
{
        private String name = "samte";

        private IIcon[] icons;

        public BlockSamTE()
        {
                super(Material.rock);
                setBlockName(SamsMod.MODID + "_" + name);
                setCreativeTab(CreativeTabs.tabBlock);
                setHardness(2F);
                setResistance(5F);
                setStepSound(soundTypeStone);
                setHarvestLevel("pickaxe", 2);
        }

        @Override
        @SideOnly(Side.CLIENT)
        public void registerBlockIcons(IIconRegister par1IconRegister)
        {
                icons = new IIcon[10];

                for (int i = 0; i < icons.length; i++)
                {
                        icons[i] = par1IconRegister.registerIcon(SamsMod.MODID +
➡":" + "samte" + i);
                }
        }

        @Override
        @SideOnly(Side.CLIENT)
        public IIcon getIcon(int par1, int par2)
        {
                return icons[par2];
        }

        @Override
        public TileEntity createNewTileEntity(World var1, int var2)
        {
                return new TileEntitySam();
        }

        @Override
        public boolean onBlockActivated(World world, int x, int y, int z,
➡EntityPlayer player, int side, float hitX, float hitY, float hitZ)
```

```
        {
                TileEntity entity = world.getTileEntity(x, y, z);

                if(entity != null)
                {
                        if(entity instanceof TileEntitySam)
                        {
                                TileEntitySam samEntity = (TileEntitySam) entity;

                                if(!world.isRemote)
                                        samEntity.editCounter();

                                return true;
                        }
                }
                return false;
        }
}
```

Something you could be wondering is why a method in the `TileEntity` is required to simply switch the `counterEnabled` variable. However, there are multiple things that are required for this to work correctly. The `editCounter` method in `TileEntitySam` should look like this:

```
public void editCounter()
{
        counterEnabled = !counterEnabled;
        markDirty();
        worldObj.markBlockForUpdate(xCoord, yCoord, zCoord);
}
```

First, the variable is switched. Then two methods are called, which make sure the client and server sync.

Sending the Data

Next, you are required to tell Minecraft what to sync. To do this, four new methods are required. One of the methods writes the required data, one reads it, and the other two simply make sure the packets—as the data sent between a client and a server is called—are usable. The four new methods in `TileEntitySam` should look as follows:

```
@Override
public void readFromNBT(NBTTagCompound tag)
{
        super.readFromNBT(tag);

        counter = tag.getInteger("counter");
        counterEnabled = tag.getBoolean("counterEnabled");
```

```
}

@Override
public void writeToNBT(NBTTagCompound tag)
{
        super.writeToNBT(tag);

        tag.setInteger("counter", counter);
        tag.setBoolean("counterEnabled", counterEnabled);
}


@Override
public void onDataPacket(NetworkManager net, S35PacketUpdateTileEntity packet)
{
        this.readFromNBT(packet.func_148857_g());
}


@Override
public Packet getDescriptionPacket()
{
        NBTTagCompound var1 = new NBTTagCompound();

        this.writeToNBT(var1);

        return new S35PacketUpdateTileEntity(xCoord, yCoord, zCoord, 1, var1);
}
```

Before these methods can be explained properly, you should know what NBT is. NBT, or Named Binary Tag, is basically a way of storing additional information for items, blocks, entities, or tile entities in Minecraft. In this case, NBT is used to store the counter and counterEnabled variables.

One thing you don't want this tile entity to do is sync the counter every single tick. This is not only way too much work, which slows down the server and the client, but it's also simply not required because the client can be trusted with counting to 20. However, in writeToNBT, the counter integer is written. One important thing to note is that writeToNBT and readFromNBT are run only when the block is marked dirty and then updated. They are also run when the server starts or stops to make sure all relevant data is loaded for the block. Because the counter is also in here, it makes sure the counter works for multiple starts. When you start the game and end it after 10 ticks and start it again, it only takes 10 more ticks to get to 20 instead of starting at 0 again.

In readFromNBT, it's important to start the method with the super. In the super of readFromNBT, the position of the tile entity is read, so it's important not to skip this line. After the super line, the counter and counterEnabled boolean are retrieved based on their NBT tag name. Both of the tag names are the same as the variable names. This isn't required, but it does make it easier to read.

In writeToNBT, it's also important to start the method with the super. In there, the position is written. After the super, the counter integer and counterEnabled boolean are written to the NBT based on their value and name.

The onDataPacket method is the method that is run when a new packet is received. Some mods may have special packets, which means that they have to do something unique. However, this is just a standard packet that contains NBT, and the packet.func_148857_g simply makes sure the NBT is read properly.

The getDescriptionPacket method is, just like onDataPacket, a method that works with packets. This one returns the packets that have to be sent. Because this tile entity does nothing more complicated than sending some basic NBT, the S35PacketUpdateTileEntity can be used, but if your mod does something more difficult, you will likely have your own custom packet, which might mean you have to do something custom in here as well.

The TileEntitySam is now finished and should look like Listing 12.5.

LISTING 12.5   Finished `TileEntitySam`

```
package com.wuppy.samsmod;

import net.minecraft.nbt.NBTTagCompound;
import net.minecraft.network.NetworkManager;
import net.minecraft.network.Packet;
import net.minecraft.network.play.server.S35PacketUpdateTileEntity;
import net.minecraft.tileentity.TileEntity;

public class TileEntitySam extends TileEntity
{
        private int counter = 0;
        private int metadata;
        private boolean counterEnabled = true;

        @Override
        public void updateEntity()
        {
                if(counterEnabled)
                {
```

```
                          counter++;

                          if(counter == 20)
                          {
                                  counter = 0;

                                  metadata = worldObj.getBlockMetadata(xCoord,
➥yCoord, zCoord) + 1;

                                      if(metadata > 9)
                                          metadata = 0;

                                      if(!worldObj.isRemote)
                                          worldObj.setBlockMetadataWithNotify(xCoord,
➥yCoord, zCoord, metadata, 2);
                                  }
                          }

                  super.updateEntity();
          }

          @Override
          public void readFromNBT(NBTTagCompound tag)
          {
                  super.readFromNBT(tag);

                  counter = tag.getInteger("counter");
                  counterEnabled = tag.getBoolean("counterEnabled");
          }

          @Override
          public void writeToNBT(NBTTagCompound tag)
          {
                  super.writeToNBT(tag);

                  tag.setInteger("counter", counter);
                  tag.setBoolean("counterEnabled", counterEnabled);
          }

          @Override
          public void onDataPacket(NetworkManager net, S35PacketUpdateTileEntity
➥packet)
          {
                  this.readFromNBT(packet.func_148857_g());
          }
```

```
@Override
public Packet getDescriptionPacket()
{
        NBTTagCompound var1 = new NBTTagCompound();

        this.writeToNBT(var1);

        return new S35PacketUpdateTileEntity(xCoord, yCoord, zCoord,
➥1, var1);
    }

    public void editCounter()
    {
        counterEnabled = !counterEnabled;
        markDirty();
        worldObj.markBlockForUpdate(xCoord, yCoord, zCoord);
    }
}
```

Figure 12.3 shows the finalized tile entity in the game.

FIGURE 12.3
Three Sam's tile entities in the game.

Summary

In this hour, you learned how to make a block that has a tile entity on it. You also learned exactly what a tile entity is, and you made a basic one that loops through the textures of the block it's on. After this, you learned how to synchronize your tile entity with the server to make sure it works properly when you start or stop the server. You also learned about a method that can change the behavior of a block on right-click.

Q&A

Q. Is there a maximum amount of tile entities that can be registered?

A. There is no exact maximum, but it's smart to keep the amount of tile entities both registered and in the world down, because they can slow down the server quite a bit.

Q. How do you add a GUI to a tile entity?

A. This is extremely difficult and beyond the scope of this book. To do this, you need to register a GUI handler, create a GUI, and create a container, as well as many other things. More information regarding GUIs and containers can be found at http://www.minecraftforge.net/wiki/Containers_and_GUIs.

Workshop

In this hour, you learned how to make one of the most complicated and useful aspects of a Minecraft mod. Tile entities can be used for all kinds of things from simple texture changes to furnaces or crafting tables. Because tile entities are complicated and useful, it's important to understand them.

Quiz

1. Why do you not want to sync for every update of the counter?

2. Will the `counter` and `counterEnabled` value stay when you restart the game?

Answers

1. It's not only slow, but also useless.

2. Yes. At the end of the game, they are saved, and when you restart the game, they will be read again.

Exercises

Make the right-clicking of the block a little better by letting it only switch off when the player is crouching using Shift. This might not seem very important, but it's useful, because sometimes a block is right-clicked right after being placed. Additionally, it's how most other mods do it and it's generally a good idea to follow unwritten rules like that.

To do this, edit the onBlockActivated method with an extra check for the player. It should look like the following:

```java
@Override
public boolean onBlockActivated(World world, int x, int y, int z, EntityPlayer
player, int side, float hitX, float hitY, float hitZ)
{
        TileEntity entity = world.getTileEntity(x, y, z);

        if(entity != null)
        {
                if(entity instanceof TileEntitySam)
                {
                        TileEntitySam samEntity = (TileEntitySam) entity;

                        if(player.isSneaking())
                        {
                                if(!world.isRemote)
                                        samEntity.editCounter();
                        }

                        return true;
                }
        }
        return false;
}
```

HOUR 13
Generating Ores

What You'll Learn in This Hour:

▶ Using Forge and an `EventHandler`
▶ Creating a `SamEventHandler`
▶ Using `OreDictionary`

Part IV, "World Generation," is all about world generation in any way you can think of. This part teaches you how to add ores, plants, and structures to your world. In this hour, you learn how to add generation for the ore created in Hour 9, "Making Your First Block." To start off Part IV, you create an `EventHandler` for generation.

Using Forge and an `EventHandler`

Forge has a lot of different events. You can use all of these events to do something unique. There are events for world generation, fuels, item dropping, sound playing, player spawning, and many other things. You could make a different class for handling each event in your mod, but generally you will create an `EventHandler` class, which contains all of the code for the events you want to use. In this book, the only event that is covered is world generation. Because the name `EventHandler` is already used by Forge itself, the name is generally preceded by the mod name.

Creating a `SamEventHandler`

To create an EventHandler for your mod, you add a variable like this to the mod class:

```
SamEventHandler handler = new SamEventHandler();
```

Because the class `SamEventHandler` hasn't been made yet, this contains an error. You fix this soon when you create the class. However, before that is done, it would be useful to register this class as a class that handles world generation. To do that, add the following line of code to the `preInit` method:

```
GameRegistry.registerWorldGenerator(handler, 0);
```

This method registers the event handler as a world generator. The first parameter is the handler variable, which was just created. The second parameter is the importance of the generator. The lower the number, the sooner it generates. It is, however, not suggested to use a number below zero. This number can be used if you want to overwrite generation from a different mod, in which case you enter a higher number. If you don't overwrite any generation from other mods, simply enter a low number to ensure others can easily go after your generation.

NOTE

Changing Names

If you ever want to change the name of a variable, class, or package—because you spelled it wrong or want to use it differently—you can use a nice feature in Eclipse. You can access this feature by placing the cursor on the variable, class, or package you want to rename and pressing Alt+Shift+R. It then selects the variable, class, or package wherever it's used and changes all occurrences simultaneously.

Now create the `SamEventHandler` class. It should look like Listing 13.1.

LISTING 13.1   Initial `SamEventHandler`

```
package com.wuppy.samsmod;

public class SamEventHandler
{

}
```

Adding the World Generation Code

When you have created this class, an error appears in your mod file under method the `registerWorldGenerator`. To fix this, hover your mouse over the error and select Let SamEventHandler Implement IWorldGenerator.

After doing this, the error in the mod file goes away, but now an error appears under `SamEventHandler` because there are unimplemented methods you need to add. After adding the unimplemented methods, the class should look like Listing 13.2.

LISTING 13.2   SamEventHandler with the IWorldGenerator

```
package com.wuppy.samsmod;

import java.util.Random;

import net.minecraft.world.World;
import net.minecraft.world.chunk.IChunkProvider;
import cpw.mods.fml.common.IWorldGenerator;

public class SamEventHandler implements IWorldGenerator
{
        @Override
        public void generate(Random random, int chunkX, int chunkZ,
➡World world, IChunkProvider chunkGenerator, IChunkProvider chunkProvider)
        {



        }
}
```

In the `generate` method, you must create a switch based on the dimension ID. For the normal world, the dimension is 0, the nether is –1 and the end is 1. The dimension ID can be found using `world.provider.dimensionId`. When you create this switch, you can check for all three dimensions and then add a method for it. This looks like Listing 13.3.

LISTING 13.3   SamEventHandler with the Three Generation Methods

```
package com.wuppy.samsmod;

import java.util.Random;

import net.minecraft.world.World;
import net.minecraft.world.chunk.IChunkProvider;
import cpw.mods.fml.common.IWorldGenerator;

public class SamEventHandler implements IWorldGenerator
{
        @Override
        public void generate(Random random, int chunkX, int chunkZ, World world,
➡IChunkProvider chunkGenerator, IChunkProvider chunkProvider)
        {
                switch(world.provider.dimensionId)
                {
                        case -1: generateNether(world, random, chunkX * 16, chunkZ *
➡16);
                        case 0: generateSurface(world, random, chunkX * 16, chunkZ *
➡16);
```

```
                case 1: generateEnd(world, random, chunkX * 16, chunkZ * 16);
            }
        }


        private void generateEnd(World world, Random random, int x, int z)
        {



        }

        private void generateSurface(World world, Random random, int x, int z)
        {



        }

        private void generateNether(World world, Random random, int x, int z)
        {



        }
    }
```

All of this code basically makes sure you can generate ores based on the dimension. Next, you add a standard method. This standard method makes it very easy to add new ores to the world. It looks like the following:

```
/**
 * Adds an Ore Spawn to Minecraft. Simply register all Ores to spawn with this
➥method in your Generation method in your IWorldGeneration extending Class
 *
 * @param The Block to spawn
 * @param The metadata of the Block
 * @param The Block where to generate in
 * @param The World to spawn in
 * @param A Random object for retrieving random positions within
➥the world to spawn the Block
 * @param An int for passing the X-Coordinate for the Generation method
 * @param An int for passing the Z-Coordinate for the Generation method
 * @param An int for setting the maximum X-Coordinate values for spawning
➥on the X-Axis on a Per-Chunk basis
 * @param An int for setting the maximum Z-Coordinate values for spawning
➥on the Z-Axis on a Per-Chunk basis
 * @param An int for setting the maximum size of a vein
 * @param An int for the Number of chances available for the Block to
➥spawn per-chunk
```

```
 * @param An int for the minimum Y-Coordinate height at which this block may spawn
 * @param An int for the maximum Y-Coordinate height at which this block may spawn
 **/
public void addOreSpawn(Block block, int metadata, Block target, World world,
➥Random random, int blockXPos, int blockZPos, int maxX, int maxZ, int
➥maxVeinSize, int chancesToSpawn, int minY, int maxY)
{
        int maxPossY = minY + (maxY - 1);
        assert maxY > minY: "The maximum Y must be greater than the Minimum Y";
        assert maxX > 0 && maxX <= 16: "addOreSpawn: The Maximum X must be
➥greater than 0 and less than 16";
        assert minY > 0: "addOreSpawn: The Minimum Y must be greater than 0";
        assert maxY < 256 && maxY > 0: "addOreSpawn: The Maximum Y must be
➥less than 256 but greater than 0";
        assert maxZ > 0 && maxZ <= 16: "addOreSpawn: The Maximum Z must be
➥greater than 0 and less than 16";

        int diffBtwnMinMaxY = maxY - minY;
        for(int x = 0; x < chancesToSpawn; x++)
        {
                int posX = blockXPos + random.nextInt(maxX);
                int posY = minY + random.nextInt(diffBtwnMinMaxY);
                int posZ = blockZPos + random.nextInt(maxZ);
                (new WorldGenMinable(block, metadata, maxVeinSize,
➥target)).generate(world, random, posX, posY, posZ);
        }
}
```

Basically, everything you need to know is in this code fragment. There are a lot of parameters, but once you fill all of them in, the block generates in the way you want it to. One useful thing about this method is that if you put an invalid value somewhere, it tells you.

This method is used in the `generateSurface` method to generate the Sam's Stone ore. Code for that is as follows:

```
addOreSpawn(SamsMod.samStone, 0, Blocks.stone, world, random, x, z, 16, 16,
➥5 + random.nextInt(5), 4, 20, 60);
```

The first parameter is the block you want to generate, and the second is the metadata. After this, you get the kind of block you want it to generate in. Then there are some standard values, which will have to be passed on, including `world`, `random`, `x`, `z`, and the two `16`s. All of these values basically make sure that the ore can generate anywhere on any chunk, which is a 16 blocks wide, 16 blocks long, and 256 blocks high area in the Minecraft world. After this are some ore-specific numbers. The `5 + random.nextInt(5)` part is the amount of ores that will generate in a single vein. It's generally a good idea to randomize this a little bit. After the vein size, a number is set for how many veins there can be in a single chunk. Finally, the last two numbers are the top and bottom y value the ore will generate in.

If you want to generate your ore in any other kind of ground type, you can simply change `Blocks.stone` into whatever the ground is made up of. Additionally, the exact same code can be used in `generateEnd` and `generateNether` to add ores in those dimensions.

▼ TRY IT YOURSELF

Nether Ore Generation

Add Sam's Stone to the nether by adding an `addOreSpawn` line to the `generateNether` method. Make sure you change `Blocks.stone` into `Blocks.netherrack`, or it will not work.

`SamEventHandler` should now look like Listing 13.4.

LISTING 13.4   Finished `SamEventHandler`

```
package com.wuppy.samsmod;

import java.util.Random;

import net.minecraft.block.Block;
import net.minecraft.init.Blocks;
import net.minecraft.world.World;
import net.minecraft.world.chunk.IChunkProvider;
import net.minecraft.world.gen.feature.WorldGenMinable;
import cpw.mods.fml.common.IWorldGenerator;

public class SamEventHandler implements IWorldGenerator
{
        @Override
        public void generate(Random random, int chunkX, int chunkZ, World world,
➥IChunkProvider chunkGenerator, IChunkProvider chunkProvider)
        {
                switch(world.provider.dimensionId)
                {
                        case -1: generateNether(world, random, chunkX * 16, chunkZ *
➥16);
                        case 0: generateSurface(world, random, chunkX * 16, chunkZ *
➥16);
                        case 1: generateEnd(world, random, chunkX * 16, chunkZ * 16);
                }
        }
```

```
    private void generateEnd(World world, Random random, int x, int z)
    {


    }

    private void generateSurface(World world, Random random, int x, int z)
    {
        addOreSpawn(SamsMod.samStone, 0, Blocks.stone, world, random, x, z, 16,
➼16, 5 + random.nextInt(5), 4, 20, 60);
    }

    private void generateNether(World world, Random random, int x, int z)
    {
        addOreSpawn(SamsMod.samStone, 0, Blocks.netherrack, world, random,
➼x, z, 16, 16, 5 + random.nextInt(5), 4, 20, 60);
    }

    /**
     * Adds an Ore Spawn to Minecraft. Simply register all Ores to spawn with
➼this method in your Generation method in your IWorldGeneration extending Class
     *
     * @param The Block to spawn
     * @param The metadata of the Block
     * @param The Block where to generate in
     * @param The World to spawn in
     * @param A Random object for retrieving random positions within
➼the world to spawn the Block
     * @param An int for passing the X-Coordinate for the Generation method
     * @param An int for passing the Z-Coordinate for the Generation method
     * @param An int for setting the maximum X-Coordinate values for spawning
➼on the X-Axis on a Per-Chunk basis
     * @param An int for setting the maximum Z-Coordinate values for spawning
➼on the Z-Axis on a Per-Chunk basis
     * @param An int for setting the maximum size of a vein
     * @param An int for the Number of chances available for the Block
➼to spawn per-chunk
     * @param An int for the minimum Y-Coordinate height at which this
➼block may spawn
     * @param An int for the maximum Y-Coordinate height at which this
➼block may spawn
     **/
    public void addOreSpawn(Block block, int metadata, Block target, World
➼world, Random random, int blockXPos, int blockZPos, int maxX, int maxZ,
➼int maxVeinSize, int chancesToSpawn, int minY, int maxY)
```

```
        {
                int maxPossY = minY + (maxY - 1);
                assert maxY > minY: "The maximum Y must be greater than the
➥Minimum Y";
                assert maxX > 0 && maxX <= 16: "addOreSpawn: The Maximum X must
➥be greater than 0 and less than 16";
                assert minY > 0: "addOreSpawn: The Minimum Y must be greater than 0";
                assert maxY < 256 && maxY > 0: "addOreSpawn: The Maximum Y must be
➥less than 256 but greater than 0";
                assert maxZ > 0 && maxZ <= 16: "addOreSpawn: The Maximum Z must be
➥greater than 0 and less than 16";


                int diffBtwnMinMaxY = maxY - minY;
                for(int x = 0; x < chancesToSpawn; x++)
                {
                        int posX = blockXPos + random.nextInt(maxX);
                        int posY = minY + random.nextInt(diffBtwnMinMaxY);
                        int posZ = blockZPos + random.nextInt(maxZ);
                        (new WorldGenMinable(block, metadata, maxVeinSize,
➥target)).generate(world, random, posX, posY, posZ);
                }
        }
}
```

Using OreDictionary

In the Exercise in Hour 9, you made the Sam's Stone ore block drop Sam's Dust when it is broken. If you haven't already, add a smelting recipe to smelt the dust into Sam's Ingot. If you don't know how to do this, look in Hour 3, "Working with Recipes and Other Small Modifications," where smelting recipes are explained.

OreDictionary is a class in Forge that can be used to allow multiple mods to use the same ingots. An example of this is copper. Many different mods add copper, and with OreDictionary, they can use copper from the different mods without having to write a recipe for each of them. It's unlikely that other mods use Sam's Ingots, but it's always better to maximize compatibility.

OreDictionary Registry

To use OreDictionary, you must register your ingot as an ore. You can do that with the following line of code in your mod file. Make sure this is written after the initialization and registry of the ingot:

```
OreDictionary.registerOre("ingotSam", new ItemStack(samingot));
```

The first parameter has to be the name you want your ingot to be registered as. Because these methods are used in several different mods and the names must be exactly the same for `OreDictionary` to function, there are some strict rules on what the name should be. For an ingot, it should always be ingot followed directly by the type of material, starting with a capital letter. For example, `ingotCopper` is correct, whereas `copperIngot` and `ingotcopper` are incorrect. The complete list of naming rules, vanilla names, and names in other mods can be found at www.minecraftforge.net/wiki/Common_Oredict_names.

The second parameter is an `ItemStack` with the item or block you want to add to the `OreDictionary`.

`OreDictionary` **Recipes**

Now your ingot is registered as `ingotSam`. However, this is only half of the work. If you want other mods, which have an ingot using the same name, to be able to use their ingots in your recipes, you need to change your recipes a little. The following is a recipe for the Sam's Pickaxe using the standard `samingot`:

```
GameRegistry.addRecipe(new ItemStack(SamsMod.sampickaxe),
        "XXX",
        " Y ",
        " Y ",
        'X', SamsMod.samingot, 'Y', Items.stick
);
```

This recipe still works fine, but it won't work with `OreDictionary`. To make it work with `OreDictionary`, the `SamsMod.samingot` should be replaced with the `OreDictionary` `String` you used to register the ingot. When you do this, the recipe should look like this:

```
GameRegistry.addRecipe(new ShapedOreRecipe(ModItems.sampickaxe,
        "XXX",
        " Y ",
        " Y ",
        'X', "ingotSam", 'Y', Items.stick
));
```

In addition to the change from the `Item` to a `String`, you also have to add `ShapedOreRecipe` within `addRecipe`. This simply makes sure that you can use `Strings` registered in `OreDictionary`. In addition to that, everything else is the same as any other recipe.

NOTE

Eclipse Navigation

You can easily access classes such as `ShapedOreRecipe` by Ctrl-clicking them. Eclipse then opens a new tab where you can see the code in that file.

Once you have found the ores, it should look similar to Figure 13.1.

FIGURE 13.1
The Ores generated in the game.

Summary

In this hour, you learned how to create the `SamEventHandler` class. This is an important class in your mod because it can not only hold generation code, but also hold code for any other kind of event. After creating this file, you learned how to use it by adding a new method to the class, which is able to generate any kind of ore in any kind of target area. You can use this method to spawn ores in stone as well as clouds in the air. After adding this method, you used it in two different places to actually generate ores with it.

Q&A

Q. Is there a maximum amount of ores you can add to generation?

A. There is no maximum, but with every ore you add to generation, the generation is slower. It can get so slow that it doesn't generate at all or takes multiple times to generate. Therefore, it's important to not waste generation.

Q. How do I add multiple ores to be generated?

A. Simply copy the line starting with `addOreSpawn` and change the ore you want to generate.

Workshop

In this hour, you created the class `SamEventHandler`, which is the backbone of everything in Part IV. Therefore, it's important to know exactly what it does and how it works.

Quiz

1. **How do you add ore generation to the end?**

2. **Will the following code make the ore very rare or very common?**

```
addOreSpawn(SamsMod.samStone, 0, Blocks.stone, world, random,
➥x, z, 2, 2, 2, 4, 3, 20);
```

Answers

1. Simply copy the line from overworld generation and change the target block from stone to endstone.

2. This code makes the block really rare. This ore is only allowed to generate in a 2×2 area in a chunk, and if it does, it only generates two ores. It also only generates in a very specific height.

Exercises

Add the Sam's Stone ore generation to the end in the obsidian spikes.

The following code does that:

```
private void generateEnd(World world, Random random, int x, int z)
{
        addOreSpawn(SamsMod.samStone, 0, Blocks.obsidian, world, random, x, z,
➥16, 16, 5 + random.nextInt(5), 4, 20, 60);
}
```

HOUR 14
Generating Plants

What You'll Learn in This Hour:

▶ Creating a custom `WorldGen` class
▶ Adding code to `SamEventHandler`

In Hour 11, "Making Your Blocks Unique," you created a plant. However, unless you some-how get seeds to the player, the plant can't be used. It is quite common for plants to be gen-erated in the world, such as cacti, grass, and flowers in vanilla Minecraft. To do this, you need a `WorldGen` class just like was used in Hour 13, "Generating Ores," to spawn the ores in the world. The only difference is that this time you must make it yourself. You use the `SamEventHandler` from the previous hour again because you don't need a new one for every event or world generation.

Creating a Custom `WorldGen` Class

The custom `WorldGen` class for the generation of Sam's Plant will be called `WorldGenSamPlant`. It's useful, but not required, to make sure the name of every world gen-eration file starts with `WorldGen`. This makes code easier to read. To create a new class, simply right-click the package your mod is in and select Create Class. After typing the name in the win-dow that pops up, click Finish. This creates a class that should look like Listing 14.1.

LISTING 14.1 Initial `WorldGenSamPlant` Class

```
package com.wuppy.samsmod;

public class WorldGenSamPlant
{

}
```

To make sure `WorldGenSamPlant` will actually work as a `WorldGen` class, it has to extend `WorldGenerator`. Once you add the `extends WorldGenerator` code, an error appears under `WorldGenerator`, which you can fix by importing it. Next, an error appears under `WorldGenSamPlant`, which you can fix by adding the unimplemented methods. After doing this, `WorldGenSamPlant` should look like Listing 14.2.

LISTING 14.2   `WorldGenSamPlant` Extending `WorldGenerator`

```
package com.wuppy.samsmod;

import java.util.Random;

import net.minecraft.world.World;
import net.minecraft.world.gen.feature.WorldGenerator;

public class WorldGenSamPlant extends WorldGenerator
{
        @Override
        public boolean generate(World world, Random rand, int x, int y, int z)
        {
                return true;
        }
}
```

Now it would be useful to actually add some block placing code to the `generate` method.

Randomizing the Location

This `generate` method will be called in the `SamEventHandler`. However, before calling it in `SamEventHandler`, it would be useful to add some code to the method in `WorldGenSamPlant` to make it actually place some blocks. A location will be provided by `SamEventHandler`, but you don't want several blocks to be placed in the same location, nor do you want only a single block. Therefore, add the following code to the `generate` method in `WorldGenSamPlant`:

```
@Override
public boolean generate(World world, Random rand, int x, int y, int z)
{
        for (int l = 0; l < 64; ++l)
        {
                int x1 = x + rand.nextInt(8) - rand.nextInt(8);
                int y1 = y + rand.nextInt(4) - rand.nextInt(4);
                int z1 = z + rand.nextInt(8) - rand.nextInt(8);
        }

        return true;
}
```

This code makes it possible for 64 plants to spawn. However, because most plants have some pretty specific generation requirements—dirt or grass below and air above—this generally results in only a few plants. Next, a random x, y, and z are obtained for each loop to make sure the plants can spawn in different locations.

NOTE

Randomization

In the preceding code fragment, you can see how the randomization is done. However, you could always do it differently. If you remove the second `rand.nextInt()`, the generation works just as well. However, it might be slightly less random.

You could also increase the numbers to make the plants more spread out. However, try to keep the numbers below 16. If you make them above 16, the generation in Minecraft world may cause you, and more likely people on a slower computer, crashes.

Checking and Placing

The next piece of code that is required is to check if the block can actually be placed in the location. It shouldn't be placed in the air or underground in stone. To do this, add the following code:

```
@Override
public boolean generate(World world, Random rand, int x, int y, int z)
{
      for (int l = 0; l < 64; ++l)
      {
            int x1 = x + rand.nextInt(8) - rand.nextInt(8);
            int y1 = y + rand.nextInt(4) - rand.nextInt(4);
            int z1 = z + rand.nextInt(8) - rand.nextInt(8);

            if (SamsMod.samPlant.canPlaceBlockAt(world, x1, y1, z1) &&
➥world.getBlock(x1, y1 - 1, z1) == Blocks.grass)
            {


            }
      }

      return true;
}
```

Now that the spawn requirements are met, add a single line of code in the `if` block, as follows:

```
world.setBlock(x1, y1, z1, SamsMod.samPlant, 0, 2);
```

This simply places a Sam's Plant Block at the random x, y, and z location.

▼ TRY IT YOURSELF

Add a Random Start Metadata

Add a random start metadata to the generation of your plant, making it possible for the plant to spawn with the highest metadata right from the start.

The code you need for it:

```
world.setBlock(x1, y1, z1, SamsMod.samPlant, rand.nextInt(3), 2);
```

Now the `WorldGenSamPlant` class is done. It should look like Listing 14.3.

LISTING 14.3   Finished `WorldGenSamPlant`

```java
package com.wuppy.samsmod;

import java.util.Random;

import net.minecraft.init.Blocks;
import net.minecraft.world.World;
import net.minecraft.world.gen.feature.WorldGenerator;

public class WorldGenSamPlant extends WorldGenerator
{
        @Override
        public boolean generate(World world, Random rand, int x, int y, int z)
        {
                for (int l = 0; l < 64; ++l)
                {
                        int x1 = x + rand.nextInt(8) - rand.nextInt(8);
                        int y1 = y + rand.nextInt(4) - rand.nextInt(4);
                        int z1 = z + rand.nextInt(8) - rand.nextInt(8);

                        if (SamsMod.samPlant.canPlaceBlockAt(world, x1, y1, z1) &&
➥world.getBlock(x1, y1 - 1, z1) == Blocks.grass)
                        {
                        world.setBlock(x1, y1, z1, SamsMod.samPlant, rand.nextInt(3),
➥2);
                        }
                }

            return true;
        }
}
```

NOTE
_____

Eclipse Code Formatting

Sometimes when you are working on code, you might forget a space or a tab or something similar in some places. When you are coding for a while and revisit a file several times, this might become quite messy. Thankfully, Eclipse has an easy way to fix this.

To format your code, simply press Ctrl+Shift+F and Eclipse takes care of it for you. However, if you do this right now, the code will look completely different from what you have made so far. It is very likely that you want to make some changes to the code formatting used. This can be done by clicking Window, Preferences, as shown in Figure 14.1.

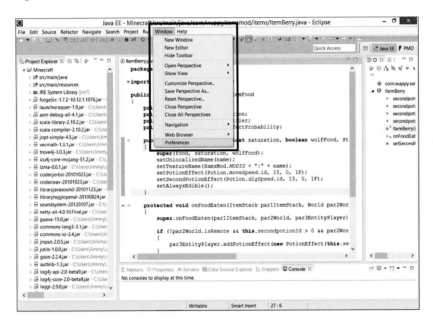

FIGURE 14.1
The Preferences option.

This opens up the Preferences window where you navigate to Java, Code Style, Formatter. When you do so, you should see a screen like Figure 14.2.

In the Formatter window, click New. The New Profile window opens, as shown in Figure 14.3. Enter a custom name for your formatting profile and then click OK in the New Profile window.

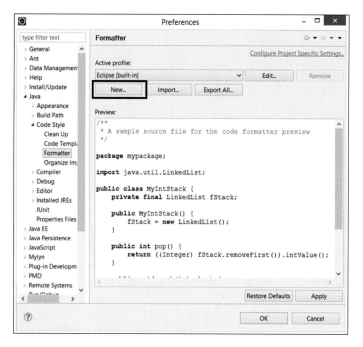

FIGURE 14.2
The Formatter window.

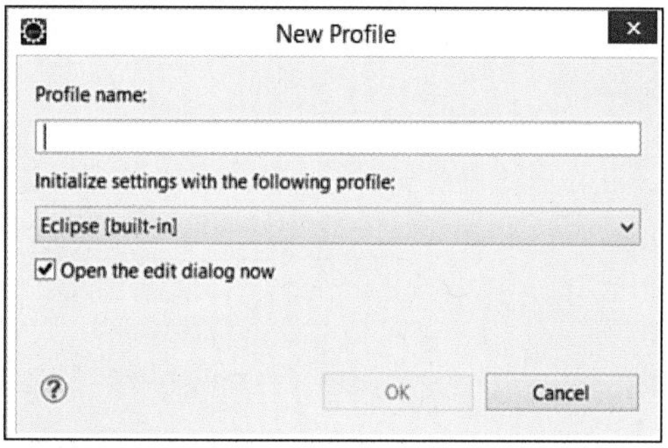

FIGURE 14.3
The New Profile window.

A new Profile 'Custom' window (where *'Custom'* is the name you just chose for your custom profile) opens, as shown in Figure 14.4. Here, you should configure your new formatting profile.

Figures 14.5 to 14.8 show the options you need to make your autoformatting look like the code shown in this book. You can, of course, change any of the options you want and make your own code look completely different.

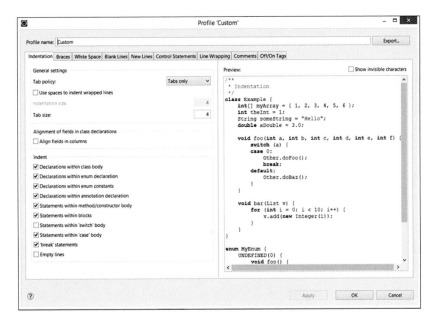

FIGURE 14.4
The formatting options.

FIGURE 14.5
The Braces options.

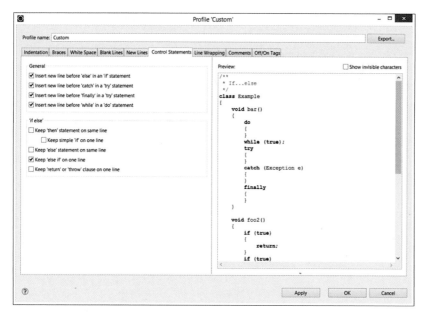

FIGURE 14.6
The Control Statement options.

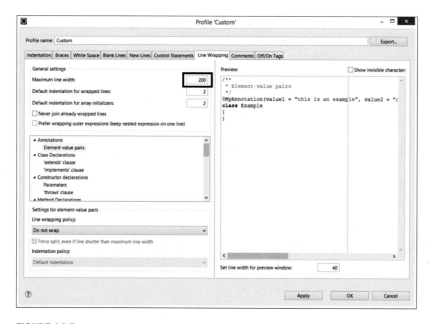

FIGURE 14.7
The Line Wrapping options.

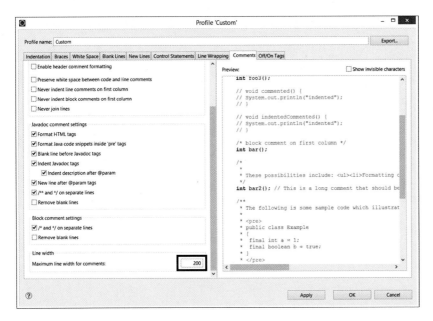

FIGURE 14.8
The Comments options.

Now click Apply and then OK, make sure your profile is selected in the window from Figure 14.2, and click Apply and OK again. When you press Ctrl+Shift+F now, the code formats the way you want it to.

Adding Code to `SamEventHandler`

Now to make sure this code is actually used, you must add it to the `SamEventHandler` class. This plant generates on grass and, therefore, several things are required for it to work. First, it only generates in the overworld. Second, it only generates around the ground level because that's the only place with grass.

The code to add generation for classes like `WorldGenSamPlant` is very similar to what's inside of the `addOreSpawn` method from the previous hour. There is a random x, y, and z and a line that calls the `generate` method in `WorldGenSamPlant`. All of this code can be added in a `for` loop to make the plant more common. The code required should look similar to this:

```
int posX = x + random.nextInt(16);
int posY = 50 + random.nextInt(35);
int posZ = z + random.nextInt(16);
new WorldGenSamPlant().generate(world, random, posX, posY, posZ);
```

This code creates an x and a z value that can be anywhere in the world. The y value can only be between 50 and 84. This height should cover most normal grass generation. After creating the location, it's used for the `generate` method in `WorldGenSamPlant`. Unlike `WorldGenMinable`, `WorldGenSamPlant` doesn't require any parameters and is, therefore, easier to use.

NOTE

Autocompletion

`WorldGenSamPlant` is a pretty long "word" to enter. If you want to make this a little bit easier, enter something like `WorldGenS` and then press Ctrl+Space. When you do this, it automatically completes the remainder of the word if there is only one word to choose from. If there are multiple options, a small menu appears, similar to what is shown in Figure 14.9. You simply select the word you want and you don't have to enter it.

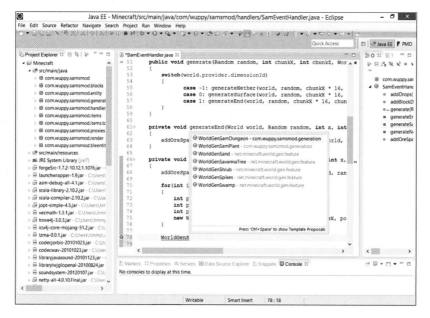

FIGURE 14.9
The Autocomplete box.

A method like `addOreSpawn` isn't required because `WorldGenSamPlant` is very specific and will never be used more than once.

The whole `SamEventHandler` looks like Listing 14.4.

LISTING 14.4   `SamEventHandler` with the `WorldGenSamPlant` Code

```java
package com.wuppy.samsmod;

import java.util.Random;

import net.minecraft.block.Block;
import net.minecraft.init.Blocks;
import net.minecraft.world.World;
import net.minecraft.world.chunk.IChunkProvider;
import net.minecraft.world.gen.feature.WorldGenMinable;
import cpw.mods.fml.common.IWorldGenerator;

public class SamEventHandler implements IWorldGenerator
{
    @Override
    public void generate(Random random, int chunkX, int chunkZ,
 ➡World world, IChunkProvider chunkGenerator, IChunkProvider chunkProvider)
    {
        switch(world.provider.dimensionId)
        {
            case -1: generateNether(world, random, chunkX * 16, chunkZ * 16);
            case 0: generateSurface(world, random, chunkX * 16, chunkZ * 16);
            case 1: generateEnd(world, random, chunkX * 16, chunkZ * 16);
        }
    }

    private void generateEnd(World world, Random random, int x, int z)
    {
        addOreSpawn(SamsMod.samStone, 0, Blocks.obsidian, world, random,
 ➡x, z, 16, 16, 5 + random.nextInt(5), 4, 20, 60);
    }

    private void generateSurface(World world, Random random, int x, int z)
    {
        addOreSpawn(SamsMod.samStone, 0, Blocks.stone, world, random,
 ➡x, z, 16, 16, 5 + random.nextInt(5), 4, 20, 60);

        int posX = x + random.nextInt(16);
        int posY = 50 + random.nextInt(35);
        int posZ = z + random.nextInt(16);
        new WorldGenSamPlant().generate(world, random, posX, posY, posZ);
    }
```

```
    private void generateNether(World world, Random random, int x, int z)
    {
        addOreSpawn(SamsMod.samStone, 0, Blocks.netherrack, world, random,
➥x, z, 16, 16, 5 + random.nextInt(5), 4, 20, 60);
    }

/**
 * Adds an Ore Spawn to Minecraft. Simply register all Ores to spawn with
➥this method in your Generation method in your IWorldGeneration extending Class
 *
 * @param The Block to spawn
 * @param The metadata of the Block
 * @param The Block where to generate in
 * @param The World to spawn in
 * @param A Random object for retrieving random positions within the
➥world to spawn the Block
 * @param An int for passing the X-Coordinate for the Generation method
 * @param An int for passing the Z-Coordinate for the Generation method
 * @param An int for setting the maximum X-Coordinate values for spawning
➥on the X-Axis on a Per-Chunk basis
 * @param An int for setting the maximum Z-Coordinate values for spawning
➥on the Z-Axis on a Per-Chunk basis
 * @param An int for setting the maximum size of a vein
 * @param An int for the Number of chances available for the Block
➥to spawn per-chunk
 * @param An int for the minimum Y-Coordinate height at which this
➥block may spawn
 * @param An int for the maximum Y-Coordinate height at which this
➥block may spawn
 **/
    public void addOreSpawn(Block block, int metadata, Block target, World
➥world, Random random, int blockXPos, int blockZPos, int maxX, int maxZ,
➥int maxVeinSize, int chancesToSpawn, int minY, int maxY)
    {
        int maxPossY = minY + (maxY - 1);
        assert maxY > minY: "The maximum Y must be greater than the
➥Minimum Y";
        assert maxX > 0 && maxX <= 16: "addOreSpawn: The Maximum X must be
➥greater than 0 and less than 16";
        assert minY > 0: "addOreSpawn: The Minimum Y must be greater than 0";
        assert maxY < 256 && maxY > 0: "addOreSpawn: The Maximum Y must be
➥less than 256 but greater than 0";
        assert maxZ > 0 && maxZ <= 16: "addOreSpawn: The Maximum Z must
➥be greater than 0 and less than 16";
```

```
        int diffBtwnMinMaxY = maxY - minY;
        for(int x = 0; x < chancesToSpawn; x++)
        {
                int posX = blockXPos + random.nextInt(maxX);
                int posY = minY + random.nextInt(diffBtwnMinMaxY);
                int posZ = blockZPos + random.nextInt(maxZ);
                (new WorldGenMinable(block, metadata, maxVeinSize,
➥target)).generate(world, random, posX, posY, posZ);
        }
    }
}
```

Just like with ore generation, it might take a little while to find your plants, but they should look something like Figure 14.10.

FIGURE 14.10
The plants generated in the game.

Summary

In this hour, you learned how to manually create a `WorldGen` class. It's important to know how to do this for creating basic generation such as plants. However, for larger structures, there is a different, faster way to do this, which you learn in the next two hours. In this hour, you also learned how to use the new `WorldGen` file in the `EventHandler`.

Q&A

Q. How rare are these plants without a `for` loop in the `SamEventHandler` class?

A. They will not always be visible on the screen when you look at the terrain, but they are not rare either.

Q. Is it bad to make `WorldGen` files generate very often?

A. It isn't exactly bad, but it does really slow down the game if there is a lot of generation going on at once.

Workshop

In this hour, you learned how to create a custom `WorldGen` class by hand. This is the only hour that covers that, so it's important to understand it.

Quiz

1. Would it be possible to paste the code from the `generateSurface` method into `generateNether` to make the plant generate in the nether?

2. What should you do when you have multiple plants that generate in the same way?

    A. Create a custom `WorldGen` file for each plant type.

    B. Create a `WorldGen` file that takes the plant type as a parameter, so multiple plants can be generated using the same class.

Answers

1. It doesn't crash if you do this, but it does slow down the game. Because the `BlockSamPlant` class contains code that makes sure it can only be placed on dirt or grass, it doesn't generate.

2. B is the best option. Having more classes doesn't make your mod slower, but it's just harder to read and useless.

Exercises

Make the Sam's Plant much more common by adding a `for` loop around the generation code.

The code:

```
for(int i = 0; i < 3; i++)
{
    int posX = x + random.nextInt(16);
    int posY = 50 + random.nextInt(35);
    int posZ = z + random.nextInt(16);
    new WorldGenSamPlant().generate(world, random, posX, posY, posZ);
}
```

Make sure the `posX`, `posY`, and `posZ` code is also included in the `for` loop or it generates the plants in the same place every time.

HOUR 15
Using MCEdit

What You'll Learn in This Hour:

▶ Why use MCEdit
▶ Getting MCEdit
▶ Using MCEdit

This hour and the next are the final hours in Part IV, "World Generation." These two hours teach you how to create a structure and how to make it generate in Minecraft with as little work as possible. In this hour, you learn how to install and use MCEdit, which is a Minecraft world editor, and in Hour 16, "Generating Your Structure," you learn how to change what you made with it into Java code.

Why Use MCEdit

You can add structures to the world in several different ways. The most commonly used ones are by coding the placement of each block by hand and using MCEdit along with a converter. In some cases, coding each individual block can be quite easy. For example, if you just want a few walls, you can easily do that by writing several `for` loops. However, when your structures become a bit more complicated, this becomes far too much work because writing code for every single wall or other features of your structure can take a long time. In this case, it's much easier to build the structure in Minecraft and then export it using MCEdit along with an exporter. The second option is what you learn in this and the following hour.

Getting MCEdit

To install MCEdit, you first have to download it. The website for MCEdit can be found at http://www.mcedit.net/. On this website, click the button on the upper left, as shown in Figure 15.1.

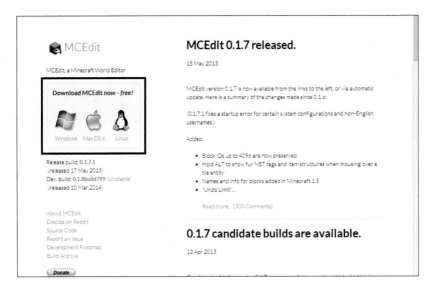

FIGURE 15.1
mcedit.net Download button.

When you click this button, a new screen opens, which looks like Figure 15.2. Download the version you need based on your operating system.

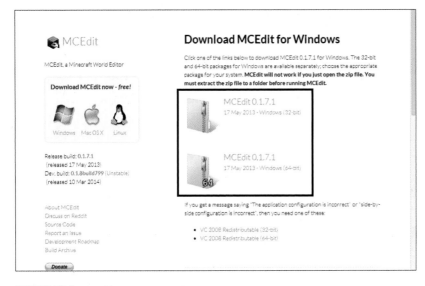

FIGURE 15.2
mcedit.net Download links.

Installing MCEdit

To use the program you just downloaded, unzip it to a location where you can find it later, then double-click the `mcedit.exe` file, and it should run. As mentioned on the website, it doesn't run from the `.zip` file. You must extract the contents to a folder before you can run the `mcedit.exe` file. If you receive an error mentioning configuration on starting the program, you should then download and install the VC redistributable, which you can also find on the website.

Once you have it working, MCEdit should look Figure 15.3.

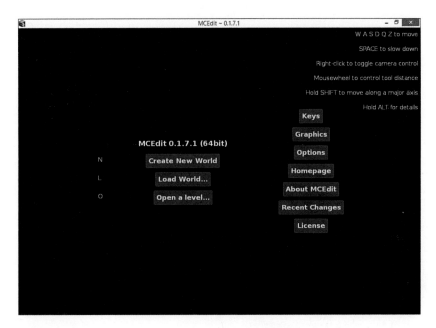

FIGURE 15.3
MCEdit start screen.

Using MCEdit

There are two ways to make and export structures in MCEdit. You can create it all in MCEdit, which is easier when you want to create large landscapes, for example. For smaller buildings, though, it's generally easier to build them in Minecraft and then open the world in MCEdit. This book only covers how to export your structure using MCEdit after building it in Minecraft. However, if you want to learn how to do more with this tool, watch one or both of the following YouTube videos: https://www.youtube.com/watch?v=Bpuq2LIUy1E by SethBling or https://www.youtube.com/watch?v=B6di0TCI8LU by Vechs.

Alternatively, if you don't want to watch a YouTube video, you can check out www.wuppy29.com/minecraft/modding-tutorials/modding-easy-structure-creation-part-2-using-mcedit/.

▼ TRY IT YOURSELF

Create the Structure

Before exporting a structure, it's a good idea to create one. In this case, the structure you must make is a dungeon. Follow these steps to create it:

1. Open Minecraft and enter a world where you can build in creative mode.

2. Build the four walls of the dungeon. It should be 8 blocks wide, 11 blocks long, and 6 blocks high.

3. Build the floor and the roof on the bottom and top of the walls.

4. Add a few obstacles inside the dungeon, such as small walls.

5. Add a block of glowstone to the top.

Figure 15.4 shows the structure that you will export using MCEdit. It doesn't have a roof in the figure for visibility, but it will in the game.

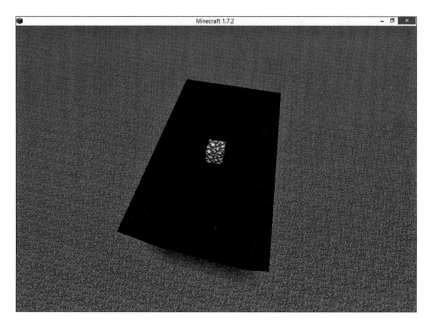

FIGURE 15.4
The structure.

This structure is built on a superflat world. It's smart to create structures you will have to export using MCEdit in a superflat world because it makes exporting in MCEdit a lot easier.

Importing a World

Now, open the world where this structure is built in MCEdit. Start MCEdit and click the Open a Level option, as shown in Figure 15.3. This opens a file browser where you can select the `level.dat` file, which is located within the save.

If you build your structure in the default installation of Minecraft, look in the following folder structure: C:\Users\[Your Username]\AppData\Roaming\.minecraft. In here you will find a Saves folder. In there should be another folder with the name of your world. Within that folder you will find the `level.dat` file. If you created the world in your Eclipse workspace, the folder should look like Figure 15.5.

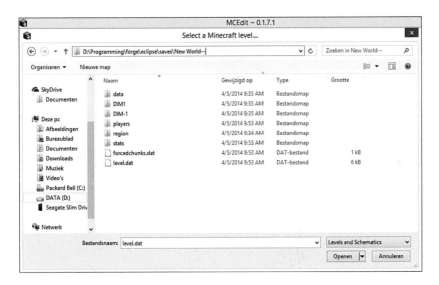

FIGURE 15.5
The folder with the `level.dat` file.

After selecting the correct file, click Open, which starts MCEdit in the World Editor mode. Figure 15.6 shows how the structure will look in MCEdit.

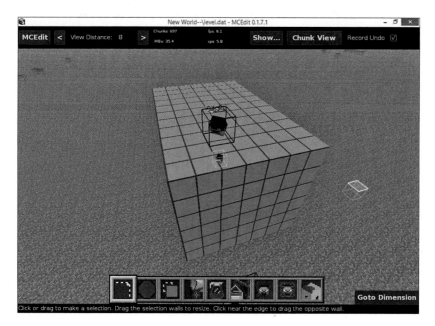

FIGURE 15.6
The structure in MCEdit.

Exporting Your Structure

As you can see, all of the Sam's Stone blocks are purple. That is because MCEdit doesn't know what the block is. This problem also persists in the converter used in the next hour, but it's easily fixed in code. You fix this problem in Hour 16.

Another thing you might notice is that there are a lot of players. That is because you get a different player almost every time you start Minecraft in Eclipse. Because of this, MCEdit thinks there are multiple players in the same place. However, you don't have to worry about players when exporting the structure.

To export the structure, use the Selection tool, which is the tool on the lower left. Drag the Selection tool from the lower left to the upper right to make sure the entire structure is contained within the selection marquee. Make sure you don't select anything outside of the structure, though. If you do, it will generate that part as well. After selecting the structure, the structure looks a little different, and a new menu appears on the left, as shown in Figure 15.7.

Now simply click the Export button and save it with a smart name, such as the name of the structure. Figure 15.8 shows the folder and filename of the structure created in this hour.

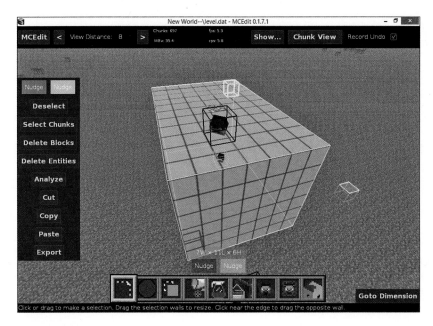

FIGURE 15.7
The structure selected.

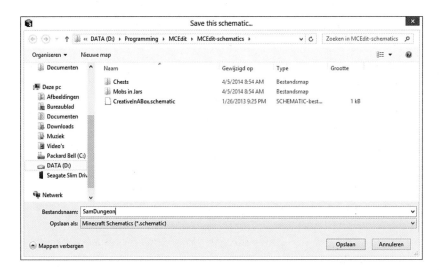

FIGURE 15.8
The exported structure.

Summary

In this hour, you learned how to install and use MCEdit. You also learned how to import a world in MCEdit and how to export a structure.

Q&A

Q. What is the largest size of structure you can export?

A. The structure size in MCEdit can be enormous, but it's not suggested to make a structure too large when it's turned into code because it takes ages to generate and sometimes won't at all. The maximum size of the structure that will normally generate depends on the user's computer, which means it's different for everyone.

Q. How will the purple blocks that aren't recognized by MCEdit be fixed?

A. The problem will be there in MCEdit and in the converter in the next hour. Thanks to the converter, it is easy to see which blocks are unknown, and they can easily be changed in the final code. It will be not much more than a simple find and replace action in Eclipse.

Workshop

In this hour, you learned how to install MCEdit and how to export a structure made in Minecraft. Complete the quiz to make sure you understand these topics completely.

Quiz

1. How do you open a world in MCEdit?

2. Where are `level.dat` files located?

Answers

1. You select the `level.dat` file in the folder where your world is stored.

2. They can be found within the Saves folder, which is either in the Forge setup or your Minecraft installation, depending on which world you want to open. In this folder, you select the save you want to find.

Exercises

Create a tree and export it using MCEdit.

HOUR 16

Generating Your Structure

What You'll Learn in This Hour:

▶ Installing the Schematic Converter
▶ Using the Schematic Converter
▶ Adding mobs to your structure

In this hour, the `.schematic` created in Hour 15, "Using MCEdit," is changed into code using a Schematic Converter. The Schematic Converter was created by Mithion and it was made for Minecraft 1.3.2. Because the structure will be for 1.7, there will be a few problems in the code, but you can easily fix those and it takes far less time than writing all of the code by hand.

Installing the Schematic Converter

Before you install the Schematic Converter, you have to download it. You can download it from www.minecraftforum.net/topic/1336152-132-updated-metadata-support-simple-schematic-to-java-file-converter/. You download a `.zip` file, which you should extract in a location where you can easily find it later. Within the `.zip` file are several folders along with a `.jar` file. To open this `.jar` file, Shift-click the folder it's in to open a command prompt and type the following command:

```
java -jar SchematicConverter.jar
```

You can easily autocomplete the SchematicConverter by pressing Tab when you have entered the first few letters.

Figure 16.1 shows how to do this.

FIGURE 16.1
The folder and command prompt.

When you run this command, the Schematic Converter should start. This looks like Figure 16.2.

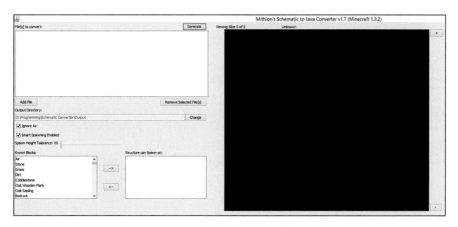

FIGURE 16.2
The Schematic Converter.

Using the Schematic Converter

The Schematic Converter isn't perfect. If you are using a small screen, it might not display as shown in Figure 16.2. There are a few other problems, but they are only small.

Now you need to import your schematic from MCEdit in the Schematic Converter. To do this, click the Add File button on the left. This opens up a file browser where you select the

`.schematic` file. If you have saved this in the standard location when you exported it with MCEdit, this is the location you installed it in and then within the MCEdit-schematics folder. This is shown in Figure 16.3.

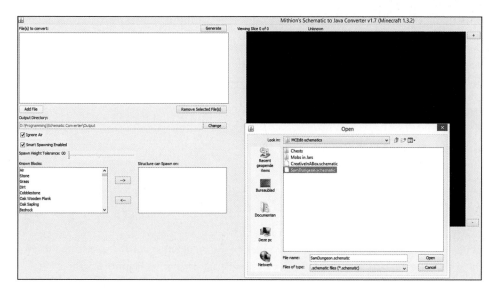

FIGURE 16.3
Opening the schematic.

Once you have opened the schematic in the converter, several things in the interface change and it looks like Figure 16.4.

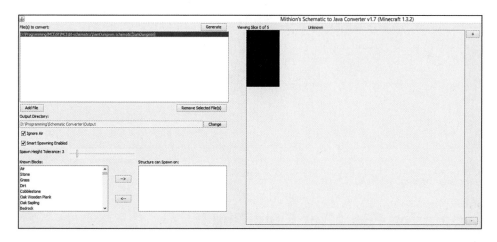

FIGURE 16.4
The converter with the schematic.

On the right is a screen that you can use to look through the blocks. Because this structure is mostly made of air and custom blocks, this menu isn't very useful. One small problem with this window is that the bottom and right row aren't showing up.

Just below the Add File button are several settings of the exported file that you might want to edit. First is the Output folder, which is where the `.java` file will be placed. There are also options for whether the program should add code for placing air blocks and whether there should be code for smart spawning. The smart spawning code can decide how high above the ground it can generate. It can also be used to select which blocks it considers as able to generate.

▼ TRY IT YOURSELF

Play with the Converter Settings

Make sure the structure only generates on top of grass.

You can do this by enabling the smart spawning and setting the slider to 0. You also have to go to the Known Blocks list, select the Grass block, and press the right arrow button.

When all of the settings are the way they should be for your structure, click the Generate button at the top. It should then add [success] at the end of the structure name. Figure 16.5 shows the settings after generating.

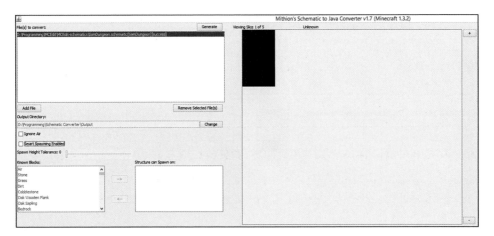

FIGURE 16.5
The converter with the right settings.

The Generation File After Exporting It

After your structure code has been generated, you will see a file with the same name as the `.schematic` in the Output folder. Even though this is a Java file, it can't directly be used in the mod because the code is a little outdated. Copy the `.java` file from the Output folder into your mod package to start working on it. Listing 16.1 shows a part of the file. Most of the `setBlock` lines have been removed from the listing because they are all the same. The full class can be found in the sample code available (after registration) on the book's website, www.informit.com/title/9780672337192. (See the introduction for full register/download instructions.)

LISTING 16.1 The Generated Code

```
/*
*** MADE BY MITHION'S .SCHEMATIC TO JAVA CONVERTING TOOL v1.6 ***
*/

package net.minecraft.src;
import java.util.Random;

public class SamDungeon extends WorldGenerator
{
        public SamDungeon() { }

        public boolean generate(World world, Random rand, int i, int j,
➥int k)
        {
                world.setBlockAndMetadata(i + 0, j + 0, k + 0, -91, 1);
                world.setBlockAndMetadata(i + 0, j + 0, k + 1, -91, 1);
                world.setBlockAndMetadata(i + 0, j + 0, k + 2, -91, 1);
                world.setBlock(i + 1, j + 1, k + 1, 0);
                world.setBlock(i + 1, j + 1, k + 2, 0);
                world.setBlock(i + 1, j + 1, k + 3, 0);
                world.setBlock(i + 1, j + 1, k + 4, 0);

                return true;
        }
}
```

Quite a few things are required to clean this file. The required changes are the following:

▶ Change the name of the class. Right now, it's called `SamDungeon`, but it's smart to follow the vanilla names for world generation classes. Therefore, rename it to `WorldGenSamDungeon`.

▶ Remove the comment at the top. This is not required, but it looks a little nicer.

▶ There is an error under `net.minecraft.src`, which you can fix by hovering over it and selecting Change Package Declaration.

▶ Remove the constructor. It's empty and, therefore, not required.

▶ Rename the i, j, and k variables to x, y, and z for readability.

▶ Change `setBlockAndMetadata` into `setBlock` using Find and Replace, which you can access with Ctrl+F.

▶ Change –91, or whichever number the converter used, into the block used for building. In the case of Sam's Dungeon, replace it with `SamsMod.samStone`.

▶ If you have a block that uses metadata, add an extra variable to the `setBlock` lines. This should be 2 everywhere. The easiest way to do this is by searching for `SamsMod.samStone, 1);` and replacing that with `SamsMod.samStone, 1, 2);`. This makes sure only the correct lines change.

▶ If your structure contains air, an error appears wherever it returns 0 as the block. The zeros have to be replaced with `Blocks.air`.

▶ If your structure contains any vanilla blocks, edit the variable used. For example, it exports the following for glowstone: `Block.glowStone.blockID`. Change this to `Blocks.glowstone`.

▶ Import all the used files using Ctrl+Shift+O or right-click, Source, Organize Imports.

`WorldGenSamDungeon` now looks like Listing 16.2.

LISTING 16.2   The Cleaned-Up `WorldGenSamDungeon`

```
package com.wuppy.samsmod;

import java.util.Random;

import net.minecraft.block.Block;
import net.minecraft.init.Blocks;
import net.minecraft.world.World;
import net.minecraft.world.gen.feature.WorldGenerator;

public class WorldGenSamDungeon extends WorldGenerator
{
        public boolean generate(World world, Random rand, int x, int y, int z)
        {
                world.setBlock(x + 0, y + 0, z + 0, SamsMod.samStone, 1, 2);
                world.setBlock(x + 0, y + 0, z + 1, SamsMod.samStone, 1, 2);
                world.setBlock(x + 0, y + 0, z + 2, SamsMod.samStone, 1, 2);
                world.setBlock(x + 4, y + 3, z + 1, Blocks.air);
                world.setBlock(x + 4, y + 3, z + 2, Blocks.air);
                world.setBlock(x + 4, y + 3, z + 3, Blocks.air);
                world.setBlock(x + 4, y + 3, z + 4, Blocks.air);

                return true;
        }
}
```

The total size of this file is close to 500 lines of code, which were easily created using the converter. This saves quite a bit of time even though the converter itself is outdated.

Making the Structure Generate

Now this class has to be called in the SamEventHandler class. The code for this is very similar to the code used to generate the plants. It is added to generateSurface because it should generate in the normal world. The code looks like this:

```
int posX = x + random.nextInt(16);
int posY = 10 + random.nextInt(40);
int posZ = z + random.nextInt(16);
new WorldGenSamDungeon().generate(world, random, posX, posY, posZ);
```

This code makes sure it can generate everywhere on a chunk, but only between the heights 10 and 49. SamEventHandler should now look like Listing 16.3.

LISTING 16.3   The Finished `SamEventHandler`

```
package com.wuppy.samsmod;

import java.util.Random;

import net.minecraft.block.Block;
import net.minecraft.init.Blocks;
import net.minecraft.world.World;
import net.minecraft.world.chunk.IChunkProvider;
import net.minecraft.world.gen.feature.WorldGenMinable;
import cpw.mods.fml.common.IWorldGenerator;

public class SamEventHandler implements IWorldGenerator
{
    @Override
    public void generate(Random random, int chunkX, int chunkZ, World world,
➥IChunkProvider chunkGenerator, IChunkProvider chunkProvider)
    {
        switch (world.provider.dimensionId)
        {
        case -1:
            generateNether(world, random, chunkX * 16, chunkZ * 16);
        case 0:
            generateSurface(world, random, chunkX * 16, chunkZ * 16);
        case 1:
            generateEnd(world, random, chunkX * 16, chunkZ * 16);
        }
    }

    private void generateEnd(World world, Random random, int x, int z)
```

```
    {
        addOreSpawn(ModBlocks.samStone, 0, Blocks.obsidian, world, random,
➡x, z, 16, 16, 5 + random.nextInt(5), 4, 20, 60);
    }

    private void generateSurface(World world, Random random, int x, int z)
    {
        addOreSpawn(ModBlocks.samStone, 0, Blocks.stone, world, random,
➡x, z, 16, 16, 5 + random.nextInt(5), 4, 20, 60);

        for (int i = 0; i < 3; i++)
        {
            int posX = x + random.nextInt(16);
            int posY = 50 + random.nextInt(35);
            int posZ = z + random.nextInt(16);
            new WorldGenSamPlant().generate(world, random, posX, posY, posZ);
        }

        int posX = x + random.nextInt(16);
        int posY = 10 + random.nextInt(40);
        int posZ = z + random.nextInt(16);
        new WorldGenSamDungeon().generate(world, random, posX, posY, posZ);
    }

    private void generateNether(World world, Random random, int x, int z)
    {
        addOreSpawn(ModBlocks.samStone, 0, Blocks.netherrack, world, random,
➡x, z, 16, 16, 5 + random.nextInt(5), 4, 20, 60);
    }

    /**
     * Adds an Ore Spawn to Minecraft. Simply register all Ores to spawn with
➡this method in your Generation method in your IWorldGeneration extending Class
     *
     * @param The
     *            Block to spawn
     * @param The
     *            metadata of the Block
     * @param The
     *            Block where to generate in
     * @param The
     *            World to spawn in
     * @param A
     *            Random object for retrieving random positions within
➡the world to spawn the Block
     * @param An
     *            int for passing the X-Coordinate for the Generation method
```

```
     * @param An
     *               int for passing the Z-Coordinate for the Generation method
     * @param An
     *               int for setting the maximum X-Coordinate values for spawning
➥on the X-Axis on a Per-Chunk basis
     * @param An
     *               int for setting the maximum Z-Coordinate values for spawning
➥on the Z-Axis on a Per-Chunk basis
     * @param An
     *               int for setting the maximum size of a vein
     * @param An
     *               int for the Number of chances available for the Block
➥to spawn per-chunk
     * @param An
     *               int for the minimum Y-Coordinate height at which this
➥block may spawn
     * @param An
     *               int for the maximum Y-Coordinate height at which this
➥block may spawn
     **/
    public void addOreSpawn(Block block, int metadata, Block target, World
➥world, Random random, int blockXPos, int blockZPos, int maxX, int maxZ,
➥int maxVeinSize, int chancesToSpawn, int minY, int maxY)
    {
        int maxPossY = minY + (maxY - 1);
        assert maxY > minY : "The maximum Y must be greater than the Minimum Y";
        assert maxX > 0 && maxX <= 16 : "addOreSpawn: The Maximum X must be
➥greater than 0 and less than 16";
        assert minY > 0 : "addOreSpawn: The Minimum Y must be greater than 0";
        assert maxY < 256 && maxY > 0 : "addOreSpawn: The Maximum Y must be
➥less than 256 but greater than 0";
        assert maxZ > 0 && maxZ <= 16 : "addOreSpawn: The Maximum Z must be
➥greater than 0 and less than 16";

        int diffBtwnMinMaxY = maxY - minY;
        for (int x = 0; x < chancesToSpawn; x++)
        {
            int posX = blockXPos + random.nextInt(maxX);
            int posY = minY + random.nextInt(diffBtwnMinMaxY);
            int posZ = blockZPos + random.nextInt(maxZ);
            (new WorldGenMinable(block, metadata, maxVeinSize,
➥target)).generate(world, random, posX, posY, posZ);
        }
    }
}
```

Adding Mobs to Your Structure

Many different structures, such as this one, are designed for entities to walk around. There are two commonly used ways to spawn entities. First is the manual spawning code and the second option is using a mob spawner.

Manual Spawning of Entities

It is possible to manually spawn a mob in your structure.

The advantages of manually spawning an entity are as follows:

▶ It's the easiest way to spawn an entity.

▶ It's the easiest way to only have a single copy of the entity.

▶ It doesn't require you to place an extra block.

The disadvantages of manually spawning an entity are as follows:

▶ If you want several entities to be in a single structure, this is annoying and unclear to code.

▶ Certain entities despawn when you get too far away from them, meaning the structure will be empty.

▶ The entities can get killed or die for many different reasons.

▶ In many cases, a single entity just isn't enough to make it an interesting or challenging structure.

How to Manually Spawn an Entity

First, you create the object of the entity you want to spawn inside your `WorldGen` class, which you can do with code like this:

```
EntityZombie entity = new EntityZombie(world);
```

In this case, the spawned entity will be a zombie, but the same code can be applied to every type of entity.

CAUTION

Spawning Locations

As you probably know, most entities do not survive for very long when they are inside of a wall. Therefore, it's important to make sure the spawn location is smart; otherwise, it will die. Additionally, make sure the entity is spawned after making the area it spawns in empty, or it may die after all.

After creating the entity, give it a location to spawn in, which you can do by adding the following line of code:

```
entity.setPosition(x + 1, y + 2, z + 1);
```

Here, the parameters are, as you might expect, the x, y, and z location of the mob. Make sure that the mob spawns in the air, which means that both the coordinates in the method as well as one block higher must be air.

Finally, you actually have to spawn this entity, which you can do by using this code:

```
world.spawnEntityInWorld(entity);
```

The full code for creating and spawning an entity should look like Listing 16.4.

LISTING 16.4   The Complete Entity Spawn Code

```
EntityZombie entity = new EntityZombie(world);
entity.setPosition(x + 1, y + 2, z + 1);
world.spawnEntityInWorld(entity);
```

Using a Mob Spawner

You can also use a mob spawner to spawn mobs in your structure.

The advantages of using a mob spawner are as follows:

- ▶ It is easy to spawn a lot of entities.
- ▶ You can make a structure, like a dungeon, in which you have to fight.

The disadvantages of using a mob spawner are as follows:

- ▶ You can't use it to only spawn a few entities at once.
- ▶ You need to place a block.
- ▶ You need to know the code name of the entity you want to spawn.
- ▶ A single spawner can only spawn a single type of entity.

How to Create a Mob Spawner

To create a working mob spawner, you first create the mob spawner block. You can do this by placing a block in the structure using the following code:

```
world.setBlock(x + 5, y + 1, z + 1, Blocks.mob_spawner);
```

This places the mob spawner block. It also places the mob spawner `TileEntity`, which does the mob spawning logic. However, you haven't set the mob type it should spawn yet. To do this, you first need to get the `TileEntity` as an object in the `WorldGen` class. Use this code:

```
TileEntityMobSpawner spawner = (TileEntityMobSpawner)world.getTileEntity(x
➥+ 5, y + 1, z + 1);
```

CAUTION

Getting the `TileEntity`

If you ever move the mob spawner in the code, try to get the `TileEntity` before placing the block. Or use different coordinates for the block placement and `getTileEntity`. This code does not work on generation, so make sure this is correct.

Now you use the spawner `TileEntity` to set the mob it will spawn. You can do this using the following code:

```
if (spawner != null)
{
    spawner.func_145881_a().setEntityName("Skeleton");
}
else
{
    System.err.println("Failed to fetch mob spawner entity at (" +
➥x + ", " + y + ", " + z + ")");
}
```

First, a check is made to make sure the spawner has actually been found. If you don't have this check, this code is likely to crash.

The code in the `if` statement simply sets the type of mob it will spawn. In this case, it spawns skeletons.

TIP

Entity Names

You can find the entity names of every single entity in the game by looking at the bottom of the class `EntityList`.

If for some reason the spawner hasn't been found, it prints it out as an error in the log. This ensures you are alerted so you can fix it.

The complete mob spawner code should look like Listing 16.5.

LISTING 16.5   Mob Spawner Code

```
world.setBlock(x + 5, y + 1, z + 1, Blocks.mob_spawner);
TileEntityMobSpawner spawner = (TileEntityMobSpawner)world.getTileEntity(x
➥+ 5, y + 1, z + 1);


if (spawner != null)
{
    spawner.func_145881_a().setEntityName("Skeleton");
}
else
{
    System.err.println("Failed to fetch mob spawner entity at (" +
➥x + ", " + y + ", " + z + ")");
}
```

Summary

In this hour, you finished the "World Generation" part of this book. You learned how to add world generation for ores, plants, and structures in the last two hours. In this hour, you learned how to install and use the converter and how to edit the exported file in such a way that it can be generated without errors into the world. Finally, you also learned about the entity spawning options and how to code them.

Q&A

Q. Is there a limit to the file size?

A. There is no actual limit, but if it becomes longer, it not only takes longer to generate, but also longer to load in Eclipse. It may even cause the game to crash if the file size is too large.

Q. Is there a limit to the amount of `WorldGen` files you can add to the generate methods?

A. No, but if there are too many, the world generation either takes an extremely long time or doesn't finish at all.

Workshop

In this hour, you learned how to create the most complicated generation yet. Use the quiz to test your comprehension to make sure you completely understand world generation.

Quiz

1. How would you code a `WorldGen` structure that is only able to generate on trees?

2. How would you make sure the structure only generates in the air?

Answers

1. You don't have to. Simply tell the converter to add the code for it.

2. Make sure the spawn height is above 80 or so and that smart spawning is disabled.

Exercises

Make a new structure or use the existing one. Make sure it only generates on lava and in the nether.

HOUR 17
Learning About Entities

What You'll Learn in This Hour:

▶ Understanding what an entity is

▶ Creating proxies

▶ Creating a basic entity

Entities are quite complicated and there are many different types of entities. Therefore, this hour is an introduction to entities, where you learn what an entity is and what the required code for a basic entity is. Hours 18 and 19, "Creating an Entity Model Using Techne" and "Coding a Mob," respectively, cover making a moving monster entity such as a zombie. Hour 20, "Creating a Throwable," covers how to create a throwable entity such as a snowball.

Understanding What an Entity Is

As mentioned in the introduction text, two examples of entities are zombies and snowballs. The meaning of the word *entity* is something that exists, whether that is material, such as a human, or immaterial, such as thunder. You can find a complete list of entities at http://minecraft. gamepedia.com/Entity#Types_of_entities. Both of these also exist as entities in Minecraft. When you look at how programmers define and use entities, they are basically pieces of data that can interact with other data. An example of this is a creeper blowing up and interacting with the world by breaking blocks.

In Minecraft, almost everything that moves is an entity, with the exception of lava and water. Every animal and monster in the game is an entity. Additionally, particles, throwables, projectiles, and weather effects are all entities in Minecraft. Every single entity in Minecraft extends the `Entity` class. However, most of them also extend an additional class such as `EntityFX`, `EntityThrowable`, or `EntityCreature`. This book covers the last two, but not the first. `EntityFX` isn't covered in this book because it requires a large knowledge of OpenGL. You can find a tutorial on a basic `EntityFX` at www.minecraftforum.net/ topic/2112525-164-custom-particles-tutorial/.

One other important thing to know about entities in Minecraft is that all of them have an x, y, and z value. All of them can also access the world, which means they can place and remove blocks. One very important method for entities is `updateEntity`. In this method, you can write code that makes the entity behave or interact.

Creating Proxies

Almost every single entity needs proxies to function. Therefore, it is required to first create the proxies and make sure they work, before starting on an actual entity.

What Are Proxies?

Proxies are important when dealing with the server and client. There is a `CommonProxy`, which has code focused on the server, and a `ClientProxy`, which contains client code. As you should know from the `@SideOnly(Side.CLIENT)` code explained in the earlier hours, there are certain pieces of code that only run on the client. If these pieces of code are run on the server, Minecraft crashes. The proxies can be seen as entire classes with the `@SideOnly` annotation above them.

However, in Forge, you must use proxies for certain client or server code, which can only run at certain times during the starting of Minecraft. This mostly includes the registering of renders, which is what this book uses proxies for.

Adding Proxies to Your Mod

The first requirement to make the proxies is to add some code to the mod file. Add the following two lines to the list of variables:

```
@SidedProxy(clientSide = "com.wuppy.samsmod.ClientProxySam", serverSide =
➥"com.wuppy.samsmod.CommonProxySam")
publicstatic CommonProxySam proxy;
```

This code contains an error under `CommonProxySam`, which you fix later by creating the file. First, it is important to know what this code does and how it works.

The `@SidedProxy` annotation contains two parameters: `clientSide` and `serverSide`. Both take a `String`, which should contain the `String` referencing the client and server proxies. The `String` will be the package, followed by the class name, separated by dots. In this case, two classes called `ClientProxySam` and `CommonProxySam` are added to the `com.wuppy.samsmod` package.

Directly under the `@SidedProxy` annotation, add the `CommonProxy` variable.

After adding this code, you add a single line of code to the `preInit` method, as follows. It also contains an error, which you fix once the `CommonProxySam` is made.

```
proxy.registerRendering();
```

It is a good idea to make this the first line in the `preInit` method. `registerRendering` contains code to register the renders, obviously, and it doesn't rely on any of the code following in `preInit`. However, there are pieces of code that do. These pieces of code could crash when the rendering isn't registered yet, so it's important to start the `preInit` with this line.

Coding the `CommonProxy`

Now, hover your mouse over the error under `CommonProxySam` and select the Create Class option. Listing 17.1 shows the file that appears.

LISTING 17.1   The Initial `CommonProxySam`

```
package com.wuppy.samsmod;

public class CommonProxySam
{

}
```

The error under `CommonProxySam` is now gone, but there is now an error under `registerRendering`. To fix this, hover your mouse over the error and select the Create Method option. After cleaning up the class a little, it should look like Listing 17.2.

LISTING 17.2   `CommonProxySam` with the `registerRendering` Method

```
package com.wuppy.samsmod;

public class CommonProxySam
{
        public void registerRendering()
        {


        }
}
```

Because all of the rendering is done on the client side, this method is empty in the `CommonProxy`.

Creating the `ClientProxy`

To create the `ClientProxySam`, right-click the `com.wuppy.samsmod` package and select New, Class. The class name will be `ClientProxySam`. Listing 17.3 shows the resulting class.

LISTING 17.3   Initial `ClientProxySam`

```
package com.wuppy.samsmod;

public class ClientProxySam
{

}
```

This class will have to extend the `CommonProxy`. It also has to override the method in the `CommonProxy`. After doing this, it looks like Listing 17.4.

LISTING 17.4   The `ClientProxy` with `registerRendering`

```
package com.wuppy.samsmod;

public class ClientProxySam extends CommonProxySam
{
        @Override
        public void registerRendering()
        {


        }
}
```

This class will stay empty for now, but it is required in Hour 19.

Creating a Basic Entity

Before creating a mob, it is important to know some of the basic code required for entities.

Every entity in Minecraft, with the exception of a `TileEntity`, has to be registered using `EntityRegistry`. For `EntitySamMob`, a mob which will be created over the next few hours, the `EntityRegistry` will look as follows:

```
EntityRegistry.registerModEntity(EntitySamMob.class, "sammob", 0, this, 80, 3,
➥true);
```

This code contains an error, which you fix shortly by creating the `EntitySamMob` class.

`registerModEntity` is the method required to register your entities. The first parameter in there is the `Entity` class you want to register.

The second parameter is the name you want to register it with. Two different mods can have the same name here, but you can't have two mobs with the same name in a single mod. Two mods can have the same mob name because the unlocalized name is not just the name you enter in here. Instead, it is `entity.[modid].[registryname].name`. This means for `EntitySamMob`, the unlocalized name is `entity.wuppy29_samsmod.sammob.name`. This is also added to the `en_US.lang` file and looks like the following:

```
entity.wuppy29_samsmod.sammob.name=Sam's Mob
```

The third parameter in `registerModEntity` is the ID of the mob. These IDs are different for every mod, meaning that there can be an endless amount of mods with a mob of ID 0. However, you can't have two mobs with the same ID in a single mod.

The fourth parameter is `this`, which makes sure the registered mob is part of this mod.

The fifth parameter is called the tracking range. This is the maximum distance this entity can be from the player where it will still update—so move and attack. If it is any further than the number in here, it does not do anything. This is generally kept at 80 for most entities.

The sixth parameter is the `updateFrequency`. When the entity is within the tracking range of the previous parameter, the entity must be updated. If this is done more frequently, the entity may behave better. However, the game will also be slower. For entities, the update frequency is generally 3, and for projectiles, which have to be more precise, it is 1.

The final parameter states if it should send velocity information with the entity when it is updating. Almost every entity should have this on `true`. The only exception is when your entity will never move.

Creating the `EntitySamMob` Class

To create the `EntitySamMob` class, simply hover your mouse over the error and select Create Class. Listing 17.5 shows the resulting class.

LISTING 17.5   Empty `EntitySamMob` Class

```
package com.wuppy.samsmod;

public class EntitySamMob
{

}
```

To make `EntitySamMob` an entity, you extend `Entity`, which you do by adding the following piece of code after `EntitySamMob`. Don't forget to import the `Entity` class.

`extends Entity`

When importing the `Entity` class, make sure you get the one in the `Minecraft` package. Once you do this, you get an error under `EntitySamMob`, which you can fix by adding the constructor. When you add the constructor, a second error appears under `EntitySamMob`, which you can fix by hovering over it and selecting Add Unimplemented Methods.

After cleaning up the class a little, it should look like Listing 17.6.

LISTING 17.6 **EntitySamMob** with the Required Methods

```
package com.wuppy.samsmod;

import net.minecraft.entity.Entity;
import net.minecraft.nbt.NBTTagCompound;
import net.minecraft.world.World;

public class EntitySamMob extends Entity
{
        public EntitySamMob(World par1World)
        {
                super(par1World);
        }

        @Override
        protected void entityInit()
        {

        }

        @Override
        protected void readEntityFromNBT(NBTTagCompound tag)
        {

        }

        @Override
        protected void writeEntityToNBT(NBTTagCompound tag)
        {

        }
}
```

Summary

In this hour, you started by learning what an entity is. Entities are frequently used in Minecraft and there are many types, so it's important to understand the basics. Next, you learned how to create proxies, which are used to register rendering code for the entities created in the following hours. Finally, you created your first `Entity` class and registered it. The entity doesn't do anything yet, but functionality will be added in Hour 19.

Q&A

Q. Is there a limit to the amount of registerable entities?

A. No. However, if there are a lot of entities to register, it will take Minecraft much longer to start.

Q. Why did I have to create the proxies even though they are empty?

A. They are empty now, but some very important code will be added in the next few hours.

Workshop

In this hour, you laid the foundation for entities. The following hours cover how to create your own entities, but it's important to completely understand the code covered in this hour. Check your comprehension by completing this quiz.

Quiz

1. What is the `ClientProxy` for?
2. Why does the method in the `CommonProxy` have to be called at the start of the `preInit` method?
3. Is it a good idea to register blocks in the `ClientProxy`?

Answers

1. It is created to run registry code on the client side only.
2. Other code in the method will rely on the code in the proxies.
3. No, this would be very bad. If the blocks are registered on the client only, it will desynchronize with the server, which can lead to crashes and many other problems.

Exercises

Create a `registerEntity` for a second mob. Make sure it has a different name and ID.

Creating an Entity Model Using Techne

What You'll Learn in This Hour:

▶ What are models?
▶ Downloading and installing Techne
▶ Using Techne

In this hour, you learn how to create a basic model in Techne, which is a modeling program made specifically for Minecraft models. In Hour 19, "Coding a Mob," this model is used in an entity to create a mob. Before creating the model in Techne, it is important to install Techne first and to understand what models in Minecraft are. Finally, you export the created model.

What Are Models?

Models in Minecraft consist of three parts. First is the shape of the model. Every single model in Minecraft is nothing but a collection of cubes. These cubes can have different sizes, lengths, rotations, and so forth. The most commonly used model is called `ModelBiped`. This is the model for the player, zombie, zombie pigman, and several others. The body itself is made from six body parts. There are also a few extra, which aren't used that often. One example of that is `bipedEars`. This is a model piece, which only gets rendered when the player is called deadmau5.

The second part is the texture. The texture can be seen as a 2D paper, which gets folded around the 3D model cubes. Every single cube used in the 3D model has six sides on the 2D texture. In Hour 8, "Creating Armor," you created textures very similar to the texture required for a model.

The final part is the moving of the model. One example of this moving is the rotating of the player's legs when it walks. Another example is that zombies always have their arms pointed forward, even though they use the same model as the player. This hour covers the creation of the model and texture. However, it does not cover moving parts. This is done with reasonably complicated trigonometric functions; to do this properly, you simply have to understand this part of math very well.

When these three parts are combined, you can have something like the player. It has a biped model, the skin you want it to have, and it moves its legs when it walks around.

NOTE

Using Models

You can use models not only for entities but also for items and blocks. This works similarly to using a model for an entity, but it's beyond the scope of this book. Information on how to do this for blocks can be found here: www.minecraftforge.net/wiki/Rendering_a_Techne_Model_as_a_Block. An explanation for items can be found here: http://ichun.us/modding-tutorial-3d-item-models-using-techne/.

Downloading and Installing Techne

To get Techne, you can download the `.application` file at http://techne.zeux.me/Techne. When you have downloaded it, paste the file in a location where you will be able to find it. Because Techne is an `.application` file, you can simply double-click it and it's ready to go. When you do this, a New Model window opens, similar to Figure 18.1. If the installation does go wrong, you should see if you have .NET Framework 4.1 or higher installed. If not, download it at www.microsoft.com/en-us/download/details.aspx?id=17718. If it still goes wrong after installing this, you should join #techne on IRC and ask questions there. How to get on IRC is explained in Hour 24, "What's Next."

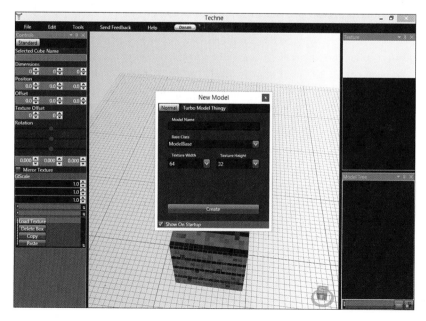

FIGURE 18.1
Techne startup window.

Using Techne

Below the Model Name you put the name for your model. You can also set the model it should start with under Base Class. For Sam's Mob, this is ModelBiped. If you want to start with a completely empty model, simply select ModelBase. The last setting you can set in the New Model window is the texture size. For most entities, a 64×32 texture works just fine, but if the entity is going to be very large, you might need a bigger texture.

Understanding the Interface

Once you have selected the settings you want, click Create. With ModelBiped selected as the starting model, Techne now looks like Figure 18.2.

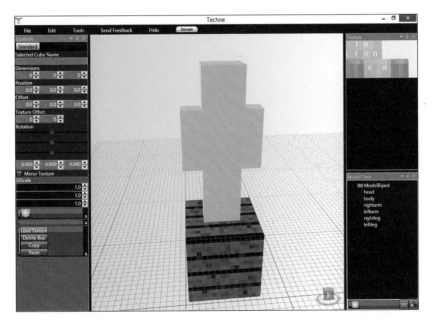

FIGURE 18.2
Techne model creation screen.

This screen is what you will be looking at most of the time. In the middle, you can look at your model from every side. Just below the model is a wood block, which you can use to visualize the in-game size of your model. On the lower right of the middle window, a cube is located where you can see from which side you are looking. To the right of that is a window called ModelTree. All of the cubes the model is made of will be in here. You can edit the name from the cube by double-clicking.

Editing Cube Properties

When you select a cube, the way most of the parts of the screen look change a bit. It will then look like Figure 18.3.

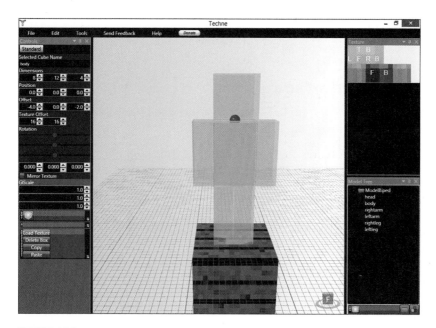

FIGURE 18.3
Techne with a selected cube.

Once you have selected a cube, all of the other pieces of the screen become active and usable. The most important part of the window, besides the part where you can actually see the model, is in the top left. Here, you can set the name, location, rotation, and several other things for each cube.

At the top is the name, which must be different for every single cube or you will experience problems. This name is used in Techne but also in the code that you export later.

Below that are the dimensions, which are the x, y, and z size of the cube.

Next there are two x, y, and z values, which might seem a little confusing. There is position and offset. It's very important to edit the correct one, or your model will likely behave strangely. The position is the location where the blue ball in the cube is located. This blue ball is the point that the cube will rotate around. This position is very important because it can make the difference between arms moving around when walking and arms falling off all the time. The blue ball can be seen as the joint of the cube. When the offset is normal, this ball is at the center of the cube. To move the joint into a logical place, such as the top left for the right arm, the offset can be used.

Texture offset is used for the location of the texture. The entire model has a single texture, which is cut up into pieces for each cube. Because each cube will likely have a different texture, texture offset must be used to make sure the cube uses the texture from the correct part of the image. The texture can be seen on the top right. The selected cube has a slightly less transparent color so you can easily see which part of the texture the cube is getting the texture from.

Rotation can be used to rotate body parts. It always rotates around the blue ball and can rotate in every direction. ModelBiped has a rotation of 0 for each value, but when the player walks around, the body parts do move. Each value you set in here is editable later in the code or by the code when Minecraft is running. However, it is a good idea to set the rotation values to the standard value in Techne.

There are two more options for your model. First, mirror texture enables you to have the same texture area for both arms and it will mirror it. Second, GlScale enables you to make each piece look larger or smaller than it actually is. This is mostly set to 1, which makes it look normal. This is just a visual aid in Techne and does not influence your model.

Adding and Removing Cubes

To add a cube, the blue cube just below GlScale can be used. This adds a new cube with size 1, 1, 1 at the origin. Below there are a few more options that you can use to remove, copy, and paste cubes.

The final option on the screen is Load Texture. You can use this to load the model texture onto the model. Because the model used up to this point is exactly the same as the ModelBiped, you can use a texture such as the zombie to show the model with the texture on it.

TRY IT YOURSELF ▼

Add the Zombie Texture

Add the zombie texture to the model. To do this, follow this list of steps:

1. Go to the location where you installed Minecraft, which is, by default, C:\Users\ [username]\AppData\Roaming\.minecraft\versions.

2. Select the version of Minecraft you want the texture from and open up the .jar file with 7zip or Winrar.

3. All textures can be found in assets/minecraft/textures. Enter these folders.

4. For the zombie texture, enter entity/zombies and select zombie.png.

5. Now copy it in a folder where you can easily find it.

6. Select the Load Texture option in Techne.

7. Select the `zombie.png` file and Techne looks like Figure 18.4.

FIGURE 18.4
Zombie in Techne.

The mob made in this hour is very similar to `ModelBiped` with the standard player texture. The only difference is that there is a cap on its head. In Techne, this model looks like Figure 18.5.

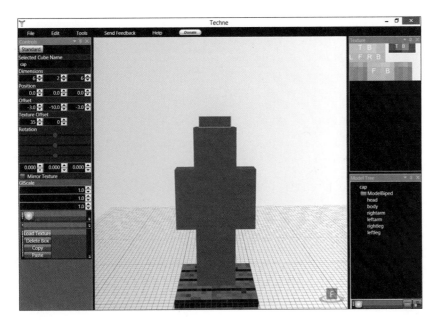

FIGURE 18.5
The Sam's Mob model.

Exporting Your Model

After creating the model, it would be nice if it was actually usable in Minecraft. You can do this by exporting it. You can export using File, Export As on the top right. The model must be exported as both a Texturemap and Java. Don't forget to save your model as a Techne file as well so you can edit it later. Figure 18.6 shows the menu where you can export.

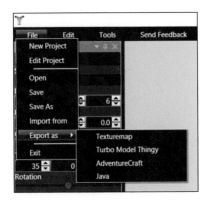

FIGURE 18.6
The Sam's Mob model.

The exported Java class for the model looks similar to Listing 18.1.

LISTING 18.1   The Exported Model

```java
// Date: 6/4/2014 1:22:20 PM
// Template version 1.1
// Java generated by Techne
// Keep in mind that you still need to fill in some blanks
// - ZeuX




package net.minecraft.src;

public class ModelModel extends ModelBase
{
  //fields
    ModelRenderer cap;
    ModelRenderer head;
    ModelRenderer body;
    ModelRenderer rightarm;
    ModelRenderer leftarm;
    ModelRenderer rightleg;
    ModelRenderer leftleg;

  public ModelModel()
  {
    textureWidth = 64;
    textureHeight = 32;

      cap = new ModelRenderer(this, 35, 0);
      cap.addBox(-3F, -10F, -3F, 6, 2, 6);
      cap.setRotationPoint(0F, 0F, 0F);
      cap.setTextureSize(64, 32);
      cap.mirror = true;
      setRotation(cap, 0F, 0F, 0F);
      head = new ModelRenderer(this, 0, 0);
      head.addBox(-4F, -8F, -4F, 8, 8, 8);
      head.setRotationPoint(0F, 0F, 0F);
      head.setTextureSize(64, 32);
      head.mirror = true;
      setRotation(head, 0F, 0F, 0F);
      body = new ModelRenderer(this, 16, 16);
      body.addBox(-4F, 0F, -2F, 8, 12, 4);
      body.setRotationPoint(0F, 0F, 0F);
```

```
        body.setTextureSize(64, 32);
        body.mirror = true;
        setRotation(body, 0F, 0F, 0F);
        rightarm = new ModelRenderer(this, 40, 16);
        rightarm.addBox(-3F, -2F, -2F, 4, 12, 4);
        rightarm.setRotationPoint(-5F, 2F, 0F);
        rightarm.setTextureSize(64, 32);
        rightarm.mirror = true;
        setRotation(rightarm, 0F, 0F, 0F);
        leftarm = new ModelRenderer(this, 40, 16);
        leftarm.addBox(-1F, -2F, -2F, 4, 12, 4);
        leftarm.setRotationPoint(5F, 2F, 0F);
        leftarm.setTextureSize(64, 32);
        leftarm.mirror = true;
        setRotation(leftarm, 0F, 0F, 0F);
        rightleg = new ModelRenderer(this, 0, 16);
        rightleg.addBox(-2F, 0F, -2F, 4, 12, 4);
        rightleg.setRotationPoint(-2F, 12F, 0F);
        rightleg.setTextureSize(64, 32);
        rightleg.mirror = true;
        setRotation(rightleg, 0F, 0F, 0F);
        leftleg = new ModelRenderer(this, 0, 16);
        leftleg.addBox(-2F, 0F, -2F, 4, 12, 4);
        leftleg.setRotationPoint(2F, 12F, 0F);
        leftleg.setTextureSize(64, 32);
        leftleg.mirror = true;
        setRotation(leftleg, 0F, 0F, 0F);
    }

    public void render(Entity entity, float f, float f1, float f2, float f3,
➥float f4, float f5)
    {
        super.render(entity, f, f1, f2, f3, f4, f5);
        setRotationAngles(f, f1, f2, f3, f4, f5, entity);
        cap.render(f5);
        head.render(f5);
        body.render(f5);
        rightarm.render(f5);
        leftarm.render(f5);
        rightleg.render(f5);
        leftleg.render(f5);
    }

    private void setRotation(ModelRenderer model, float x, float y, float z)
    {
        model.rotateAngleX = x;
        model.rotateAngleY = y;
        model.rotateAngleZ = z;
```

```
  }

  public void setRotationAngles(float f, float f1, float f2, float f3,
➥float f4, float f5, Entity entity)
  {
    super.setRotationAngles(f, f1, f2, f3, f4, f5, entity);
  }

}
```

You have to do a little bit of work when this model is added to Eclipse in Hour 19 because there are several errors now.

The texture, when exported from Techne, looks like Figure 18.7.

FIGURE 18.7
The Exported Sam's Mob texture.

This might look really unclear, but which cube refers to which part in the texture can be seen within Techne. The color of each area is also the same as the direction cube at the bottom of the model view in Techne. The easiest way to texture a mob is to import the texture in Techne and see how it looks. When you edit the texture file you load, Techne should automatically update it for you so you can see the changes.

After editing the texture, the mob looks like Figure 18.8.

FIGURE 18.8
The Finished Sam's Mob texture.

The .techne file itself can be found in the sample files for this book (see the introduction for instructions on downloading the files).

In Hour 19, you use these files to make the mob actually work.

NOTE

Other Modeling Software

Techne is the only commonly used modeling software that can export models to the Minecraft code format. However, Forge also allows you to use `.obj` files. This extension is supported by most modern modeling programs, including Blender and Maya. If you use an `.obj` file, you have to use a class called `AdvancedModelLoader` to use the model.

Summary

In this hour, you first learned what models are in Minecraft and how you can use them. Next, you learned about Techne, which is a tool in which you can easily make models. You learned how to install Techne, how the interface works, and how you can create your own models with it. Additionally, you exported your model from Techne into a `.png` and a `.java` file, which you can use to code and texture your mob.

Q&A

Q. Is there a maximum number of model cubes there can be?

A. No, there is no maximum, but when there are more cubes, it takes longer to render, so try to balance performance and appearance.

Q. Can models like this be used for other purposes than just mobs?

A. Yes. They can also be used for blocks and items.

Workshop

In this hour, you learned about models and how to create them in Techne. Many different mods use models, so it's important to understand these well. Complete the quiz to test your understanding.

Quiz

1. Why do you have to use Techne?

2. What do you need to export from Techne?

Answers

1. Because it's simply easier. You could write the model by hand, but that would take a really long time. Techne makes it easy to visualize your model.

2. You need to export the texture and the code. However, don't forget to save the model as a `.techne` file or you will not be able to edit it later.

Exercises

Edit `ModelBiped` in such a way that it only has a single leg in the middle of the body.

HOUR 19

Coding a Mob

What You'll Learn in This Hour:

▶ Rendering the mob
▶ Making the mob spawn
▶ Making `EntitySamMob` a mob

In this hour, you combine what you did in Hours 17 and 18, "Learning About Entities" and "Creating an Entity Model Using Techne," respectively, to create a mob. This hour covers combining that code and adding some more to make the entity work like a mob.

To create a mob, a lot of classes have to be made. First, you need a mod file, which you have already made. You also need a `CommonProxy` and `ClientProxy`, as created in Hour 17. Additionally, you require an `Entity`, `Model`, and `Render` class. This hour covers all of the files, starting with the `Model`.

Rendering the Mob

One very important aspect of a mob is that it is visible. To do this, you create the `Model` and the `Render` files. You also add a line of code to the `ClientProxy`.

Finishing the Model Class

In Hour 18, you created a model in Techne from which the code was also exported. Now it's time to add this model to your workspace. To do this, right-click your package in Eclipse and select New, Class. The name for the class is `ModelSamMob`. It's a good idea to have a very similar name for all of the classes related to the same mob. The mob that you create in this hour has `EntitySamMob`, `ModelSamMob`, and `RenderSamMob` as its classes, which you create throughout this hour. This way, it's easy to see which classes belong to which mob, in the case of having multiple mobs in a single mod.

NOTE

About Techne

You are not forced to use Techne. It is perfectly possible to write models yourself. If you do, you must write all the code yourself, which can take quite a lot of time.

Next, copy the code from the exported `.java` file and paste it in `ModelSamMob`. This code has quite a few problems. To fix all of the problems, work through the following list:

▶ Remove the comment at the top. It doesn't add anything and it might make your class harder to read.

▶ Change the package declaration. The exported file has as the package `net.minecraft.src`, which you should change to the package this class is in. When you hover your mouse over it, you can select Change Package Declaration to change it into the correct package.

▶ Change the class and constructor name from `ModelModel` into `ModelSamMob`, or whatever your `Model` file is named. You can do this easily by hovering your mouse over the error under `ModelModel` and selecting Rename Type.

▶ Import all of the used files using Ctrl+Shift+O or by right-clicking and then selecting Source, Organize Imports.

CAUTION

Techne Is Not Perfect

Just like almost everything else that exists, Techne isn't perfect. It is possible for your exported code to contain some errors. If you try to use the exported Techne code for a different version than Techne made it for, you may run into problems.

Another thing you might want to check is if the line `[bodypart].mirror = true;` isn't used before the body parts are initialized. This can sometimes happen and results in crashes.

The class should now look like Listing 19.1 and should not have any errors left.

LISTING 19.1   The Finished `ModelSamMob`

```
package com.wuppy.samsmod.render;

import net.minecraft.client.model.ModelBase;
import net.minecraft.client.model.ModelRenderer;
import net.minecraft.entity.Entity;

public class ModelSamMob extends ModelBase
{
    // fields
```

```
ModelRenderer cap;
ModelRenderer head;
ModelRenderer body;
ModelRenderer rightarm;
ModelRenderer leftarm;
ModelRenderer rightleg;
ModelRenderer leftleg;

public ModelSamMob()
{
        textureWidth = 64;
        textureHeight = 32;

        cap = new ModelRenderer(this, 35, 0);
        cap.addBox(-3F, -10F, -3F, 6, 2, 6);
        cap.setRotationPoint(0F, 0F, 0F);
        cap.setTextureSize(64, 32);
        cap.mirror = true;
        setRotation(cap, 0F, 0F, 0F);
        head = new ModelRenderer(this, 0, 0);
        head.addBox(-4F, -8F, -4F, 8, 8, 8);
        head.setRotationPoint(0F, 0F, 0F);
        head.setTextureSize(64, 32);
        head.mirror = true;
        setRotation(head, 0F, 0F, 0F);
        body = new ModelRenderer(this, 16, 16);
        body.addBox(-4F, 0F, -2F, 8, 12, 4);
        body.setRotationPoint(0F, 0F, 0F);
        body.setTextureSize(64, 32);
        body.mirror = true;
        setRotation(body, 0F, 0F, 0F);
        rightarm = new ModelRenderer(this, 40, 16);
        rightarm.addBox(-3F, -2F, -2F, 4, 12, 4);
        rightarm.setRotationPoint(-5F, 2F, 0F);
        rightarm.setTextureSize(64, 32);
        rightarm.mirror = true;
        setRotation(rightarm, 0F, 0F, 0F);
        leftarm = new ModelRenderer(this, 40, 16);
        leftarm.addBox(-1F, -2F, -2F, 4, 12, 4);
        leftarm.setRotationPoint(5F, 2F, 0F);
        leftarm.setTextureSize(64, 32);
        leftarm.mirror = true;
        setRotation(leftarm, 0F, 0F, 0F);
        rightleg = new ModelRenderer(this, 0, 16);
        rightleg.addBox(-2F, 0F, -2F, 4, 12, 4);
        rightleg.setRotationPoint(-2F, 12F, 0F);
        rightleg.setTextureSize(64, 32);
```

```
            rightleg.mirror = true;
            setRotation(rightleg, 0F, 0F, 0F);
            leftleg = new ModelRenderer(this, 0, 16);
            leftleg.addBox(-2F, 0F, -2F, 4, 12, 4);
            leftleg.setRotationPoint(2F, 12F, 0F);
            leftleg.setTextureSize(64, 32);
            leftleg.mirror = true;
            setRotation(leftleg, 0F, 0F, 0F);
    }

    public void render(Entity entity, float f, float f1,
➥float f2, float f3, float f4, float f5)
    {
            super.render(entity, f, f1, f2, f3, f4, f5);
            setRotationAngles(f, f1, f2, f3, f4, f5, entity);
            cap.render(f5);
            head.render(f5);
            body.render(f5);
            rightarm.render(f5);
            leftarm.render(f5);
            rightleg.render(f5);
            leftleg.render(f5);
    }

    private void setRotation(ModelRenderer model, float x, float y, float z)
    {
            model.rotateAngleX = x;
            model.rotateAngleY = y;
            model.rotateAngleZ = z;
    }

    public void setRotationAngles(float f, float f1, float f2,
➥float f3, float f4, float f5, Entity entity)
    {
            super.setRotationAngles(f, f1, f2, f3, f4, f5, entity);
    }
}
```

Moving Body Parts

Once you have finished this hour, you will have a fully functional mob. It will walk around and attack enemies. When vanilla mobs move around, their legs and, in some cases, arms move. If body parts don't properly move, these mobs will look really weird when they move around.

So to make sure this mob doesn't look weird, the body parts should rotate when the player is moving. You can do this using setRotationAngles. In this method, you can set a rotation to every body part using basic trigonometry.

Because this model is almost exactly the same as `ModelBiped`, which is used for normal entities such as players, the rotations from that class can easily be copied into here. The code
from `ModelBiped` has some different variable names, which you change to the ones in
`ModelSamMob`. You can remove some lines, such as those that set the rotation for sneaking or
holding things like a bow, because the mob won't do that.

You also add two lines. These two lines make sure that the cap rotates the exact same way as the
head. This ensures that the cap doesn't clip into the head. Because the rotation point of the head
and the cap are the same, the rotations of the head can be copied to the rotations of the cap.

`setRotationAngles` in `ModelSamMob` should now look like Listing 19.2.

LISTING 19.2 `setRotationAngles` Added to `ModelSamMob`

```
public void setRotationAngles(float f, float f1, float f2, float f3,
➥float f4, float f5, Entity entity)
{
    this.head.rotateAngleY = f3 / (180F / (float)Math.PI);
    this.head.rotateAngleX = f4 / (180F / (float)Math.PI);

    this.cap.rotateAngleX = this.head.rotateAngleX;
    this.cap.rotateAngleY = this.head.rotateAngleY;

    this.rightarm.rotateAngleX = MathHelper.cos(f * 0.6662F +
➥(float)Math.PI) * 2.0F * f1 * 0.5F;
    this.leftarm.rotateAngleX = MathHelper.cos(f * 0.6662F) * 2.0F * f1 * 0.5F;
    this.rightarm.rotateAngleZ = 0.0F;
    this.leftarm.rotateAngleZ = 0.0F;
    this.rightleg.rotateAngleX = MathHelper.cos(f * 0.6662F) * 1.4F * f1;
    this.leftleg.rotateAngleX = MathHelper.cos(f * 0.6662F +
➥(float)Math.PI) * 1.4F * f1;
    this.rightleg.rotateAngleY = 0.0F;
    this.leftleg.rotateAngleY = 0.0F;

    this.rightarm.rotateAngleY = 0.0F;
    this.leftarm.rotateAngleY = 0.0F;
    float f6;
    float f7;

    if (this.onGround > -9990.0F)
    {
        f6 = this.onGround;
        this.body.rotateAngleY = MathHelper.sin(MathHelper.sqrt_float(f6)
➥* (float)Math.PI * 2.0F) * 0.2F;
        this.rightarm.rotationPointZ = MathHelper.sin(this.body.rotateAngleY)
➥* 5.0F;
        this.rightarm.rotationPointX = -MathHelper.cos(this.body.rotateAngleY)
➥* 5.0F;
```

```
        this.leftarm.rotationPointZ = -MathHelper.sin(this.body.rotateAngleY)
➥* 5.0F;
        this.leftarm.rotationPointX = MathHelper.cos(this.body.rotateAngleY)
➥* 5.0F;
        this.rightarm.rotateAngleY += this.body.rotateAngleY;
        this.leftarm.rotateAngleY += this.body.rotateAngleY;
        this.leftarm.rotateAngleX += this.body.rotateAngleY;
        f6 = 1.0F - this.onGround;
        f6 *= f6;
        f6 *= f6;
        f6 = 1.0F - f6;
        f7 = MathHelper.sin(f6 * (float)Math.PI);
        float f8 = MathHelper.sin(this.onGround * (float)Math.PI) *
➥-(this.head.rotateAngleX - 0.7F) * 0.75F;
        this.rightarm.rotateAngleX = (float)((double)this.rightarm.
➥rotateAngleX - ((double)f7 * 1.2D + (double)f8));
        this.rightarm.rotateAngleY += this.body.rotateAngleY * 2.0F;
        this.rightarm.rotateAngleZ = MathHelper.sin(this.onGround *
➥(float)Math.PI) * -0.4F;
    }
    this.rightarm.rotateAngleZ += MathHelper.cos(f2 * 0.09F) * 0.05F + 0.05F;
    this.leftarm.rotateAngleZ -= MathHelper.cos(f2 * 0.09F) * 0.05F + 0.05F;
    this.rightarm.rotateAngleX += MathHelper.sin(f2 * 0.067F) * 0.05F;
    this.leftarm.rotateAngleX -= MathHelper.sin(f2 * 0.067F) * 0.05F;

    super.setRotationAngles(f, f1, f2, f3, f4, f5, entity);
}
```

Coding the `Render` Class

Now that the `Model` class is finished, it is time to create the `Render` class. To do this, again, right-click the package and select New, Class. Use the name `RenderSamMob`. When you create the file, it should look similar to Listing 19.3.

LISTING 19.3   Initial RenderSamMob Class

```
package com.wuppy.samsmod;

public class RenderSamMob
{

}
```

Now make it extend `RenderLiving`, which makes sure it renders like a living entity, fix the imports, and add the required constructor and method by hovering your mouse over the errors and selecting the fixes. At this point, `RenderSamMob` should look like Listing 19.4.

LISTING 19.4   `RenderSamMob` Extending `RenderLiving`

```
package com.wuppy.samsmod;

import net.minecraft.client.model.ModelBase;
import net.minecraft.client.renderer.entity.RenderLiving;
import net.minecraft.entity.Entity;
import net.minecraft.util.ResourceLocation;

public class RenderSamMob extends RenderLiving
{
        public RenderSamMob(ModelBase par1ModelBase, float par2)
        {
                super(par1ModelBase, par2);
        }

        @Override
        protected ResourceLocation getEntityTexture(Entity entity)
        {
                return null;
        }
}
```

Now change the null in `getEntityTexture` with the following piece of code:

```
new ResourceLocation(SamsMod.MODID, "textures/models/sammob.png")
```

This gets the texture located in the `SamsMod` textures folder. In there should be a folder called textures. Within that folder is another one called models—in this folder, place the mob texture created in the previous hour. The name of the file is, in this case, `sammob.png`. In most cases, it's best to give the texture the same name as the mob in code. The texture looks like Figure 19.1.

FIGURE 19.1
The entity texture.

Rendering the Mob

Now the `Render` and `Model` classes are finished, which means you can now actually render the mob. To do this, add the following line of code to the `ClientProxy`:

```
RenderingRegistry.registerEntityRenderingHandler(EntitySamMob.class, new
➥RenderSamMob(new ModelSamMob(), 0.5F));
```

To register a mob, you have to access the `RenderingRegistry` class. For an entity, the required method is called `registerEntityRenderingHandler`. This method takes two parameters. The first parameter is the `Entity` class it is supposed to register a render for.

Second, it needs the class it will render with. In this case, that class is `RenderSamMob`. `RenderSamMob` takes two parameters as well. The first parameter is the model it should render, which is `ModelSamMob` in this example. The second parameter is the shadow size. If you make this larger, the shading circle under the mob will be made larger as well. 0.5F is the default value for models similar to the player.

The `ClientProxy` should now look like Listing 19.5.

LISTING 19.5   `ClientProxySam` with the `RenderingRegistry`

```
package com.wuppy.samsmod;

import cpw.mods.fml.client.registry.RenderingRegistry;

public class ClientProxySam extends CommonProxySam
{
        @Override
        public void registerRendering()
        {
                RenderingRegistry.registerEntityRenderingHandler(EntitySamMob.
➥class, new RenderSamMob(new ModelSamMob(), 0.5F));
        }
}
```

Even though you didn't add any code to the `CommonProxy`, do not remove it, because without it, the `ClientProxy` doesn't work.

Making the Mob Spawn

There are two ways to make a mob spawn. There are spawn eggs, which enable you to spawn a mob with an item, and there are natural spawns, which make sure that, for example, cows walk on grassy areas.

Adding a Mob Egg

It is smart to give every single mob you have a spawn egg. Doing this makes it much easier to test. In some cases, it also helps the user. The best part about mob eggs, however, is that it only requires a little bit of code and it doesn't use any new items. The new spawn eggs are added to the vanilla mob egg.

To add your mob to a spawn egg, add the following code to the mod class:

```
static int startEntityId = 300;

@SuppressWarnings("unchecked")
public static void registerEntityEgg(Class<? extends Entity> entity,
➥int primaryColor, int secondaryColor)
{
        int id = getUniqueEntityId();
        EntityList.IDtoClassMapping.put(id, entity);
        EntityList.entityEggs.put(id, new EntityEggInfo(id, primaryColor,
➥secondaryColor));
}

public static int getUniqueEntityId()
{
        do
        {
                startEntityId++;
        }
        while (EntityList.getStringFromID(startEntityId) != null);

        return startEntityId;
}
```

To use this code, call the registerEntityEgg method. The parameters are the entity you want to register, the egg's base color, and the color of the spots on the egg. The method calls getUniqueEntityId, which looks through the entity egg list to find an empty spot, at which point that number is returned to registerEntityEgg. In this method, the mob is registered with an egg.

Adding EntitySamMob to the spawn eggs is really easy now. Add the following line of code to the preInit method after registering the mob, and an entity egg will show up with EntitySamMob in the game:

```
registerEntityEgg(EntitySamMob.class, 0xd8bb9d, 0xa63c1a);
```

The colors are in hexadecimal, which is required here. In Java, hexadecimal numbers such as this one, usually only used for colors, are preceded by 0x to tell Java it's a hexadecimal color. These values don't include an alpha value.

Figure 19.2 shows the spawn egg created earlier.

FIGURE 19.2
The spawn egg in the game.

Adding Natural Spawns

To add a mob to the natural spawn list, you must use a method called `addSpawn` in
`EntityRegistry`. You can use the following code to add a spawn for `EntitySamMob` in the
desert. You have to add this code to the `preInit` method after registering the entity. The following code has an error under `EntitySamMob`:

```
EntityRegistry.addSpawn(EntitySamMob.class, 10, 1, 3, EnumCreatureType.monster,
➥BiomeGenBase.desert);
```

The first parameter is the `Entity` class you want to add to the spawn. The second parameter,
10 in this case, is the frequency at which this mob will try to be spawned. If you change this to a
higher number, the mob shows up more often.

The third and fourth parameters are together. The third is the minimum amount of Sam's Mobs
that can spawn at once and the fourth is the maximum. With these numbers, you can make
mobs always spawn in groups or always alone.

The fifth parameter is the `EnumCreatureType` you want it to spawn as. The creature type you
put here decides several things. It decides where it can spawn, how many there can be at any
given time, and if they can spawn at peaceful difficulty.

The final parameter is a unique one. `addSpawn` can take infinite parameters. The final
parameter can contain hundreds of `BiomeGenBase` biomes. This means that if you add
`, BiomeGenBase.desertHills` behind the desert part, the mob spawns both in the desert and
the desert hills. However, if you want your mob to spawn in every existing biome, this can't be

used. First, the code required for that would be enormous, but, more important, the mobs won't spawn in biomes added by other mods. However, there is a workaround; this method can be used differently in such a way that it spawns in every registered biome. The code for that is as follows. The following code has an error under EntitySamMob.

```
for (int i = 0; i < BiomeGenBase.getBiomeGenArray().length; i++)
{
        if (BiomeGenBase.getBiomeGenArray()[i] != null)
        {
                EntityRegistry.addSpawn(EntitySamMob.class, 10, 1, 3,
➥EnumCreatureType.monster, BiomeGenBase.getBiomeGenArray()[i]);
        }
}
```

This piece of code loops through the entire biome gen array, which holds all the biomes, and checks to see if anything is registered at that index. If there is, the mob is added to it. The null check can't be skipped or the code crashes at launch.

Making EntitySamMob a Mob

So far, EntitySamMob has gotten a render, a model, spawning, and many other things. However, EntitySamMob is nothing more than an empty entity now. The previous spawn code also contained an error mentioning EntitySamMob isn't an EntityLiving. To make EntitySamMob both an EntityLiving as well as a mob, it should extend EntityMob. When you add this, you can then remove the three empty methods in EntitySamMob, at which point it looks like Listing 19.6.

LISTING 19.6   EntitySamMob Extending EntityMob

```
package com.wuppy.samsmod;

import net.minecraft.entity.monster.EntityMob;
import net.minecraft.world.World;

public class EntitySamMob extends EntityMob
{
        public EntitySamMob(World par1World)
        {
                super(par1World);
        }
}
```

You can do a lot of things with an EntityMob. It would be impossible to cover everything possible with entities, but the following sections cover some of the most important pieces.

Adding AI to the Mob

Minecraft contains many `EntityAI` classes, which you can use to make your mob move in a natural way. It is possible for a mob to have many different `EntityAI` classes to choose from; a number can be assigned to it that tells the mob which one to use at which time. A lower number makes it more likely to do a certain AI. For example, zombies normally wander around, but as soon as they have a target player to attack, this doesn't happen anymore. There can also be two different AIs at the same number—at which point the mob will likely do either one or the other based on checks within the AI classes. For example, a zombie normally looks around, but as soon as a target player is near, it looks at the player. Both of these `EntityAI` options are at the same number, but only one of the two can happen at any given time. Listing 19.7 contains the AI for `EntitySamMob`.

LISTING 19.7 `EntitySamMob` AI Code

```
public EntitySamMob(World par1World)
{
        super(par1World);
        this.getNavigator().setBreakDoors(true);
        this.tasks.addTask(0, new EntityAISwimming(this));
        this.tasks.addTask(2, new EntityAIAttackOnCollide(this,
➡EntityPlayer.class, 1.0D, false));
        this.tasks.addTask(3, new EntityAIWander(this, 1.0D));
        this.tasks.addTask(4, new EntityAIWatchClosest(this, EntityPlayer.class,
➡8.0F));
        this.tasks.addTask(4, new EntityAILookIdle(this));
        this.targetTasks.addTask(1, new EntityAIHurtByTarget(this, true));
        this.targetTasks.addTask(2, new EntityAINearestAttackableTarget(this,
➡EntityPlayer.class, 0, true));
}
```

This code contains three different things. First, there is the line about breaking doors. This simply makes sure that Sam's Mob can break doors when chasing a player just like zombies do.

Second, there are five AI tasks. The one with priority 0, the highest, is `EntityAISwimming`. If this one is not at priority 0, the mob will likely drown because it will be doing other things when it's in the water. This AI only runs when the mob is in the water, so it does not affect it on the land.

Third, there is `AttackOnCollide`, which takes four parameters. The first parameter is `this`, then the entity it should attack, the speed at which it will attack, and, finally, `false`. This AI doesn't make the entity move toward the target entity, but it only hurts the player when it collides with the entity.

If it doesn't have to swim or hurt a player when it's colliding, it walks around randomly using EntityAIWander. It also either looks at the closest target using EntityAIWatchClosest or just looks around using EntityAILookIdle.

The final new thing is the targetTasks. These tasks actually tell the entity which way to move. This generally has EntityAIHurtByTarget as the first task. After that, EntityAINearestAttackableTarget can be used several times. Some mobs only attack the player, whereas other mobs attack players, villagers, and others. In this case, it only chases EntityPlayer if it's close enough.

There are many different EntityAI classes and you can also create your own. Additionally, you can combine them differently to make a mob work differently.

TRY IT YOURSELF ▼

Attack Villagers

Make EntitySamMob attack villagers. To do this, add two more EntityAIs to the tasks and one to the targetTasks.

First, add an EntityAIAttackOnCollide for the EntityVillager.

Then, add an EntityAINearestAttackableTarget for the villager to the targetTasks.

After adding these, the constructor should look like this:

```
public EntitySamMob(World par1World)
{
        super(par1World);
        this.getNavigator().setBreakDoors(true);
        this.tasks.addTask(0, new EntityAISwimming(this));
        this.tasks.addTask(2, new EntityAIAttackOnCollide(this,
➥EntityPlayer.class, 1.0D, false));
        this.tasks.addTask(2, new EntityAIAttackOnCollide(this,
➥EntityVillager.class, 1.0D, false));
        this.tasks.addTask(3, new EntityAIWander(this, 1.0D));
        this.tasks.addTask(4, new EntityAIWatchClosest(this,
➥EntityPlayer.class, 8.0F));
        this.tasks.addTask(4, new EntityAIWatchClosest(this,
➥EntityVillager.class, 8.0F));
        this.tasks.addTask(4, new EntityAILookIdle(this));
        this.targetTasks.addTask(1, new EntityAIHurtByTarget(this, true));
        this.targetTasks.addTask(2, new EntityAINearestAttackableTarget(this,
➥EntityPlayer.class, 0, true));
        this.targetTasks.addTask(2, new EntityAINearestAttackableTarget(this,
➥EntityVillager.class, 0, true));
}
```

Adding Base Values

Base values for an entity are quite important. They contain information about the max health, speed, following range, and a few others. You can set these values in the following method:

```
protected void applyEntityAttributes()
{
        super.applyEntityAttributes();
}
```

For EntitySamMob, only a single attribute is set, making the method look like the following:

```
protected void applyEntityAttributes()
{
        super.applyEntityAttributes();
        this.getEntityAttribute(SharedMonsterAttributes.attackDamage).
➥setBaseValue(3.0D);
}
```

First, you get one of the entity attributes from SharedMonsterAttributes, which can be attackDamage, maxHealth, followRange, knockbackResistance, and movementSpeed. All of them have default values, but they can all be changed if required for your mob. For example, a zombie has a lower movementSpeed than most other mobs.

Adding Drops

Most mobs drop an item or a block when they die. There are two methods that can be used to drop things. getDropItem is a method that will drop something almost every time the mob is killed. dropRareDrop is a method that runs very infrequently. For EntitySamMob, these two methods are as follows:

```
protected Item getDropItem()
{
    return SamsMod.samdust;
}

protected void dropRareDrop(int par1)
{
    switch (this.rand.nextInt(2))
    {
        case 0:
            this.dropItem(SamsMod.samsword, 1);
            break;
        case 1:
            this.dropItem(Item.getItemFromBlock(SamsMod.samTE), 1);
    }
}
```

Now when the mob dies, it often drops Sam's Dust and sometimes a sword or the tile entity. The finished `EntitySamMob` should now look like Listing 19.8.

LISTING 19.8 EntitySamMob Finished

```
package com.wuppy.samsmod;

import net.minecraft.entity.SharedMonsterAttributes;
import net.minecraft.entity.ai.EntityAIAttackOnCollide;
import net.minecraft.entity.ai.EntityAIHurtByTarget;
import net.minecraft.entity.ai.EntityAILookIdle;
import net.minecraft.entity.ai.EntityAINearestAttackableTarget;
import net.minecraft.entity.ai.EntityAISwimming;
import net.minecraft.entity.ai.EntityAIWander;
import net.minecraft.entity.ai.EntityAIWatchClosest;
import net.minecraft.entity.monster.EntityMob;
import net.minecraft.entity.passive.EntityVillager;
import net.minecraft.entity.player.EntityPlayer;
import net.minecraft.init.Items;
import net.minecraft.item.Item;
import net.minecraft.world.World;

public class EntitySamMob extends EntityMob
{
        public EntitySamMob(World par1World)
        {
                super(par1World);
                this.getNavigator().setBreakDoors(true);
                this.tasks.addTask(0, new EntityAISwimming(this));
                this.tasks.addTask(2, new EntityAIAttackOnCollide(this,
➡EntityPlayer.class, 1.0D, false));
                this.tasks.addTask(2, new EntityAIAttackOnCollide(this,
➡EntityVillager.class, 1.0D, false));
                this.tasks.addTask(3, new EntityAIWander(this, 1.0D));
                this.tasks.addTask(4, new EntityAIWatchClosest(this,
➡EntityPlayer.class, 8.0F));
                this.tasks.addTask(4, new EntityAIWatchClosest(this,
➡EntityVillager.class, 8.0F));
                this.tasks.addTask(4, new EntityAILookIdle(this));
                this.targetTasks.addTask(1, new EntityAIHurtByTarget(this, true));
                this.targetTasks.addTask(2, new EntityAINearestAttackableTarget(
➡this, EntityPlayer.class, 0, true));
                this.targetTasks.addTask(2, new EntityAINearestAttackableTarget(
➡this, EntityVillager.class, 0, true));
        }
```

```
     protected void applyEntityAttributes()
     {
          super.applyEntityAttributes();
          this.getEntityAttribute(SharedMonsterAttributes.
➥attackDamage).setBaseValue(3.0D);
     }

     protected Item getDropItem()
     {
          return SamsMod.samdust;
     }

     protected void dropRareDrop(int par1)
     {
          switch (this.rand.nextInt(2))
          {
           case 0:
                this.dropItem(SamsMod.samsword, 1);
                break;
           case 1:
                this.dropItem(Item.getItemFromBlock(SamsMod.samTE), 1);
          }
     }
}
```

Figure 19.3 shows the resulting entity.

FIGURE 19.3
EntitySamMob in the game.

Summary

In this hour, you learned how to combine the classes and resources made in the previous two hours to create a fully functional entity. By now, you should know how to import the Techne model into Minecraft, and you should have a basic understanding of how body parts can be moved. You also learned how to create a basic Render class and how to make sure Minecraft renders your entity using the Model and Render classes. Finally, you learned how to customize your entity with AI, attributes, and drops.

Q&A

Q. Can there be more than one item or block dropped every time when a mob dies?

A. Yes. However, to do this, you would have to find the method in which getDropItem is called, overwrite it, and add a second item drop.

Q. Are there any other kinds of entities?

A. Yes there are. There are throwables, which are covered in the next hour, but also entities such as cows. Those work very much the same as mobs covered in this hour, but you have to change the `EnumCreatureType` and the extended class from Mob into Animal.

Q. Does Minecraft programming in general require a lot of math knowledge, in particular trigonometry?

A. No, math isn't used that much when making mods for Minecraft. Math is only required when you do rotations and custom rendering.

Workshop

In this hour, you learned about entities and coding mobs. Entities are very important for most mods because there is a lot you can do with them. Use the quiz to make sure you fully understand these topics.

Quiz

1. What does the number before the `EntityAI` do?

2. What happens when you don't set a value for the entity attributes?

Answers

1. It sets the importance of the `AI`; the lower the number, the more likely it is to run.

2. It uses the default values.

Exercises

Change the speed of the mob by editing one of the entity attributes.

You would add this code to the `applyEntityAttributes` method:

```
this.getEntityAttribute(SharedMonsterAttributes.movementSpeed).setBaseValue(1.0D);
```

HOUR 20
Creating a Throwable

What You'll Learn in This Hour:
- ▶ Registering a throwable entity
- ▶ Creating the `Entity` class
- ▶ Using the entity
- ▶ Rendering the entity

In this hour, you again create an entity. However, this time, the entity won't move around and work without influence of the player, but will be thrown by the player. This might sound quite complicated, but Minecraft already has throwables, such as snowballs, so most of the code is already written for you.

Registering a Throwable Entity

Before creating a new entity file, you have to register it just like a mob. The following code contains an error under `EntitySamThrowable` and has to be added to the `preInit` method:

```
EntityRegistry.registerModEntity(EntitySamThrowable.class, "samthrow", 1,
➥this, 80, 3, true);
```

Because a throwable doesn't spawn normally, an `addSpawn` isn't required for this entity.

CAUTION

The Entity Register Number

The third parameter in `registerModEntity` is the ID of the entity you are registering. As you should know, this is unique for every mod, which means that different mods can have an entity with ID 0. However, you can't have a single mod with the same ID twice, so make sure it's different for every entity if you don't want to run into problems.

Creating the `Entity` Class

Now hover your mouse over `EntitySamThrowable` and select Create Class. Listing 20.1 shows the resulting class.

LISTING 20.1   Initial `EntitySamThrowable`

```
package com.wuppy.samsmod;


public class EntitySamThrowable
{


}
```

Now make this class extend `EntityThrowable`. After doing that and importing `EntityThrowable`, it asks you to add a constructor. There are three different choices, and you must add all of them. You also must add the unimplemented method called `onImpact`. After adding these, `EntitySamThrowable` looks like Listing 20.2.

LISTING 20.2   `EntitySamThrowable` Extending `EntityThrowable`

```
package com.wuppy.samsmod;

import net.minecraft.entity.EntityLivingBase;
import net.minecraft.entity.projectile.EntityThrowable;
import net.minecraft.util.MovingObjectPosition;
import net.minecraft.world.World;

public class EntitySamThrowable extends EntityThrowable
{
    public EntitySamThrowable(World par1World)
    {
        super(par1World);
    }

    public EntitySamThrowable(World par1World, EntityLivingBase
➥par2EntityLivingBase)
    {
        super(par1World, par2EntityLivingBase);
    }

    public EntitySamThrowable(World par1World, double par2, double par4,
➥double par6)
    {
        super(par1World, par2, par4, par6);
    }
```

```
@Override
protected void onImpact(MovingObjectPosition position)
{


}
}
```

To make these throwables fly in the same way as an Experience bottle in Minecraft does, add the following three methods:

```
protected float getGravityVelocity()
{
    return 0.07F;
}


protected float func_70182_d()
{
    return 0.7F;
}


protected float func_70183_g()
{
    return -20.0F;
}
```

The first one makes sure the entity falls down at a reasonable speed. The other two numbers have to do with the rotation of the entity.

You could edit details of a throwable by overwriting methods in EntityThrowable, but for this book only onImpact is used, which is what you want in almost all of the cases.

As the name suggests, onImpact is a method that is run when the throwable registers an impact with something like a block. You can add code that makes the throwable unique. The throwable you create in this hour is very simple. When it collides with a block, there is an explosion. First, add the basic onImpact code, which makes the method look like the following:

```
@Override
protected void onImpact(MovingObjectPosition position)
{
        if (!this.worldObj.isRemote)
        {
                this.setDead();
        }
}
```

First, there is a check that makes sure the code inside the brackets is only run on the server. This is always required because this.setDead() should only be called on the server.

Before the throwable is killed, it has to create an explosion. That is done by adding the following line in the `if` statement before `this.setDead()`:

```
worldObj.newExplosion(this, position.blockX, position.blockY,
➥position.blockZ, 3F, true, true);
```

The first parameter is the entity that is exploding. The next three are the x, y, and z positions of the collided block. `3F` is the power of the explosion. When this is larger, more blocks are broken. The final two Booleans decide whether or not the explosion should contain fire and smoke, respectively.

▼ TRY IT YOURSELF

Create a Large Random Explosion

Make a large explosion with some randomness in it. Make sure it has a force between 5 and 7.

The following code should do this:

```
worldObj.newExplosion(this, position.blockX, position.blockY, position.blockZ,
➥5 + rand.nextInt(3), true, true);
```

EntitySamThrowable should now look like Listing 20.3.

LISTING 20.3   **EntitySamThrowable Finished**

```
package com.wuppy.samsmod;

import net.minecraft.entity.EntityLivingBase;
import net.minecraft.entity.projectile.EntityThrowable;
import net.minecraft.util.MovingObjectPosition;
import net.minecraft.world.World;

public class EntitySamThrowable extends EntityThrowable
{
    public EntitySamThrowable(World par1World)
    {
        super(par1World);
    }

    public EntitySamThrowable(World par1World, EntityLivingBase
➥par2EntityLivingBase)
    {
        super(par1World, par2EntityLivingBase);
    }

    public EntitySamThrowable(World par1World, double par2,
➥double par4, double par6)
    {
```

```
        super(par1World, par2, par4, par6);
}

@Override
protected void onImpact(MovingObjectPosition position)
{
        if (!this.worldObj.isRemote)
        {
                worldObj.newExplosion(this, position.blockX,
➥position.blockY, position.blockZ, 5 + rand.nextInt(3), true, true);


                this.setDead();
        }
}

@Override
protected float getGravityVelocity()
{
    return 0.07F;
}

@Override
protected float func_70182_d()
{
    return 0.7F;
}

@Override
protected float func_70183_g()
{
    return -20.0F;
}
}
```

Using the Entity

Right now, the throwable is finished and ready for use, but there is no way to spawn it or even test it in any way. This throwable will be spawned by an item. To do that, a new item must be created. You can do that by adding the following line of code to the mod class:

```
public static Item samthrow;
```

And this to the preInit method:

```
samthrow = new ItemSamThrow("samthrow");
GameRegistry.registerItem(samthrow, "SamThrowable");
```

This error contains an error under `ItemSamThrow`, which you have seen frequently. You can fix the error by creating the `Item` class, which initially looks like Listing 20.4.

LISTING 20.4   The Initial `ItemSamThrow`

```
package com.wuppy.samsmod;

import net.minecraft.item.Item;

public class ItemSamThrow extends Item
{


}
```

An error under `ItemSamThrow` in the mod class still remains, which you can easily fix by adding a constructor with a `String` parameter. Next, add the standard lines of code to this constructor, which include the unlocalized name, texture name, and Creative tab. After adding this, it should look like Listing 20.5.

LISTING 20.5   `ItemSamThrow` with the Constructor

```
package com.wuppy.samsmod;

import net.minecraft.creativetab.CreativeTabs;
import net.minecraft.item.Item;

public class ItemSamThrow extends Item
{
        public ItemSamThrow(String name)
        {
                setCreativeTab(CreativeTabs.tabMisc);
                setUnlocalizedName(SamsMod.MODID + "_" + name);
                setTextureName(SamsMod.MODID + ":" + name);
        }
}
```

The localization in the `en_US.lang` file looks like the following:

```
item.wuppy29_samsmod_samthrow.name=Sam's Throwable
```

And the texture, which will be saved as `samthrow.png` in the items folder, looks like Figure 20.1.

FIGURE 20.1
The Sam's throwable texture.

Making the Item Throw the Entity

In Minecraft, items are thrown when they are right-clicked. To do this, you use the
`onItemRightClick` method. To make this item throw normally, one item of the `ItemStack`
should be removed when it's right-clicked, but only if the player isn't in Creative mode. The code
for the `onItemRightClick` is as follows:

```
@Override
public ItemStack onItemRightClick(ItemStack par1ItemStack, World par2World,
➥EntityPlayer par3EntityPlayer)
{
    if (!par3EntityPlayer.capabilities.isCreativeMode)
    {
        --par1ItemStack.stackSize;
    }

    return par1ItemStack;
}
```

Also note that the `ItemStack` is returned at the end. That is required because the return type of
`onItemRightClick` is an `ItemStack`.

Except for decreasing the `ItemStack`, it would also be useful if the entity was actually spawned.
To add the code, a check has to be made to make sure that the entity is spawned on the server,
which is done by the `isRemote` variable in World. After making sure the method only runs
on the server, the entity has to be spawned using `spawnEntityInWorld`. The entire
`onItemRightClick` should look as follows:

```
@Override
public ItemStack onItemRightClick(ItemStack par1ItemStack, World par2World,
➥EntityPlayer par3EntityPlayer)
{
    if (!par3EntityPlayer.capabilities.isCreativeMode)
    {
        --par1ItemStack.stackSize;
    }

    if (!par2World.isRemote)
    {
```

```
        par2World.spawnEntityInWorld(new EntitySamThrowable(par2World,
    ➥par3EntityPlayer));
    }

    return par1ItemStack;
}
```

The `EntitySamThrowable` made earlier takes two parameters, which make sure it is spawned in the right location.

Rendering the Entity

Now when you right-click the item, a white box will spawn. To make it look like the thrown item, a `Render` class is required.

Thankfully, Minecraft has a class called `RenderSnowball`, which renders throwables exactly like this one should. However, there is one small problem: `RenderSnowball` takes an item parameter, the item that the throwable has to be renderd as. Up to this point, rendering is done in the `registerRendering` method, which is called at the start of the `preInit` phase. However, at this point, the required item, `samthrow`, isn't initialized yet and is, therefore, null, which results in crashes. To fix this, you add a second method to both the Common and Client proxy. You must also call this method in the mod class. It's important to add the following line to the `preInit` method after initializing and registering the items:

`proxy.registerItemRenders();`

The `CommonProxy` looks like Listing 20.6 with the new method.

LISTING 20.6 **CommonProxySam with the `registerItemRenders` Method**

```
package com.wuppy.samsmod;

public class CommonProxySam
{
        public void registerRendering()
        {


        }

        public void registerItemRenders()
        {


        }
}
```

The `ClientProxy` looks like Listing 20.7.

LISTING 20.7   `ClientProxySam` with the New Method

```
package com.wuppy.samsmod;

import net.minecraft.client.renderer.entity.RenderSnowball;
import cpw.mods.fml.client.registry.RenderingRegistry;

public class ClientProxySam extends CommonProxySam
{
        @Override
        public void registerRendering()
        {
                RenderingRegistry.registerEntityRenderingHandler(
➥EntitySamMob.class, new RenderSamMob(new ModelSamMob(), 0.5F));
        }

        @Override
        public void registerItemRenders()
        {
                RenderingRegistry.registerEntityRenderingHandler(
➥EntitySamThrowable.class, new RenderSnowball(SamsMod.samthrow));
        }
}
```

The `RenderingRegistry` for the throwable has already been added. It takes two parameters, first the `Entity` class, which will be rendered, and second, the `Render` class, which will render the entity. In this case, the `Render` class is `RenderSnowball` and requires one parameter, which is the item it will look like. Now when you start the game and throw one of the entities, it will look the way it should.

The throwable item should look like Figure 20.2.

FIGURE 20.2
The throwable item in the game.

Figure 20.3 displays what happens when you right-click the throwable item, which spawns the entity.

FIGURE 20.3
The throwable entity in the game.

Once the entity in Figure 20.3 touches the ground, something like what is shown in Figure 20.4 happens.

FIGURE 20.4
The aftermath.

Summary

In this hour, you learned how to create a throwable entity. You learned about the `Entity` class itself, how to spawn an entity using `onItemRightClick` in the `Item` class, and, finally, how to render the entity. You also learned how to make explosions appear in Minecraft, which is a lot of fun. `onItemRightClick` is an important method for an item because you can do a lot of customization.

Q&A

Q. Why use `RenderSnowball` instead of a custom `Render` class?

A. `RenderSnowball` is used here because it does exactly what is required for the rendering of the throwable. It's not required to make a custom one.

Q. How does `RenderSnowball` **work?**

A. It takes the texture based on the item and then renders it at the position of the entity by using OpenGL.

Q. Because there two methods in the proxies now, couldn't you simply move the first method below the item initialization?

A. You could, but this is cleaner and, therefore, better.

Workshop

In this hour, you learned about throwables. A lot of mods require throwables because they can be used for many different things, so it's important to understand them well. Test your comprehension with the quiz.

Quiz

1. **Why do you have to check if you are on a server before spawning the throwable?**

2. **What would happen if you added the** `RenderingRegistry` **for the throwable before initializing the item?**

Answers

1. This is done because of the way the client and the server work in Minecraft. If your code changes anything, except for rendering, it's likely it will have to run on the server.

2. The game would crash with a null pointer exception.

Exercises

Change the item's `onRightClick` method in such a way that it doesn't spawn one, but two throwables.

The following method will do that:

```
@Override
public ItemStack onItemRightClick(ItemStack par1ItemStack, World par2World,
➥EntityPlayer par3EntityPlayer)
{
    if (!par3EntityPlayer.capabilities.isCreativeMode)
    {
        --par1ItemStack.stackSize;
    }
```

```
    if (!par2World.isRemote)
    {
        par2World.spawnEntityInWorld(new EntitySamThrowable(par2World,
➥par3EntityPlayer));
         par2World.spawnEntityInWorld(new EntitySamThrowable(par2World,
➥par3EntityPlayer));
    }

    return par1ItemStack;
}
```

Editing Vanilla Minecraft

What You'll Learn in This Hour:

▶ How to change Minecraft indirectly

▶ Other events

▶ Giving your armor egg-throwing abilities

In the last 20 hours, you learned almost everything there is to do in Minecraft. However, some mods require more than just adding things. In some cases, it is required to completely overwrite a feature in Minecraft. Thankfully, there are many different ways to do this.

How to Change Minecraft Indirectly

You can overwrite features in Minecraft in many different ways. It is possible to simply remove the vanilla version of something and completely replace it, slightly tweak a few details of a feature, or use techniques like reflection or bytecode manipulation to edit the features directly in code. Reflection and bytecode manipulation aren't covered in this book because they are both really complicated and are large enough to write an entire book about. You can find basic information on reflection at http://docs.oracle.com/javase/tutorial/reflect/. To find out more information about bytecode manipulation and how to implement it in Forge, go to http://asm.ow2.org/doc/tutorial.html and www.minecraftforum.net/topic/1854988.

Removing Entities

Thanks to Forge, it's really easy to remove a vanilla entity. You can simply remove the spawn of the mob:

```
for (int i = 0; i < BiomeGenBase.getBiomeGenArray().length; i++)
{
        if (BiomeGenBase.getBiomeGenArray()[i] != null)
        {
                EntityRegistry.removeSpawn(EntityZombie.class,
➥EnumCreatureType.monster, BiomeGenBase.getBiomeGenArray()[i]);
        }
}
```

removeSpawn is a method in EntityRegistry that takes three parameters. The first is the entity, which has to be removed. The second is the type of entity it is, and the third is the biome it has to be removed from. Because this code loops through every possible biome, EntityZombie will be completely removed from the game. This can be very useful if you want to edit certain features of the zombie. Some are editable using Forge events, but if that isn't possible, you can remove a mob using this code and then add your modified one in its place.

Changing an Entity Without Replacing

An example of how you can change the behavior of an entity without having to replace it with a custom entity is by using a Forge event called LivingDropsEvent, which can be used to make an entity drop new items or blocks on death.

In an earlier hour, an EventHandler was created for world generation. To register this class as one that calls events such as this one, add the following line of code to the bottom of the preInit method:

```
MinecraftForge.EVENT_BUS.register(handler);
```

This enables the handler, an object of SamEventHandler, to interact with events like LivingDropsEvent.

In the SamEventHandler class, you can add a method like this:

```
@SubscribeEvent
public void addDrops(LivingDropsEvent event)
{

}
```

@SubscribeEvent is required above any event that isn't implemented using an interface such as IWorldGenerator. These methods can have any method name, but there can always be only one parameter, which is the event you want to use. In this case, the event is LivingDropsEvent, which is used to add the dropping of Sam's Boots to a zombie when it dies, but it can be used for any kind of entity, item, or block.

```
@SubscribeEvent
public void addDrops(LivingDropsEvent event)
{
        if(event.entity instanceof EntityZombie)
                event.drops.add(new EntityItem(event.entity.worldObj,
➥event.entity.posX, event.entity.posY, event.entity.posZ, new
➥ItemStack(SamsMod.samboots)));
}
```

`LivingDropsEvent` has several objects that must be included here. First, it has an object called `entity`, which can be used to check which kind of entity is killed as well as the position of that entity. `LivingDropsEvent` also has an object called `drops`, which is an `EntityItem` array of the items and blocks that should be dropped when the entity object dies. To add a drop, use `drops.add`. A single parameter is required: `EntityItem`.

`EntityItem` is a class that takes five parameters: first, the world, which can be passed on by accessing the `worldObj` in the entity. The next three parameters are the location where the `EntityItem` should be dropped. You can find the positions for this in the entity object using `posX`, `posY`, and `posZ`. The last parameter is an `ItemStack` of what will be dropped. In this case, the new `ItemStack` is Sam's Boots.

TRY IT YOURSELF ▼

Randomize the Drops

Randomize the drops of the zombie on death. Make it only drop Sam's Boots once every 10 times. Also make a second random drop that enables the dropping of Sam's Helmet once every 15 times. The `Random` you have to use for this can be found in `World`.

First, create an `if` statement within the code shown previously. This `if` statement should contain a `rand.nextInt(10)`, which means there are 10 options. Then, a check should be made if it equals 10, making the code within this statement run once every 10 times.

Next add a tab in front of the `events.drops.add` line shown previously, which makes sure this code is within the `if` statement you just wrote.

Now add another `if` statement below the one you just created, but within the `instanceof` `EntityZombie` one. This should have a `rand.nextInt(15)`, making it less likely to happen.

Finally, copy the code for the `samboots` drop, paste it within the `if` statement and change it into `samhelmet`.

The following code should be your result:

```
@SubscribeEvent
public void addDrops(LivingDropsEvent event)
{
        if(event.entity instanceof EntityZombie)
                if(event.entity.worldObj.rand.nextInt(10) == 0)
                        event.drops.add(new EntityItem(event.entity.worldObj,
➥event.entity.posX, event.entity.posY, event.entity.posZ, new
➥ItemStack(SamsMod.samboots)));
                if(event.entity.worldObj.rand.nextInt(15) == 0)
                        event.drops.add(new EntityItem(event.entity.worldObj,
➥event.entity.posX, event.entity.posY, event.entity.posZ, new
➥ItemStack(SamsMod.samhelmet)));
}
```

The entire `SamEventHandler` should now look similar to Listing 21.1.

LISTING 21.1   **SamEventHandler with LivingDropsEvent**

```java
package com.wuppy.samsmod;

import java.util.Random;

import net.minecraft.block.Block;
import net.minecraft.entity.item.EntityItem;
import net.minecraft.entity.monster.EntityZombie;
import net.minecraft.init.Blocks;
import net.minecraft.item.ItemStack;
import net.minecraft.world.World;
import net.minecraft.world.chunk.IChunkProvider;
import net.minecraft.world.gen.feature.WorldGenMinable;
import net.minecraftforge.event.entity.living.LivingDropsEvent;
import cpw.mods.fml.common.IWorldGenerator;
import cpw.mods.fml.common.eventhandler.SubscribeEvent;

public class SamEventHandler implements IWorldGenerator
{
        @SubscribeEvent
        public void addDrops(LivingDropsEvent event)
        {
                if(event.entity instanceof EntityZombie)
                        if(event.entity.worldObj.rand.nextInt(10) == 0)
                                event.drops.add(new EntityItem(event.entity.
➥worldObj, event.entity.posX, event.entity.posY, event.entity.posZ, new
➥ItemStack(SamsMod.samboots)));
                        if(event.entity.worldObj.rand.nextInt(15) == 0)
                                event.drops.add(new EntityItem(event.entity.
➥worldObj, event.entity.posX, event.entity.posY, event.entity.posZ, new
➥ItemStack(SamsMod.samhelmet)));
        }

        @Override
        public void generate(Random random, int chunkX, int chunkZ, World world,
➥IChunkProvider chunkGenerator, IChunkProvider chunkProvider)
        {
                switch(world.provider.dimensionId)
                {
                        case -1: generateNether(world, random, chunkX * 16,
➥chunkZ * 16);
                        case 0: generateSurface(world, random, chunkX * 16,
➥chunkZ * 16);
                        case 1: generateEnd(world, random, chunkX * 16,
➥chunkZ * 16);
                }
        }

        private void generateEnd(World world, Random random, int x, int z)
```

```
        {
                addOreSpawn(SamsMod.samStone, 0, Blocks.obsidian, world, random,
➥x, z, 16, 16, 5 + random.nextInt(5), 4, 20, 60);
        }

    private void generateSurface(World world, Random random, int x, int z)
    {
                addOreSpawn(SamsMod.samStone, 0, Blocks.stone, world, random, x, z,
➥16, 16, 5 + random.nextInt(5), 4, 20, 60);

            for(int i = 0; i < 3; i++)
            {
                int posX = x + random.nextInt(16);
                int posY = 50 + random.nextInt(35);
                int posZ = z + random.nextInt(16);
                new WorldGenSamPlant().generate(world, random, posX, posY,
➥posZ);
            }


            int posX = x + random.nextInt(16);
            int posY = 10 + random.nextInt(40);
            int posZ = z + random.nextInt(16);
            new WorldGenSamDungeon().generate(world, random, posX, posY, posZ);
    }

    private void generateNether(World world, Random random, int x, int z)
    {
                addOreSpawn(SamsMod.samStone, 0, Blocks.netherrack, world,
➥random, x, z, 16, 16, 5 + random.nextInt(5), 4, 20, 60);
    }

  /**
    * Adds an Ore Spawn to Minecraft. Simply register all Ores to spawn with
➥this method in your Generation method in your IWorldGeneration extending Class
    *
    * @param The Block to spawn
    * @param The metadata of the Block
    * @param The Block where to generate in
    * @param The World to spawn in
    * @param A Random object for retrieving random positions within the
➥world to spawn the Block
    * @param An int for passing the X-Coordinate for the Generation method
    * @param An int for passing the Z-Coordinate for the Generation method
    * @param An int for setting the maximum X-Coordinate values for spawning
➥on the X-Axis on a Per-Chunk basis
    * @param An int for setting the maximum Z-Coordinate values for spawning
➥on the Z-Axis on a Per-Chunk basis
```

```
    * @param An int for setting the maximum size of a vein
    * @param An int for the Number of chances available for the Block to
➡spawn per-chunk
    * @param An int for the minimum Y-Coordinate height at which this
➡block may spawn
    * @param An int for the maximum Y-Coordinate height at which this
➡block may spawn
    **/
    public void addOreSpawn(Block block, int metadata, Block target, World
➡world, Random random, int blockXPos, int blockZPos, int maxX, int maxZ,
➡int maxVeinSize, int chancesToSpawn, int minY, int maxY)
    {
        int maxPossY = minY + (maxY - 1);
        assert maxY > minY: "The maximum Y must be greater than the Minimum Y";
        assert maxX > 0 && maxX <= 16: "addOreSpawn: The Maximum X must
➡be greater than 0 and less than 16";
        assert minY > 0: "addOreSpawn: The Minimum Y must be greater than 0";
        assert maxY < 256 && maxY > 0: "addOreSpawn: The Maximum Y must be
➡less than 256 but greater than 0";
        assert maxZ > 0 && maxZ <= 16: "addOreSpawn: The Maximum Z must
➡be greater than 0 and less than 16";

        int diffBtwnMinMaxY = maxY - minY;
        for(int x = 0; x < chancesToSpawn; x++)
        {
            int posX = blockXPos + random.nextInt(maxX);
            int posY = minY + random.nextInt(diffBtwnMinMaxY);
            int posZ = blockZPos + random.nextInt(maxZ);
            (new WorldGenMinable(block, metadata, maxVeinSize,
➡target)).generate(world, random, posX, posY, posZ);
        }
    }
}
```

Editing Block Drops

Adding new block drops works very similar to adding new entity drops. The event required is called `HarvestDropsEvent`, which is located inside of `BlockEvent`. A method that adds the dropping of Sam's Berries to the red flowers in Minecraft looks like the following:

```
@SubscribeEvent
public void addBlockDrops(BlockEvent.HarvestDropsEvent event)
{
        if(event.block == Blocks.red_flower)
                event.drops.add(new ItemStack(SamsMod.berry));
}
```

Unlike `LivingDropsEvent`, `HarvestDropsEvent` has a drops `ArrayList` for `ItemStacks`, which makes it easier to add drops to a block than an entity.

Other Events

Now you have seen two events used in the code. However, there are many more, which you can find in the event packages of Forge and Forge Mod Loader (FML), and they all work similar to this. Every event in Forge works as follows:

- ▶ You need a method with any name you want.

- ▶ It needs to have an `@SubscribeEvent` annotation above it.

- ▶ The only allowed parameter is the event you want to use.

- ▶ The class this method is in must be registered as an `Event` class. If you are using a Forge event, you must register it, as shown earlier, which is like this:

  `MinecraftForge.EVENT_BUS.register(handler);`

- ▶ If you want to use an FML event instead, you register the handler like this:

  `FMLCommonHandler.instance().bus().register(handler);`

NOTE

`EventHandler` Registry

A single `EventHandler` can be registered as both an FML and a Forge Event class at the same time. You don't need two different classes for it.

Events can also be used for many other things than just changing drops. It's possible to completely overwrite the way a certain structure generates, change the way food works in Minecraft, and many other examples—and all of that without editing any of the classes in Minecraft.

Giving Your Armor Egg-Throwing Abilities

Another interesting thing you can do with events is make the player throw eggs when right-clicking with an empty hand as long as it has a full set of armor on. This feature will be added to the armor created in Hour 8, "Creating Armor."

To do this, use an event called `PlayerInteractEvent`. This is an event located in an fml folder, which means this event class has to be registered using the FML `EVENT_BUS`, as shown previously.

The method inside of the `SamEventHandler` looks like this:

```
@SubscribeEvent
public void throwEggs(PlayerInteractEvent event)
{
}
```

Within this method, you must check several things before the egg is thrown. The code within this method should do something like this:

1. Is the player right-clicking?

2. Does the player have nothing in his hand?

3. Does the player have the correct armor on?

4. Throw the egg.

First, you can do the right-clicking check using the action variable from within the event. If you enter `PlayerInteractEvent`, you will see that there are three possible actions: `RIGHT_CLICK_AIR`, `RIGHT_CLICK_BLOCK`, and `LEFT_CLICK_BLOCK`. To make sure the throwing of the egg only happens when you right-click, it has to be one of the right-click actions. You can do this by adding the following `if` statement to the method:

```
@SubscribeEvent
public void throwEggs(PlayerInteractEvent event)
{
        if (event.action == PlayerInteractEvent.Action.RIGHT_CLICK_AIR ||
➥event.action == PlayerInteractEvent.Action.RIGHT_CLICK_BLOCK)
        {


        }
}
```

Now you need to perform a second check to make sure the player doesn't have an item in his hand. To do this, you access the `EntityPlayer`. Thankfully, the event has this variable. In `EntityPlayer` is a method called `getCurrentEquippedItem`, which returns the item the player is holding or null. Because you don't want the player to hold anything when doing this, the currently equipped item must be null, which you can check using the following `if` statement:

```
@SubscribeEvent
public void throwEggs(PlayerInteractEvent event)
{
        if (event.action == PlayerInteractEvent.Action.RIGHT_CLICK_AIR ||
➥event.action == PlayerInteractEvent.Action.RIGHT_CLICK_BLOCK)
```

```
    {
        if (event.entityPlayer.getCurrentEquippedItem() == null)
        {


        }
    }
}
```

There is one final thing you must check. This one is a little more complicated, though. You must check every piece of armor and check if it's part of the Sam's Armor set.

You can check the armor using `entityPlayer.getCurrentArmor`, which takes a single integer parameter ranging from 0 to 3 and corresponds with the numbers used when creating the armor items. Because there are four slots, it is a good idea to create a `for` loop, which loops from 0 to 3. You can do that using this `for` loop:

```
for (int i = 0; i < 4; i++)
{

}
```

Now you have to actually check the returned item from `getCurrentArmor`. You can do this in several ways. You can check if the returned item is the same as any of the armor parts. However, you could also make this a lot better by using a feature existing in Java called `instanceof`. `instanceof` is a Java operator that can be used to check if the object before the operator is an instance (so if it extends) the class after the operator. Because all of the items in the Sam's Armor set are made in `ItemSamArmor`, you can use the following check:

```
if (event.entityPlayer.getCurrentArmor(i).getItem() instanceof ItemSamArmor)
{
}
```

However, it's also possible for the item to be null. If that happens, this method crashes your game. This would be very bad because this runs whenever the player right-clicks—meaning the player couldn't play the game at all. To prevent this crash, this code has to be run after checking if the current armor isn't null. That should look like this:

```
if (event.entityPlayer.getCurrentArmor(i) == null)
{
    return;
}
else if (event.entityPlayer.getCurrentArmor(i).getItem() instanceof ItemSamArmor)
{

}
```

Now a `boolean` must be created that holds the information if the full suit is on.

This can be quite difficult because it shouldn't be set to `true` if only a single piece of armor is Sam's Armor. Every single piece must be part of Sam's Armor. Otherwise, it shouldn't spawn the egg. There are several ways to do this and the following code is one of the possible solutions:

```
boolean fullSuit = true;


for (int i = 0; i < 4; i++)
{
        if (event.entityPlayer.getCurrentArmor(i) == null)
        {
                fullSuit = false;
                return;
        }
        else if (!(event.entityPlayer.getCurrentArmor(i).getItem() instanceof
➥ItemSamArmor))
        {
                fullSuit = false;
        }
}
```

The `boolean` is initialized as `true`. It then loops through each of the armor pieces as shown before. If any of the armor pieces is empty, it turns `false`. If any of the items isn't an instance of `ItemSamArmor`, notice the exclamation mark around the statement; it turns to `false` as well.

Now the `boolean` `fullSuit` is only `true` if the player is wearing the full suit, which means the egg can be spawned using the following code:

```
if (fullSuit)
{
        event.entityPlayer.worldObj.spawnEntityInWorld(new
➥EntityEgg(event.entityPlayer.worldObj, event.entityPlayer));
}
```

The entire `PlayerInteractEvent` method should now look like Listing 21.2.

LISTING 21.2   The Full Egg Throwing Code

```
@SubscribeEvent
public void throwEggs(PlayerInteractEvent event)
{
        if (event.action == PlayerInteractEvent.Action.RIGHT_CLICK_AIR ||
➥event.action == PlayerInteractEvent.Action.RIGHT_CLICK_BLOCK)
        {
                if (event.entityPlayer.getCurrentEquippedItem() == null)
                {
```

```
                boolean fullSuit = true;

                for (int i = 0; i < 4; i++)
                {
                        if (event.entityPlayer.getCurrentArmor(i) == null)
                        {
                              fullSuit = false;
                              return;
                        }
                        else if (!(event.entityPlayer.getCurrentArmor(i).
➥getItem() instanceof ItemSamArmor))
                        {
                              fullSuit = false;
                        }
                }

                if (fullSuit)
                {
                        event.entityPlayer.worldObj.spawnEntityInWorld(new
➥EntityEgg(event.entityPlayer.worldObj, event.entityPlayer));
                }
        }
    }
}
```

Now, when you right-click and meet all the requirements, the player throws an egg, as shown in Figure 21.1.

FIGURE 21.1
The player throwing an egg with the full armor on.

Summary

In this hour, you learned how to edit Minecraft indirectly. You can do this by, for example, removing entities from the game or editing certain features using events, reflection, and bytecode manipulation. You also learned how to implement the first two. You can easily remove entities by removing every natural spawn. You can use events in a class registered in the EVENT_BUS. They are easy to use and there is a lot that can be done with them.

Q&A

Q. Why would you avoid editing Minecraft classes directly?

A. This increases the compatibility with other mods. When two mods edit the same class, it's likely that one or both will crash. With events, this problem is completely removed.

Q. Is there a limit to the amount of events you can subscribe to?

A. There isn't, but if you add more, the game becomes slower.

Q. Can you have multiple subscriptions to the same event?

A. Yes, but if you have two in the same mod, it is best to just place them in a single method.

Workshop

In this hour, you learned about editing Minecraft indirectly. This is quite important for mods, so make sure you understand them by completing this quiz.

Quiz

1. What is the difference between the drops `ArrayList` in `LivingDropsEvent` and `HarvestDropEvent`?

2. What would happen if you don't register your `Event` class to the `EVENT_BUS`?

Answers

1. `LivingDropsEvent` requires `EntityItems`, whereas `HarvestDropEvent` requires `ItemStacks`.

2. Absolutely nothing. None of the subscribed events in your class will run, and, therefore, nothing will happen.

Exercises

Use an event called `LivingJumpEvent` in `LivingEvent` to print out "jump" to the console when an entity jumps.

The following code will do that:

```
@SubscribeEvent
public void printJump(LivingEvent.LivingJumpEvent event)
{
        System.out.println("jump");
}
```

This method might seem useless, but if you check for a player jumping and then check if the player wears a certain type of boots, this method can be used to, for example, heal the player when jumping.

HOUR 22
Structuring Your Mod

What You'll Learn in This Hour:

▶ Why it is important to structure your mod

▶ How to structure your mod

The mod created up to this point is basically done now. All there is left to do is clean up the mod and then release it in Hour 23, "Releasing Your Mod." It might seem useless to clean up your mod because it costs a lot of time. However, it can be really helpful because it speeds up development time and makes it easier to fix bugs.

Why It Is Important to Structure Your Mod

Structuring your mod and, with that, cleaning up your code are really useful. They help you by making your code easier to read. When your code is easier to read, it is much easier to add new things. It also makes it much easier to find out where your mistake is when there is a bug or an update. Additionally, if you make your mod open source, which is generally a good idea, it also helps others because they can easily understand your code and possibly even help you with updating or fixing certain pieces in it.

How to Structure Your Mod

You have already done several things to structure your mod and make it easier to read and find bugs. For example, grouping all block and item variables in your mod file and adding an @Override to each method. However, more is required to make it look really clean.

Cleaning the Package

When you look at the classes in the package, it should look similar to Figure 22.1.

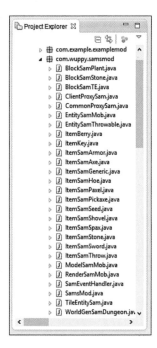

FIGURE 22.1
The classes in the package.

This doesn't look organized at all. To make this look better, subpackages can be made. Some commonly used subpackages are blocks, items, generation, and render. After fully cleaning this up, the list of packages looks like Figure 22.2.

Everything is this hour is optional. For example, the amount of packages, the names, and the files in each of the packages can be different for everyone. It really depends on your personal preferences. However, the suggested way to do this is shown in Figure 22.2. You can move files around by dragging them from package to package.

Commonly, the amount of classes in a package is at least three, because a subpackage for each class would only make it harder to read the code.

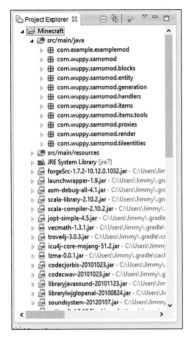

FIGURE 22.2
The classes organized in subpackages.

CAUTION

Changing Proxies

When you change the package or filename for either of the proxies, you must change the
`@SidedProxy` line in your mod file to make sure they can still be found. For this mod, that line
should now look like this:

```
@SidedProxy(clientSide = "com.wuppy.samsmod.proxies.ClientProxySam",
▶serverSide = "com.wuppy.samsmod.proxies.CommonProxySam")
```

One other thing to note is that there is a package called `items.tools`. This means that the subpackage `items` has another subpackage called `tools`. In this case, this is useful because there
are many different tools, and this way, they are also properly organized.

NOTE

Packages in Folders

Packages are represented by folders on your system. So far, all the code written was located in the
folder com/wuppy/samsmod (or whatever your package was called). Adding all of these subpackages also means there will now be several folders in the samsmod folder.

Cleaning the Mod Class

The mod class has gotten new code almost every hour in this book. Even if you kept this class as clean as possible, it will still look very crowded and get harder and harder to read. If you kept the class reasonably clean, it should look similar to Listing 22.1.

LISTING 22.1   The `SamsMod` Class

```
package com.wuppy.samsmod;

import net.minecraft.block.Block;
import net.minecraft.enchantment.Enchantment;
import net.minecraft.entity.Entity;
import net.minecraft.entity.EntityList;
import net.minecraft.entity.EntityList.EntityEggInfo;
import net.minecraft.entity.EnumCreatureType;
import net.minecraft.init.Blocks;
import net.minecraft.init.Items;
import net.minecraft.item.Item;
import net.minecraft.item.Item.ToolMaterial;
import net.minecraft.item.ItemArmor.ArmorMaterial;
import net.minecraft.item.ItemStack;
import net.minecraft.util.WeightedRandomChestContent;
import net.minecraft.world.biome.BiomeGenBase;
import net.minecraftforge.common.ChestGenHooks;
import net.minecraftforge.common.DungeonHooks;
import net.minecraftforge.common.MinecraftForge;
import net.minecraftforge.common.util.EnumHelper;

import com.wuppy.samsmod.blocks.BlockSamPlant;
import com.wuppy.samsmod.blocks.BlockSamStone;
import com.wuppy.samsmod.blocks.BlockSamTE;
import com.wuppy.samsmod.entity.EntitySamMob;
import com.wuppy.samsmod.entity.EntitySamThrowable;
import com.wuppy.samsmod.handlers.SamEventHandler;
import com.wuppy.samsmod.items.ItemBerry;
import com.wuppy.samsmod.items.ItemKey;
import com.wuppy.samsmod.items.ItemSamArmor;
import com.wuppy.samsmod.items.ItemSamGeneric;
import com.wuppy.samsmod.items.ItemSamSeed;
import com.wuppy.samsmod.items.ItemSamStone;
import com.wuppy.samsmod.items.ItemSamThrow;
import com.wuppy.samsmod.items.tools.ItemSamAxe;
import com.wuppy.samsmod.items.tools.ItemSamHoe;
import com.wuppy.samsmod.items.tools.ItemSamPaxel;
import com.wuppy.samsmod.items.tools.ItemSamPickaxe;
import com.wuppy.samsmod.items.tools.ItemSamShovel;
import com.wuppy.samsmod.items.tools.ItemSamSpax;
```

```
import com.wuppy.samsmod.items.tools.ItemSamSword;
import com.wuppy.samsmod.proxies.CommonProxySam;
import com.wuppy.samsmod.tileentities.TileEntitySam;

import cpw.mods.fml.common.Mod;
import cpw.mods.fml.common.Mod.EventHandler;
import cpw.mods.fml.common.SidedProxy;
import cpw.mods.fml.common.event.FMLInitializationEvent;
import cpw.mods.fml.common.event.FMLPreInitializationEvent;
import cpw.mods.fml.common.registry.EntityRegistry;
import cpw.mods.fml.common.registry.GameRegistry;

@Mod(modid = SamsMod.MODID, version = SamsMod.VERSION)
public class SamsMod
{
    public static final String MODID = "wuppy29_samsmod";
    public static final String VERSION = "1.0";

    //Blocks
    public static Block samStone;
    public static Block samPlant;
    public static Block samTE;

    //Items
    public static Item key;
    public static Item berry;
    public static Item samseed;
    public static Item samdust;
    public static Item samingot;
    public static Item samthrow;

    //tools
    public static Item sampickaxe;
    public static Item samaxe;
    public static Item samhoe;
    public static Item samshovel;
    public static Item samsword;

    public static Item sampaxel;
    public static Item samspax;

    ToolMaterial samium = EnumHelper.addToolMaterial("samium", 3, 1000,
➥9.5F, 3.5F, 10);

    //armor
    public static Item samhelmet;
    public static Item samchest;
    public static Item samleggings;
```

```java
    public static Item samboots;

    ArmorMaterial samarmor = EnumHelper.addArmorMaterial("samarmor", 20,
➥new int[] { 3, 7, 6, 3 }, 10);

    SamEventHandler handler = new SamEventHandler();

    @SidedProxy(clientSide = "com.wuppy.samsmod.proxies.ClientProxySam",
➥serverSide = "com.wuppy.samsmod.proxies.CommonProxySam")
    public static CommonProxySam proxy;


    @EventHandler
    public void preInit(FMLPreInitializationEvent event)
    {
        proxy.registerRendering();

        //Block init
        samStone = new BlockSamStone();
        samPlant = new BlockSamPlant();
        samTE = new BlockSamTE();

        GameRegistry.registerBlock(samStone, ItemSamStone.class,
➥"SamStone");
        GameRegistry.registerBlock(samPlant, "SamPlant");
        GameRegistry.registerBlock(samTE, "SamTE");

        GameRegistry.registerTileEntity(TileEntitySam.class, "TE_samTE");

        //Item init
        key = new ItemKey();
        berry = new ItemBerry(3, 0.3F, true, "berry");
        samseed = new ItemSamSeed(samPlant);
        samdust = new ItemSamGeneric("samdust");
        samingot = new ItemSamGeneric("samingot");
        samthrow = new ItemSamThrow("samthrow");

        //tools
        sampickaxe = new ItemSamPickaxe(samium, "sampickaxe");
        samaxe = new ItemSamAxe(samium, "samaxe");
        samhoe = new ItemSamHoe(samium, "samhoe");
        samshovel = new ItemSamShovel(samium, "samshovel");
        samsword = new ItemSamSword(samium, "samsword");

        sampaxel = new ItemSamPaxel(samium, "sampaxel");
        samspax = new ItemSamSpax(samium, "samspax");

        //armor
```

```
samhelmet = new ItemSamArmor(samarmor, 0, "samhelmet");
samchest = new ItemSamArmor(samarmor, 1, "samchestplate");
samleggings = new ItemSamArmor(samarmor, 2, "samleggings");
samboots = new ItemSamArmor(samarmor, 3, "samboots");


//Item registry
GameRegistry.registerItem(key, "Key");
GameRegistry.registerItem(berry, "Berry");
GameRegistry.registerItem(samseed, "SamSeed");
GameRegistry.registerItem(samdust, "SamDust");
GameRegistry.registerItem(samingot, "SamIngot");
GameRegistry.registerItem(samthrow, "SamThrowable");

//tools
GameRegistry.registerItem(sampickaxe, "SamPickaxe");
GameRegistry.registerItem(samaxe, "SamsAxe");
GameRegistry.registerItem(samhoe, "SamsHoe");
GameRegistry.registerItem(samshovel, "SamsShovel");
GameRegistry.registerItem(samsword, "SamsSword");

GameRegistry.registerItem(sampaxel, "SamsPaxel");
GameRegistry.registerItem(samspax, "SamsSpax");

//armor
GameRegistry.registerItem(samhelmet, "SamsHelmet");
GameRegistry.registerItem(samchest, "SamsChest");
GameRegistry.registerItem(samleggings, "SamsLeggings");
GameRegistry.registerItem(samboots, "SamsBoots");


proxy.registerItemRenders();


EntityRegistry.registerModEntity(EntitySamMob.class, "sammob", 0, this,
  80, 3, true);
EntityRegistry.registerModEntity(EntitySamThrowable.class, "samthrow",
  1, this, 80, 3, true);

for (int i = 0; i < BiomeGenBase.getBiomeGenArray().length; i++)
{
        if (BiomeGenBase.getBiomeGenArray()[i] != null)
        {
                EntityRegistry.addSpawn(EntitySamMob.class,
  10, 1, 3, EnumCreatureType.monster, BiomeGenBase.getBiomeGenArray()[i]);
        }
}
```

```
    registerEntityEgg(EntitySamMob.class, 0xd8bb9d, 0xa63c1a);

    GameRegistry.registerWorldGenerator(handler, 0);

    MinecraftForge.EVENT_BUS.register(handler);
}


@EventHandler
public void init(FMLInitializationEvent event)
{
    //Recipes
    GameRegistry.addRecipe(new ItemStack(Items.apple),
        "XXX",
        "XXX",
        "XXX",
        'X', Blocks.leaves
    );
    GameRegistry.addRecipe(new ItemStack(Items.arrow),
        "YZ",
        "X ",
        'X', Items.flint, 'Y', Items.stick, 'Z', Blocks.leaves
    );
    GameRegistry.addShapelessRecipe(new ItemStack(Items.dye, 2, 1),
        Items.redstone, new ItemStack(Items.dye, 1, 1)
    );
    GameRegistry.addSmelting(Blocks.stone, new ItemStack(Blocks.stonebrick),
➥0.1F);

    ItemStack enchantedSwordItemStack = new ItemStack(Items.stone_sword);
    enchantedSwordItemStack.addEnchantment(Enchantment.sharpness, 1);

    GameRegistry.addShapelessRecipe(enchantedSwordItemStack,
        Items.flint, Items.stone_sword
    );

    //Dungeon changes
    DungeonHooks.removeDungeonMob("Spider");
    DungeonHooks.addDungeonMob("Creeper", 100);
    ChestGenHooks.removeItem(ChestGenHooks.DUNGEON_CHEST, new
➥ItemStack(Items.saddle));
    ChestGenHooks.addItem(ChestGenHooks.DUNGEON_CHEST, new
➥WeightedRandomChestContent(new ItemStack(Blocks.cobblestone), 25, 50, 10));
}

static int startEntityId = 300;
```

```
    @SuppressWarnings("unchecked")
    public static void registerEntityEgg(Class<? extends Entity> entity,
➥int primaryColor, int secondaryColor)
    {
            int id = getUniqueEntityId();
            EntityList.IDtoClassMapping.put(id, entity);
            EntityList.entityEggs.put(id, new EntityEggInfo(id,
➥primaryColor, secondaryColor));
    }

    public static int getUniqueEntityId()
    {
            do
            {
                    startEntityId++;
            }
            while (EntityList.getStringFromID(startEntityId) != null);

            return startEntityId;
    }
}
```

The easiest way to clean up this enormous mod file is by cutting it up into pieces. This is commonly done using classes called `ModBlocks`, `ModItems`, and so on. `ModBlocks` for `SamsMod` looks like Listing 22.2.

LISTING 22.2 ModBlocks for SamsMod

```
package com.wuppy.samsmod.blocks;

import com.wuppy.samsmod.items.ItemSamStone;

import cpw.mods.fml.common.registry.GameRegistry;
import net.minecraft.block.Block;

public class ModBlocks
{
    public static Block samStone;
    public static Block samPlant;
    public static Block samTE;

    public static void loadBlocks()
    {
            samStone = new BlockSamStone();
            samPlant = new BlockSamPlant();
            samTE = new BlockSamTE();
```

```
            GameRegistry.registerBlock(samStone, ItemSamStone.class, "SamStone");
            GameRegistry.registerBlock(samPlant, "SamPlant");
            GameRegistry.registerBlock(samTE, "SamTE");
    }
}
```

You should then remove the code in this new class from the mod class. In its place, add the following line:

```
ModBlocks.loadBlocks();
```

When you do this, every reference to the block objects is broken. The code is trying to reference, for example, samStone in the SamsMod class, but it's not located there. Instead, it's in ModBlocks. That means that wherever block objects in your mod are referenced, this should be changed from the mod class into ModBlocks. An example of this is the ItemSamSeed initialization line:

```
samseed = new ItemSamSeed(samPlant);
```

This tries to access samPlant in SamsMod, which isn't there anymore. Change this code to the following code:

```
samseed = new ItemSamSeed(ModBlocks.samPlant);
```

When moving all of the code to other classes, such as ModBlocks, ModItems, ModEntities, and so on, some things may have to change in your code. For example, in ModItems, the armor and tool material must be made static and ModEntities requires the mod class to be passed to register the entities. The exact code can be found in the sample files for this book (see the introduction for information on how to access the files).

After cleaning everything up, SamsMod looks like Listing 22.3.

LISTING 22.3 SamsMod Cleaned Up

```
package com.wuppy.samsmod;

import net.minecraft.init.Blocks;
import net.minecraft.init.Items;
import net.minecraft.item.ItemStack;
import net.minecraft.util.WeightedRandomChestContent;
import net.minecraftforge.common.ChestGenHooks;
import net.minecraftforge.common.DungeonHooks;
import net.minecraftforge.common.MinecraftForge;

import com.wuppy.samsmod.blocks.ModBlocks;
import com.wuppy.samsmod.entity.ModEntities;
import com.wuppy.samsmod.handlers.RecipeHandler;
```

```java
import com.wuppy.samsmod.handlers.SamEventHandler;
import com.wuppy.samsmod.items.ModItems;
import com.wuppy.samsmod.proxies.CommonProxySam;
import com.wuppy.samsmod.tileentities.TileEntitySam;

import cpw.mods.fml.common.Mod;
import cpw.mods.fml.common.Mod.EventHandler;
import cpw.mods.fml.common.SidedProxy;
import cpw.mods.fml.common.event.FMLInitializationEvent;
import cpw.mods.fml.common.event.FMLPreInitializationEvent;
import cpw.mods.fml.common.registry.GameRegistry;

@Mod(modid = SamsMod.MODID, version = SamsMod.VERSION)
public class SamsMod
{
    public static final String MODID = "wuppy29_samsmod";
    public static final String VERSION = "1.0";

    SamEventHandler handler = new SamEventHandler();

    @SidedProxy(clientSide = "com.wuppy.samsmod.proxies.ClientProxySam",
➥serverSide = "com.wuppy.samsmod.proxies.CommonProxySam")
    public static CommonProxySam proxy;

    @EventHandler
    public void preInit(FMLPreInitializationEvent event)
    {
        proxy.registerRendering();

        ModBlocks.loadBlocks();

        GameRegistry.registerTileEntity(TileEntitySam.class, "TE_samTE");

        ModItems.loadItems();

        proxy.registerItemRenders();

        ModEntities.loadEntities(this);

        GameRegistry.registerWorldGenerator(handler, 0);

        MinecraftForge.EVENT_BUS.register(handler);
    }

    @EventHandler
    public void init(FMLInitializationEvent event)
    {
        RecipeHandler.registerRecipes();
```

```
        //Dungeon changes
        DungeonHooks.removeDungeonMob("Spider");
        DungeonHooks.addDungeonMob("Creeper", 100);
        ChestGenHooks.removeItem(ChestGenHooks.DUNGEON_CHEST, new
➥ItemStack(Items.saddle));
        ChestGenHooks.addItem(ChestGenHooks.DUNGEON_CHEST, new
➥WeightedRandomChestContent(new ItemStack(Blocks.cobblestone), 25, 50, 10));
    }
}
```

As you will notice, not every single line of code is now in a different class. Everything done in this hour is done to increase the readability of the code; adding many classes with only a few lines of code does not improve that.

Summary

In this hour, you learned why it's important to clean up your mod. After that, you learned you can do this by creating subpackages for certain types of classes. This makes it easier to read because the code you are looking for is grouped. Additionally, your code can become easier to read by creating multiple classes, which does the work of the, at this point, large mod class.

Q&A

Q. Would it be a good idea to split up the mod class in a different `init` class for everything?

A. No. If you do that the initial version is easier to read.

Q. Is there a maximum amount of subpackages a mod can have?

A. No, but if there are too many, it makes the mod harder to read.

Workshop

In this hour, you learned how to make your mod easier to read and, therefore, to code with. This is important because it can increase productivity and correctness of the mod. Test your comprehension with the quiz.

Quiz

1. What is a reasonable amount of classes for a package?

2. Why is it so useful to create subpackages and to cut up the mod class in other classes?

Answers

1. At least two is a good idea, but there is no exact rule for this.

2. It makes it easier to read for yourself. This directly makes development faster and decreases the chance for bugs. Additionally, if you make it open source, which is covered in the next hour, it also helps others by making it easier to read for them.

Exercises

If you haven't done it already, follow the instructions in this hour to structure your mod as well.

HOUR 23
Releasing Your Mod

What You'll Learn in This Hour:

▶ Exporting your mod with Forge

▶ Making your mod public

Your mod is now ready for release so others can use the mod as well. However, several things are required before users are able to actually use the mod. First, you must turn the code in Eclipse into computer code that Minecraft can use without the help of an Integrated Development Environment (IDE). Next, you must add an `mcmod.info` file to provide information to the user. Finally, it's a good idea to make sure users are actually able to find the mod.

Exporting Your Mod with Forge

To export your mod using Forge, open up the folder where you installed Forge. Make sure you are in the folder containing the `gradlew` file. Now open up a command prompt or terminal and run the following command:

```
gradlew build
```

This turns your `.java` files, which are readable by humans, into `.class` files. The `.class` files aren't readable by humans, but they are readable by PCs. These classes are used in Minecraft. The command should take around a minute to complete, at which point a new folder will have been created called build. Within build, there are many different folders, one of which is called libs. Open the libs folder and then open the `modid-1.0.jar` file using the zip opener of your choice. In this `.jar` file, you should see several folders and files.

This file is the one that will be used by your users. The `.jar` file contains a folder called META-INF. In this folder you will find a file called `MANIFEST.MF`. This file is used to give metadata to the `.jar` file and comes by default with Java. This shouldn't be edited, but should be kept exactly as it is right now.

Another folder is com, which contains the code for your mod. However, it also contains the `ExampleMod`, which should be removed. To do that, delete the examplemod folder inside of the com folder. Alternatively, if you don't want to remove this every time you build it, you can delete the `examplemod` package from Eclipse before exporting your mod.

The assets folder contains all of the textures and `lang` files created and used in Eclipse.

Creating the `mcmod.info` File

Finally, there is a file called `mcmod.info`, which, by default, looks like Listing 23.1.

LISTING 23.1 The Default `mcmod.info`

```
[
{
  "modid": "examplemod",
  "name": "Example Mod",
  "description": "Example placeholder mod.",
  "version": "1.0",
  "mcversion": "1.7.10",
  "url": "",
  "updateUrl": "",
  "authors": ["ExampleDude"],
  "credits": "The Forge and FML guys, for making this example",
  "logoFile": "",
  "screenshots": [],
  "dependencies": []
}
]
```

This file needs to be changed a little bit. It's not required to do this, but it's shown in the Mods tab of Minecraft, so it is a good idea to add some basic information. You don't have to go all out and create things like a logo image, but the `modid`, `name`, `description`, `version`, `mcversion`, and `authors` information pieces are quite important. Listing 23.2 shows the `mcmod.info` filled in for Sam's Mod.

LISTING 23.2 `mcmod.info` Filled in for Sam's Mod

```
[
{
  "modid": "wuppy29_samsmod",
  "name": "Sams Mod",
  "description": "A mod created for the book Sams Teach Yourself Minecraft Mod
➥Development in 24 Hours containing all of the basics of coding for Minecraft.",
  "version": "1.0",
  "mcversion": "1.7.10",
  "url": "",
  "updateUrl": "",
```

```
    "authors": ["Wuppy29"],
    "credits": "The people who created Minecraft, Forge and Pearson
➥Education for making this book possible.",
    "logoFile": "",
    "screenshots": [],
    "dependencies": []
}
]
```

NOTE

Screenshots

It is possible to add screenshots in your `mcmod.info` file. You can find an example of this in the Forge `mcmod.info`. One important consideration is that you must ensure that the image looks good on all formats yourself because Forge doesn't do that for you.

Figure 23.1 shows the `mcmod.info` file displayed within the Mods menu of Minecraft.

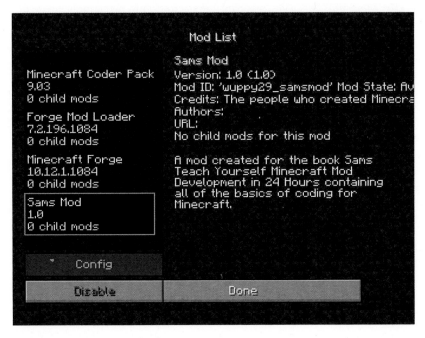

FIGURE 23.1
The mod in the game with the information provided in the `mcmod.info` file.

Making Your Mod Public

Now your mod is ready to be released. The only thing left to do is change the name of the .jar file. Initially, it's called `modid-1.0.jar`. The recommended way to save this class is [Mod name]-[Minecraft version]-[Mod version]. For the first release of the Sam's Mod, the file will be called `Sams Mod-1.7.10-1.0.jar`.

At this point, you can do two things. The first and fastest option is to start placing your mod on the various useful websites immediately. The other option is to first get a second opinion on the mod before releasing it. This can help you because the user might find bugs or provide comments or suggestions about certain features in your mod. If you don't know someone who plays Minecraft with mods, you could also ask on Internet Relay Chat (IRC), which is an online chatting program. Hour 24, "What's Next," shows you how to connect to this. Some useful channels are #Direwolf20 and #FTB. However, getting a second opinion isn't required.

Uploading to the Most Used Website

The first, and most important, website you should place your mod on is one you have very likely already visited if you play Minecraft. This website is called minecraftforum.net. Simply create an account and post your mod in the following subforum: www.minecraftforum.net/forum/51-minecraft-mods/. This is where a lot of people come to look for new Minecraft mods, and it's the place to start getting your mod out there.

It is a good idea to put the name of the mod in the title. In the post itself, it is smart to mention what the idea of the mod is, have some images of what it looks like, and provide a download link. You can upload your mod to almost any file-hosting service such as dropbox.com. One other thing that a lot of people enjoy is when your mod is open source. Just like everything else in this hour, this is not required, but is suggested nonetheless. The most commonly used way to provide the source code is to create a repository on GitHub.

Setting Up a GitHub Repository

To set up a GitHub repository, you must first set up GitHub on your computer. You can do this using the GitHub application for Windows (https://windows.github.com/) or Mac (https://mac.github.com/). Alternatively, you can set up Git, which works on every system. This is a command-line-like program, which can be used just like the GitHub application, but requires you to manually write the commands and doesn't come with a good-looking interface. You can find out how to set up Git at https://help.github.com/articles/set-up-git#platform-all.

Once you have Git setup, you have to set up a repo, which you can easily do by following the instructions at https://help.github.com/articles/create-a-repo. (A repo is an online source repository that can usually be accessed by everybody.)

Next, you need to get the code onto your GitHub repo. You could just upload the entire forge folder, but that is not legal. Instead, you should only upload the source and resources. You can do this either by writing an extensive `gitignore` file or by making a different folder for your local copy of the GitHub repo and manually copying the right folders in there. You can find an example of a GitHub repo with Minecraft source at https://github.com/wuppy29/WuppyMods.

Other Websites

In addition to the best-known website, there are some other commonly used websites where you might want to add your mod.

Adding Your Mod to modlist.mcf.li

modlist.mcf.li is a website that contains, as the name suggests, a modlist. It doesn't do much more than provide a list of mods with links for where to get them and some basic information, such as Minecraft version, name, and description, but it's a nice way to get a little more publicity. The modlist is often visited by people who want to get a few extra mods. There is also an Android app that contains all of the content on the website.

Using planetminecraft

planetminecraft.com is very similar to the Minecraft forums, but has a larger focus on showing creations, such as mods and maps for players to use, and it's less of a forum.

Even More Websites

Obviously there are many different websites where you can place your mods. However, it would be impossible and a bit pointless to cover all of them in this hour. The previous few are the most commonly used and are, therefore, also the most important. You shouldn't place your mod on too many websites, though. The most important part of modding is having fun—not getting the highest amount of downloads or views.

Summary

In this hour, you learned how to export your mod using Forge. Next, you learned how to edit the exported file in such a way that it's ready for release. You do this by removing the `ExampleMod` from it and adding some information to the `mcmod.info` file. Next, you learned that it is a good idea to make your mod open source, and, finally, you learned about several websites where you might want to place your mod.

Q&A

Q. Is there a way to automatically change the name from modid-1.0 into something more useful?

A. Yes, you can do this in the `build.gradle` file. Listing 23.3 shows the default file.

LISTING 23.3   Standard `build.gradle` File

```
buildscript {
    repositories {
        mavenCentral()
        maven {
            name = "forge"
            url = "http://files.minecraftforge.net/maven"
        }
        maven {
            name = "sonatype"
            url = "https://oss.sonatype.org/content/repositories/snapshots/"
        }
    }
    dependencies {
        classpath 'net.minecraftforge.gradle:ForgeGradle:1.2-SNAPSHOT'
    }
}

apply plugin: 'forge'

version = "1.0"
group= "com.yourname.modid" // http://maven.apache.org/guides/mini/
➥guide-naming-conventions.html
archivesBaseName = "modid"

minecraft {
    version = "1.7.10-10.13.0.1152"
    assetDir = "eclipse/assets"
}
processResources
{
    // replace stuff in mcmod.info, nothing else
    from(sourceSets.main.resources.srcDirs) {
        include 'mcmod.info'


        // replace version and mcversion
        expand 'version':project.version, 'mcversion':project.minecraft.version
    }
```

```
    // copy everything else, that's not the mcmod.info
    from(sourceSets.main.resources.srcDirs) {
        exclude 'mcmod.info'
    }
}
```

The `version` and `archivesBaseName` are the two variables used to save the `.jar` file for your mod.

Q. Is there a way to export my mod without using the command prompt?

A. Unfortunately, there isn't and there likely won't be one.

Workshop

In this hour, you learned how to turn your mod from something only you can use in Eclipse into something everybody can download and enjoy. Even though you don't have to do this very often, it's the most important thing to do when you want your mod to be used by others. It's better to have a working mod with only a few features than a huge one that doesn't even work. Test your comprehension to make sure you can export a fully functional mod.

Quiz

1. **Why should you make your mod open source?**

2. **Where will the information written in the `mcmod.info` show up?**

Answers

1. It can help your mod development because others can help you fix bugs, but it also helps others by having some source code to look at when modding.

2. This information shows up on the Mods menu in Minecraft.

Exercises

Create a post for your mod on minecraftforum.net with some basic information about the mod, a few screenshots, and a download link.

What's Next

What You'll Learn in This Hour:

▶ Using IRC

▶ Using open source mods

▶ Learning Java

In the last 23 hours, you learned how to set up everything you need to start modding, you created the actual mod, and then you exported it and released it to be used by people. This is all this book will teach you, but there is still one hour left. In this hour, you learn how to continue without this book and create new content yourself.

Using IRC

Internet Relay Chat (IRC) is an online chat program that is used by a lot of Minecraft modders to gain support from each other. In addition to being useful, it's also just a lot of fun to talk with other Minecraft modders.

Installing IRC

You can access IRC through a web client, but some channels don't allow that to prevent spammers. Therefore, it's a good idea to download a program on your PC. This is not only required to connect to certain channels, but it's simply easier to use. You can use many different clients, but this book covers HexChat. You can download HexChat from http://hexchat.github.io/downloads.html. Then, simply install HexChat by following the instructions in the downloaded file.

TIP

Other IRC Clients

Many Minecraft modders use HexChat, but there are other alternatives, such as mIRC, Mibbit, or KiwiIRC for PCs as well as countless others for mobile phones.

Adding the Required Settings

When you start HexChat for the first time, the Network List window opens. Do everything in the following list to make sure you can use it.

1. Click Add in the Network List window. This makes a new network called New Network.

2. Change this name to `EsperNet`.

3. Click Edit.

4. When the HexChat: Edit EsperNet dialog box opens, click Add.

5. Enter `irc.esper.net/6667`. This is the server you will use to chat with others.

NOTE

Other Networks

You can use many different networks for IRC. The one that is commonly used in the Minecraft community is EsperNet because it's easy to create your own channels on it.

Another commonly used, and slightly more professional, IRC network is freenode, which is stricter than EsperNet.

6. Close the HexChat: Edit EsperNet window.

7. Type your username in the Nick Name, Second Choice, Third Choice, and User Name text boxes.

8. Click Connect on the bottom right.

9. When you connect to EsperNet, enter the following command: **/msg NickServ register <password> <email>**, where <password> and <email> are your personal email address and password. This sends you an email with another command you have to paste into HexChat.

10. Check your inbox. You should receive an email that contains a command that you must paste into HexChat.

11. Return to the HexChat: Edit EsperNet window and select the Connect to This Network Automatically check box.

12. From the Login Method drop-down, select /MSG NickServ + Password. In the Password text box, enter the password that you just registered with. This ensures you don't have to register each time you log on; the next time you log on, it will be taken care of automatically.

13. Finally, click Close and you will have your IRC program set up.

Joining Channels

Now the required settings are complete, and you can start talking with people in interesting channels. One of the most important channels for Minecraft mod development with Forge is #minecraftforge. To join this channel, enter `/join #minecraftforge` in the writing area at the bottom of the screen just to the right of your username. This causes you to enter the channel, where you can chat with all kinds of people. You might want to right-click the #minecraftforge channel on the left side of the screen and select Autojoin and Settings, Hide Join/Part Messages, but that is not required.

CAUTION

Be Careful with Your Information

When chatting on the Internet, it's a good policy to never divulge personal information—for example, your home address, phone number, current location—and to never agree to meet in person those you have met on the Internet. Most of the people you'll interact with on the channels are nice, but it's best to err on the side of caution.

There are many other interesting channels you might want to join. There are channels about Minecraft mod development as well as channels about playing Minecraft. Some suggested channels are #Direwolf20, #FTB, #MinecraftForgeTuts, and #ModJam. You might also be interested in #Moddingbook, a channel created just for this book—where you can talk with other readers as well as me.

Figure 24.1 displays all the settings I'm using.

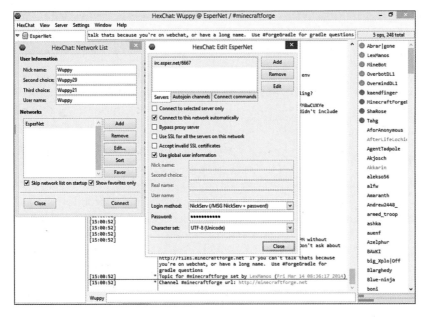

FIGURE 24.1
HexChat setup.

NOTE

Other Communities

There are many other communities on the EsperNet IRC. You can easily access other channels by writing `/join #[channelname]` in the writing area at the bottom of the screen just to the right of your User Name. It might be interesting to look around a bit and see if there is a channel for your interests or game. The easiest way to find out new channels is by trying a name, or by asking people. Sometimes websites about a topic contain the name of an IRC channel as well if they have one.

Using Open Source Mods

One of the easiest ways to learn how to code something in Minecraft is by looking through actual code, understanding how it works, and then modifying it to your needs.

Finding Open Source Mods

There are several ways to find open source mods. First, if you want source code for a specific mod, you can look for it on their forum threads. However, not every mod is open source, so this might be a problem.

Another way to find open source mods is by looking at this website: www.minecraftforge.net/wiki/List_of_Open_Source_Forge_Mods. This page lists Forge mods that are open source. Another website where you can find open source mods is modlist.mcf.li. If you search for open source mods, it displays an almost complete list of mods that you can use.

One more website that can be used to find open source mods is on modlist.mcf.li. You learned about this website in Hour 23, "Releasing Your Mod." When a mod is open source, it has a little icon to the right of its name.

In addition to mods, you can also look at the Minecraft source code to see if it contains the features you want; that can be found in the ForgeSrc library in your workspace.

Understanding the Code

It might not be easy to understand code from other people. However, most mods contain comments or at least packages and filenames, which can be helpful to find out where you have to look and what does what. In addition, knowing what to look for helps you search for what you need to find. Before going into the source code of the mod, take a look at which feature of it you want to learn about. Then either go to the corresponding block or item file where that code should be located. If you really can't find it, just start in the main class and work your way down from there.

TIP

Commenting Code

When you write code, it's helpful to include comments before code snippets, identifying what the following code does or any other information that would be helpful for the reader to know about the code. This could be helpful to you when you go back to the same code weeks later and don't quite remember what it was for. But, it's also helpful when other people are reading your code.

Don't overdo comments, though, or you risk decreasing the code's readability.

Using the Code

Now you know how to find new code and how to understand it. However, it's also important to know how to use the code.

What You Cannot Do with the Code

You can't just copy someone else's code. If you do that, the original modder might not like it. This could result in the modder changing the mod to closed source, and that is something nobody would enjoy. Therefore, it's important to respect the wishes of the mod creator when looking through the code. Some mods have a license in the source, which you must follow, but even if they don't, you still shouldn't just copy the code. That is disrespectful to the original creator, and it also means that your mod is unoriginal and, as a result of that, boring.

What You Can Do with the Code

The thing you can and should do with the code is learn from it. You can use the code to find out how others write code. With this information, you can improve your own mods. When modding, it's always a good idea to start with something that is already made and then adapt it to what you need. You should always look for the license on the code, though. Some open source mods allow this, but others don't.

CAUTION

Copying Code

Even though it usually isn't illegal to copy code, it isn't nice. If you ever do copy code from another mod, be sure to give credit where it is due. When modders are respectful to each other when modding, the community can really grow. If this doesn't happen, problems can occur, and nobody likes problems.

Before you use open source code, be sure to look at the license it uses to make sure what you want to do is allowed.

Learning Java

One of the best things you can possibly do to continue learning after completing this book is to learn Java. If you haven't learned Java yet, I highly recommend you learn Java now. You could learn Java using several different resources. One free option is the following playlist on YouTube made by thenewboston: https://www.youtube.com/playlist?list=PLFE2CE09D83EE3E28. This source is good because it's free. Although it isn't always completely accurate, it's one of the best free sources out there.

Another more accurate source that might be better to learn from is *Sams Teach Yourself Java in 24 Hours* by Rogers Cadenhead.

When you follow any source on how to learn Java, you will notice that you already know some of the basics. However, if you want to become really good at modding Minecraft, you need to know more than just the basics of Java.

You don't require a large knowledge of Java to create Minecraft mods. However, if you want to create truly unique and interesting mods, you do need to know Java—and the more Java you know, the better mods you can create. In addition, if you ever need to update your mods to a new version of Minecraft by yourself, you need to know Java well. Because of this, it's a very good idea to learn Java—and the sooner you learn it, the better off you'll be.

Summary

In this hour, you learned how to install IRC and how to join some of the most important channels for Minecraft mod development. You then learned how to use other open source mods to gain knowledge on how to make your mods better. Finally, you learned that it's a good idea to learn Java so you can develop mods without help.

Q&A

Q. Why do you use HexChat?

A. HexChat is one of the many different IRC clients. All of them have their advantages and disadvantages, and the best client might be different for different people. You need an IRC program on your PC to connect to certain channels, and HexChat is usually considered the best.

Q. Why can't I just copy code from other mods?

A. Usually, mod creators will not like it. However, in some cases it can be considered plagiarism if you don't follow the rules in the licenses provided by the modders. Moreover, it will make your mod unoriginal.

Workshop

In this hour, you learned how to continue your mod development after completing this book. Make sure you know how to do that by completing this final quiz.

Quiz

1. Why do you need to learn Java?

2. Why do you have to register with NickServ before joining #minecraftforge?

Answers

1. You need to be good at Java to make better mods and be able to mod without further help.

2. You are only able to join #minecraftforge when you have registered your username. This is used to stop spammers from joining the channel.

Exercises

Join #Moddingbook on IRC and say hello to me. I'm called Wuppy on IRC.

APPENDIX A
Additional Code Fragments

This appendix provides a variety of code fragments that you might need when writing your mod. It includes custom blocks, entity AI, and the code for a completely custom dimension.

Configs

Configs can be used to make your mod more configurable. Listing A.1 shows an example of a Config class.

LISTING A.1 A Config Example

```
package com.wuppy.samsmod;

import net.minecraftforge.common.config.Configuration;
import cpw.mods.fml.common.event.FMLPreInitializationEvent;

public class Config
{
        public static boolean spawnSamDungeon = true;

        public static void loadConfig(FMLPreInitializationEvent event)
        {
                Configuration config = new Configuration(event.
➡getSuggestedConfigurationFile());

                config.load();

                spawnSamDungeon = config.get(Configuration.CATEGORY_GENERAL,
➡"spawnSamDungeon", true).getBoolean(true);

                config.save();
        }
}
```

This method is called at the start of the `preInit` method in the mod file with the following line of code:

```
Config.loadConfig(event);
```

The `boolean` is used in the generation of the Sam Dungeon, which you created in Hour 16, "Generating Your Structure," in the `SamEventHandler` like this:

```
if (Config.spawnSamDungeon)
{
        int posX = x + random.nextInt(16);
        int posY = 10 + random.nextInt(40);
        int posZ = z + random.nextInt(16);
        new WorldGenSamDungeon().generate(world, random, posX, posY, posZ);
}
```

Rotating Blocks

If you want a block like wood in your mod, which rotates based on how you place it, it requires you to code your block like Listing A.2.

LISTING A.2   Rotatable Blocks Example

```
package com.wuppy.samsmod.blocks;

import net.minecraft.block.BlockLog;
import net.minecraft.block.BlockRotatedPillar;
import net.minecraft.block.material.Material;
import net.minecraft.client.renderer.texture.IIconRegister;
import net.minecraft.creativetab.CreativeTabs;
import net.minecraft.util.IIcon;

import com.wuppy.samsmod.SamsMod;

import cpw.mods.fml.relauncher.Side;
import cpw.mods.fml.relauncher.SideOnly;

public class BlockRotateExample extends BlockRotatedPillar
{
        public BlockRotateExample()
        {
                super(Material.rock);
                setResistance(1.0F);
                setBlockName(SamsMod.MODID + "_" + "rotateExample");
                setCreativeTab(CreativeTabs.tabBlock);
        }
```

```
    @SideOnly(Side.CLIENT)
    private IIcon[] iconArray;

    @SideOnly(Side.CLIENT)
    @Override
    public void registerBlockIcons(IIconRegister par1IconRegister)
    {
            iconArray = new IIcon[2];
            for (int i = 0; i < this.iconArray.length; ++i)
            {
                    this.iconArray[i] = par1IconRegister.registerIcon(
➥SamsMod.MODID + ":" + (this.getUnlocalizedName().substring(5)) + i);
            }
    }

    @SideOnly(Side.CLIENT)
    @Override
    protected IIcon getTopIcon(int p_150161_1_)
    {
            return iconArray[1];
    }

    @SideOnly(Side.CLIENT)
    @Override
    protected IIcon getSideIcon(int p_150163_1_)
    {
            return iconArray[0];
    }
}
```

Custom Block Rendering

It is likely that you want a block with a custom shape. To get this done, you need a block like Listing A.3 for that.

LISTING A.3   Custom Render Block Class

```
package com.wuppy.samsmod.blocks;

import java.util.Random;

import com.wuppy.samsmod.SamsMod;

import net.minecraft.block.Block;
import net.minecraft.block.material.Material;
import net.minecraft.client.renderer.texture.IIconRegister;
```

```java
import net.minecraft.creativetab.CreativeTabs;
import net.minecraft.init.Items;
import net.minecraft.item.Item;
import net.minecraft.world.IBlockAccess;
import net.minecraft.world.World;
import cpw.mods.fml.relauncher.Side;
import cpw.mods.fml.relauncher.SideOnly;

public class BlockCustomRenderWoodExample extends Block
{
        public BlockCustomRenderWoodExample()
        {
                super(Material.wood);
                setHardness(2.0F);
                setStepSound(soundTypeWood);
                setBlockName(SamsMod.MODID + "_" + "customwood");
                setCreativeTab(CreativeTabs.tabBlock);
                setHarvestLevel("axe", 1);
        }

        @Override
        public void setBlockBoundsBasedOnState(IBlockAccess world,
    int x, int y, int z)
        {
                setBlockBounds(0.33f, 0.33f, 0.33f, 0.66f, 0.66f, 0.66f);
        }

        @Override
        public boolean isOpaqueCube()
        {
                return false;
        }

        @Override
        public boolean renderAsNormalBlock()
        {
                return false;
        }

        @Override
        public int getRenderType()
        {
                return RenderCustomWoodExample.renderId;
        }

        @Override
        public boolean shouldSideBeRendered(IBlockAccess par1IBlockAccess,
    int par2, int par3, int par4, int par5)
```

```java
{
        return true;
}


/**
 * Returns the ID of the items to drop on destruction.
 */
@Override
public Item getItemDropped(int par1, Random par2Random, int par3)
{
        return Items.stick;
}


/**
 * ejects contained items into the world, and
➥notifies neighbors of an update, as appropriate
 */
@Override
public void breakBlock(World world, int x, int y, int z,
➥Block block, int meta)
{
    byte b0 = 4;
    int i1 = b0 + 1;

    if (world.checkChunksExist(x - i1, y - i1, z - i1, x + i1,
➥y + i1, z + i1))
        {
        for (int j1 = -b0; j1 <= b0; ++j1)
        {
            for (int k1 = -b0; k1 <= b0; ++k1)
            {
                for (int l1 = -b0; l1 <= b0; ++l1)
                {
                    Block blockleave = world.getBlock(x + j1, y + k1, z +
➥l1);

                    if (blockleave.isLeaves(world, x + j1, y + k1, z + l1))
                    {
                        blockleave.beginLeavesDecay(world, x +
➥j1, y + k1, z + l1);
                    }
                }
            }
        }
    }
}


@SideOnly(Side.CLIENT)
@Override
/**
```

```
        * When this method is called, your block should register all
➡the icons it needs with the given IconRegister. This
        * is the only chance you get to register icons.
        */
       public void registerBlockIcons(IIconRegister par1IconRegister)
       {
               blockIcon = par1IconRegister.registerIcon(SamsMod.MODID + ":" +
➡(this.getUnlocalizedName().substring(5)));
       }
}
```

As the name suggests, this block also works as wood. The only method related to that in here is breakBlock.

This block will be a small cube when not connected to anything. As soon as other blocks or leaves are nearby, it will connect to them, forming branches. Listing A.4 shows the RenderCustomWoodExample class.

LISTING A.4 The Custom Render Class

```
package com.wuppy.samsmod.blocks;

import net.minecraft.block.Block;
import net.minecraft.client.renderer.RenderBlocks;
import net.minecraft.client.renderer.Tessellator;
import net.minecraft.init.Blocks;
import net.minecraft.world.IBlockAccess;

import org.lwjgl.opengl.GL11;

import cpw.mods.fml.client.registry.ISimpleBlockRenderingHandler;
import cpw.mods.fml.client.registry.RenderingRegistry;

public class RenderCustomWoodExample implements ISimpleBlockRenderingHandler
{
       public static int renderId = RenderingRegistry.getNextAvailableRenderId();

       @Override
       public void renderInventoryBlock(Block block, int metadata, int modelID,
➡RenderBlocks renderer)
       {
               if (modelID == renderId)
               {
                       renderer.setRenderBounds(0.15f, 0f, 0.15f, 0.85f, 1f, 0.85f);
                       renderInvBlock(renderer, block, metadata);
               }
       }
}
```

```java
    @Override
    public boolean renderWorldBlock(IBlockAccess world, int x, int y,
int z, Block block, int modelID, RenderBlocks renderer)
    {
            if (modelID == renderId)
            {
                //middle for every wood block
                renderer.setRenderBounds(0.33f, 0.33f, 0.33f, 0.66f,
0.66f, 0.66f);

                renderer.renderStandardBlock(block, x, y, z);

                //top
                if(world.getBlock(x, y + 1, z) ==
ModBlocks.customWoodExample)
                {
                    renderer.setRenderBounds(0.33f, 0.66f, 0.33f,
0.66f, 1f, 0.66f);

                    renderer.renderStandardBlock(block, x, y, z);
                }


                if(world.getBlock(x, y + 1, z) == Blocks.leaves)
                {
                    renderer.setRenderBounds(0.33f, 0.66f, 0.33f,
0.66f, 1.15f, 0.66f);

                    renderer.renderStandardBlock(block, x, y, z);
                }



                //bottom
                if(!world.isAirBlock(x, y - 1, z))
                {
                    renderer.setRenderBounds(0.33f, 0f, 0.33f,
0.66f, 0.33f, 0.66f);

                    renderer.renderStandardBlock(block, x, y, z);
                }


                //left
                if(world.getBlock(x + 1, y, z) ==
ModBlocks.customWoodExample)
                {
                    renderer.setRenderBounds(0.33f, 0.33f, 0.33f,
1f, 0.66f, 0.66f);

                    renderer.renderStandardBlock(block, x, y, z);
                }
```

```
            if(world.getBlock(x + 1, y, z) == Blocks.leaves)
            {
                    renderer.setRenderBounds(0.33f, 0.33f,
➡0.33f, 1.15f, 0.66f, 0.66f);
                    renderer.renderStandardBlock(block, x, y, z);
            }


            //right
            if(world.getBlock(x - 1, y, z) ==
➡ModBlocks.customWoodExample)
            {
                    renderer.setRenderBounds(0f, 0.33f, 0.33f,
➡0.33f, 0.66f, 0.66f);
                    renderer.renderStandardBlock(block, x, y, z);
            }

            if(world.getBlock(x - 1, y, z) == Blocks.leaves)
            {
                    renderer.setRenderBounds(-0.15f, 0.33f,
➡0.33f, 0.33f, 0.66f, 0.66f);
                    renderer.renderStandardBlock(block, x, y, z);
            }


            //front
            if(world.getBlock(x, y, z + 1) ==
➡ModBlocks.customWoodExample)
            {
                    renderer.setRenderBounds(0.33f, 0.33f,
➡0.33f, 0.66f, 0.66f, 1f);
                    renderer.renderStandardBlock(block, x, y, z);
            }


            if(world.getBlock(x, y, z + 1) == Blocks.leaves)
            {
                    renderer.setRenderBounds(0.33f, 0.33f,
➡0.33f, 0.66f, 0.66f, 1.15f);
                    renderer.renderStandardBlock(block, x, y, z);
            }


            //behind
            if(world.getBlock(x, y, z - 1) ==
➡ModBlocks.customWoodExample)
            {
```

```
                          renderer.setRenderBounds(0.33f, 0.33f, 0f,
➡0.66f, 0.66f, 0.33f);
                                  renderer.renderStandardBlock(block, x, y, z);
                  }


                  if(world.getBlock(x, y, z - 1) == Blocks.leaves)
                  {
                          renderer.setRenderBounds(0.33f, 0.33f,
➡-0.15f, 0.66f, 0.66f, 0.33f);
                                  renderer.renderStandardBlock(block, x, y, z);
                  }
          }
          return true;
      }


      @Override
      public int getRenderId()
      {
          return renderId;
      }


      public static void renderInvBlock(RenderBlocks renderblocks,
➡Block block, int meta)
      {
          Tessellator tessellator = Tessellator.instance;
          GL11.glTranslatef(-0.5F, -0.5F, -0.5F);
          tessellator.startDrawingQuads();
          tessellator.setNormal(0.0F, -1F, 0.0F);
          renderblocks.renderFaceYNeg(block, 0.0D, 0.0D,
➡0.0D, block.getIcon(0, meta));
          tessellator.draw();
          tessellator.startDrawingQuads();
          tessellator.setNormal(0.0F, 1.0F, 0.0F);
          renderblocks.renderFaceYPos(block, 0.0D, 0.0D, 0.0D,
➡block.getIcon(1, meta));
          tessellator.draw();
          tessellator.startDrawingQuads();
          tessellator.setNormal(0.0F, 0.0F, -1F);
          renderblocks.renderFaceXPos(block, 0.0D, 0.0D, 0.0D,
➡block.getIcon(2, meta));
          tessellator.draw();
          tessellator.startDrawingQuads();
          tessellator.setNormal(0.0F, 0.0F, 1.0F);
          renderblocks.renderFaceXNeg(block, 0.0D, 0.0D, 0.0D,
➡block.getIcon(3, meta));
          tessellator.draw();
          tessellator.startDrawingQuads();
```

```
            tessellator.setNormal(-1F, 0.0F, 0.0F);
            renderblocks.renderFaceZNeg(block, 0.0D, 0.0D, 0.0D,
➡block.getIcon(4, meta));
            tessellator.draw();
            tessellator.startDrawingQuads();
            tessellator.setNormal(1.0F, 0.0F, 0.0F);
            renderblocks.renderFaceZPos(block, 0.0D, 0.0D, 0.0D,
➡block.getIcon(5, meta));
            tessellator.draw();
            GL11.glTranslatef(0.5F, 0.5F, 0.5F);
    }


    @Override
    public boolean shouldRender3DInInventory(int modelId)
    {
            return false;
    }
}
```

This custom `Render` class also has to be registered in your `ClientProxy` using this code:

```
RenderingRegistry.registerBlockHandler(new RenderCustomWoodExample());
```

Custom Tree Generation

When you create blocks for a custom tree, you likely also want to generate it. Listing A.5 shows WorldGenCustomTreeExample.

LISTING A.5   A Custom Tree Generation Class

```
package com.wuppy.samsmod.generation;

import java.util.Random;

import net.minecraft.block.Block;
import net.minecraft.init.Blocks;
import net.minecraft.world.World;
import net.minecraft.world.gen.feature.WorldGenerator;

import com.wuppy.samsmod.blocks.ModBlocks;

public class WorldGenCustomTreeExample extends WorldGenerator
{
        int height;
        Block wood = ModBlocks.customWood;
        Block leaf = Blocks.leaves;
```

```java
public boolean generate(World world, Random random, int x, int y, int z)
{
        if (world.rand.nextInt(10) == 0)
        {
                while (world.isAirBlock(x, y - 1, z) && y > 55)
                {
                        --y;
                }
                if (!world.isAirBlock(x, y, z))
                        return false;

                height = 2 + random.nextInt(5);

                for (int i = 0; i < height; i++)
                {
                        world.setBlock(x, y + i, z, wood);
                }

                int top = 1 + random.nextInt(3);

                int left = 2 + random.nextInt(3);
                int right = 2 + random.nextInt(3);
                int front = 2 + random.nextInt(3);
                int back = 2 + random.nextInt(3);

                for (int i = 0; i < top; i++)
                {
                        setBlock(world, x, y + i, z, wood);

                        if (i > 0)
                        {
                                setBlock(world, x + 1, y + i, z, leaf);
                                setBlock(world, x - 1, y + i, z, leaf);
                                setBlock(world, x, y + i, z + 1, leaf);
                                setBlock(world, x, y + i, z - 1, leaf);
                                setBlock(world, x, y + i + 1, z, leaf);
                        }
                }

                for (int i = 0; i < left; i++)
                {
                        setBlock(world, x + i, y, z, wood);
                        setBlock(world, x + i, y + 1, z, leaf);
                        if (i > 0)
                        {
                                setBlock(world, x + i, y, z + 1, leaf);
                                setBlock(world, x + i, y, z - 1, leaf);
                        }
```

```
            }
            for (int i = 0; i < right; i++)
            {
                    setBlock(world, x - i, y, z, wood);
                    setBlock(world, x - i, y + 1, z, leaf);
                    if (i > 0)
                    {
                            setBlock(world, x - i, y, z + 1, leaf);
                            setBlock(world, x - i, y, z - 1, leaf);
                    }
            }
            for (int i = 0; i < front; i++)
            {
                    setBlock(world, x, y, z + i, wood);
                    setBlock(world, x, y + 1, z + i, leaf);
                    if (i > 0)
                    {
                            setBlock(world, x - 1, y, z + i, leaf);
                            setBlock(world, x + 1, y, z + i, leaf);
                    }
            }
            for (int i = 0; i < back; i++)
            {
                    setBlock(world, x, y, z - i, wood);
                    setBlock(world, x, y + 1, z - i, leaf);
                    if (i > 0)
                    {
                            setBlock(world, x - 1, y, z - i, leaf);
                            setBlock(world, x + 1, y, z - i, leaf);
                    }
            }

            setBlock(world, x + left, y, z, leaf);
            setBlock(world, x - right, y, z, leaf);
            setBlock(world, x, y, z + front, leaf);
            setBlock(world, x, y, z - back, leaf);

            return true;
        }
        else
            return false;
    }

    public void setBlock(World world, int x, int y, int z, Block block)
    {
            world.setBlock(x, y + height, z, block);
    }
}
```

Automatic Update Checking

When you update your mod, you likely want people to know about it. The following code can help you tell the player your mod has updated by printing it in the console. Listing A.6 shows the `UpdateChecker` class.

LISTING A.6 The Class Update Checker

```java
package com.wuppy.samsmod;

import java.io.BufferedReader;
import java.io.IOException;
import java.io.InputStream;
import java.io.InputStreamReader;
import java.net.HttpURLConnection;
import java.net.URL;

public class UpdateChecker
{
    public static String updates = "";
    public static boolean outdated = false;

    public static void checkForUpdates()
    {
        int currentVersion = SamsMod.modVersion;
        int nextVersion = getNewest();

        if (currentVersion < nextVersion)
        {
            updates = getUpdate(nextVersion);
            outdated = true;
        }
        else
        {
            outdated = false;
        }
    }

    public static int getNewest()
    {
        try
        {
            URL url = new URL("http://wuppy29.com/
➡minecraft/mods/sm/newest.txt");
            HttpURLConnection connection = (HttpURLConnection)
➡url.openConnection();
            connection.setRequestMethod("POST");
```

```
                    connection.setRequestProperty("Content-Type",
➡"application/x-www-form-urlencoded");
                    connection.setRequestProperty("Content-Language","en-US");
                    connection.setRequestProperty("User-Agent","Mozilla/5.0
➡(Windows NT 5.1) AppleWebKit/535.11 (KHTML, like Gecko)
➡Chrome/17.0.963.56 Safari/535.11");

                    connection.setUseCaches(false);
                    connection.setDoInput(true);
                    connection.setDoOutput(true);

                    InputStream is = connection.getInputStream();
                    BufferedReader br = new BufferedReader(new
➡InputStreamReader(is));
                    String line;
                    StringBuffer response = new StringBuffer();

                    while ((line = br.readLine()) != null)
                    {
                            response.append(line);

                    }
                    br.close();

                    return Integer.parseInt(response.toString());
            }
            catch (IOException e)
            {
                    e.printStackTrace();
            }


            return -1;
        }

    private static String getUpdate(int version)
        {
            try
            {
                    URL url = new URL("http://wuppy29.com/minecraft/
➡mods/sm/" + version + ".txt");
                    HttpURLConnection connection = (HttpURLConnection)
➡url.openConnection();
                    connection.setRequestMethod("POST");
                    connection.setRequestProperty("Content-Type",
➡"application/x-www-form-urlencoded");
                    connection.setRequestProperty("Content-Language", "en-US");
                    connection.setRequestProperty("User-Agent", "Mozilla/5.0
```

```
➥(Windows NT 5.1) AppleWebKit/535.11 (KHTML, like Gecko) Chrome/17.0.963.56
➥Safari/535.11");

                    connection.setUseCaches(false);
                    connection.setDoInput(true);
                    connection.setDoOutput(true);

                    InputStream is = connection.getInputStream();
                    BufferedReader br = new BufferedReader(new
➥InputStreamReader(is));
                    String line;
                    StringBuffer response = new StringBuffer();

                    while ((line = br.readLine()) != null)
                    {
                            response.append(line);

                    }
                    br.close();

                    return response.toString();
            }
            catch (IOException e)
            {
                    e.printStackTrace();
            }


            return "Error";
        }
}
```

modVersion is a number that starts at 1 and increases every time a new version comes out.
There is a file called newest.txt for the mod, which contains the newest version number. If
that number is higher than the modVersion in the code, it will go to [versionnumber].txt
and get the changes. I keep all of this on my website, but you could also keep it on dropbox or
something similar.

The following event code will print out the changes to the chat:

```
@SubscribeEvent
public void checkUpdate(PlayerEvent.PlayerLoggedInEvent event)
{
        if (UpdateChecker.outdated)
        {
                event.player.addChatComponentMessage(new ChatComponentText(
➥"SamsMod is outdated."));
```

```
                event.player.addChatComponentMessage(new ChatComponentText(
➥"Changelog: "));
                event.player.addChatComponentMessage(new ChatComponentText(
➥UpdateChecker.updates));
        }
}
```

Custom Creative Tabs

When you have a lot of items or blocks, it might be useful to create custom `CreativeTabs` to make the vanilla ones easier to use and your stuff easier to find. To do this, the following line should be called by the mod file:

```
public static CreativeTabs exampleTab = new ExampleTab(CreativeTabs.
➥getNextID(), "example_tab");
```

The `ExampleTab` class should look like Listing A.7.

LISTING A.7 The Custom Creative Tab Class

```
package com.wuppy.samsmod;

import net.minecraft.creativetab.CreativeTabs;
import net.minecraft.item.Item;

import com.wuppy.samsmod.items.ModItems;

import cpw.mods.fml.relauncher.Side;
import cpw.mods.fml.relauncher.SideOnly;

public class ExampleTab extends CreativeTabs
{
        public ExampleTab(int par1, String par2Str)
        {
                super(par1, par2Str);
        }

        @Override
        @SideOnly(Side.CLIENT)
        public Item getTabIconItem()
        {
                return ModItems.sampickaxe;
        }
}
```

Custom TNT

TNT is a combination of a block and an entity. Listing A.8 shows the TNT block.

LISTING A.8   An Example of a Custom TNT Block

```
package com.wuppy.samsmod.blocks;

import net.minecraft.block.BlockTNT;
import net.minecraft.client.renderer.texture.IIconRegister;
import net.minecraft.creativetab.CreativeTabs;
import net.minecraft.entity.EntityLiving;
import net.minecraft.util.IIcon;
import net.minecraft.world.Explosion;
import net.minecraft.world.World;

import com.wuppy.samsmod.SamsMod;
import com.wuppy.samsmod.entity.EntityExampleTNTPrimed;

import cpw.mods.fml.relauncher.Side;
import cpw.mods.fml.relauncher.SideOnly;

public class BlockTNTExample extends BlockTNT
{
        public BlockTNTExample()
        {
                super();
                setHardness(0.0F);
                setStepSound(soundTypeGrass);
                setBlockName(SamsMod.MODID + "_" + "exampletnt");
                setCreativeTab(CreativeTabs.tabBlock);
        }

        @SideOnly(Side.CLIENT)
        private IIcon[] icons;

        @SideOnly(Side.CLIENT)
        @Override
        public void registerBlockIcons(IIconRegister par1IconRegister)
        {
                icons = new IIcon[3];

                for (int i = 0; i < icons.length; i++)
                {
                        icons[i] = par1IconRegister.registerIcon(SamsMod.MODID +
➡":" + (this.getUnlocalizedName().substring(5)) + i);
                }
        }
```

```java
@Override
public IIcon getIcon(int par1, int par2)
{
        switch (par1)
        {
        case 0:
                return icons[0];
        case 1:
                return icons[1];
        default:
                return icons[2];
        }
}

/**
 * Called upon the block being destroyed by an explosion
 */
@Override
public void onBlockDestroyedByExplosion(World par1World, int par2,
int par3, int par4, Explosion par5Explosion)
{
        if (!par1World.isRemote)
        {
                EntityExampleTNTPrimed entitytntprimed = new
EntityExampleTNTPrimed(par1World, (double) ((float) par2 + 0.5F), (double)
((float) par3 + 0.5F), (double) ((float) par4 + 0.5F),
par5Explosion.getExplosivePlacedBy());
                entitytntprimed.fuse = par1World.rand.nextInt(
entitytntprimed.fuse / 4) + entitytntprimed.fuse / 8;
                par1World.spawnEntityInWorld(entitytntprimed);
        }
}

/**
 * Called right before the block is destroyed by a player. Args:
world, x, y, z, metaData
 */
@Override
public void onBlockDestroyedByPlayer(World par1World, int par2, int par3,
int par4, int par5)
{
        this.detonate(par1World, par2, par3, par4, par5, (EntityLiving)
null);
}

public void detonate(World par1World, int par2, int par3, int par4,
int par5, EntityLiving par6EntityLiving)
{
```

```
                if (!par1World.isRemote)
                {
                        if ((par5 & 1) == 1)
                        {
                                EntityExampleTNTPrimed entitytntprimed = new
➡EntityExampleTNTPrimed(par1World, (double) ((float) par2 + 0.5F), (double)
➡((float) par3 + 0.5F), (double) ((float) par4 + 0.5F), par6EntityLiving);
                                par1World.spawnEntityInWorld(entitytntprimed);
                                par1World.playSoundAtEntity(entitytntprimed,
➡"random.fuse", 1.0F, 1.0F);
                        }
                }
        }
}
```

Listing A.9 shows the entity of the TNT block.

LISTING A.9   The TNT Entity

```
package com.wuppy.samsmod.entity;

import net.minecraft.entity.EntityLivingBase;
import net.minecraft.entity.item.EntityTNTPrimed;
import net.minecraft.world.World;

public class EntityExampleTNTPrimed extends EntityTNTPrimed
{
    /** How long the fuse is */
    public int fuse;

    public EntityExampleTNTPrimed(World par1World)
    {
        super(par1World);
        this.fuse = 0;
        this.preventEntitySpawning = true;
        this.setSize(0.98F, 0.98F);
        this.yOffset = this.height / 2.0F;
    }

    public EntityExampleTNTPrimed(World par1World, double par2, double par4,
➡double par6, EntityLivingBase entityLivingBase)
    {
        this(par1World);
        this.setPosition(par2, par4, par6);
        float f = (float)(Math.random() * Math.PI * 2.0D);
        this.motionX = (double)(-((float)Math.sin((double)f)) * 0.02F);
        this.motionY = 0.20000000298023224D;
```

```java
        this.motionZ = (double)(-((float)Math.cos((double)f)) * 0.02F);
        this.fuse = 80;
        this.prevPosX = par2;
        this.prevPosY = par4;
        this.prevPosZ = par6;
    }


    /**
     * Called to update the entity's position/logic.
     */
    @Override
    public void onUpdate()
    {
        this.prevPosX = this.posX;
        this.prevPosY = this.posY;
        this.prevPosZ = this.posZ;
        this.motionY -= 0.03999999910593033D;
        this.moveEntity(this.motionX, this.motionY, this.motionZ);
        this.motionX *= 0.9800000190734863D;
        this.motionY *= 0.9800000190734863D;
        this.motionZ *= 0.9800000190734863D;

        if (this.onGround)
        {
            this.motionX *= 0.699999988079071D;
            this.motionZ *= 0.699999988079071D;
            this.motionY *= -0.5D;
        }

        if (this.fuse-- <= 0)
        {
            this.setDead();

            if (!this.worldObj.isRemote)
            {
                this.explode();
            }
        }
        else
        {
            this.worldObj.spawnParticle("smoke", this.posX, this.posY +
0.5D, this.posZ, 0.0D, 0.0D, 0.0D);
        }
    }

    private void explode()
    {
        float f = 8.0F;
```

```
        this.worldObj.createExplosion(this, this.posX, this.posY,
➥this.posZ, f, true);
    }
}
```

Listing A.10 shows the class required to render the entity.

LISTING A.10 RenderExampleTNTPrimed

```
package com.wuppy.samsmod.render;

import net.minecraft.client.renderer.RenderBlocks;
import net.minecraft.client.renderer.entity.RenderTNTPrimed;
import net.minecraft.entity.Entity;
import net.minecraft.init.Blocks;

import org.lwjgl.opengl.GL11;

import com.wuppy.samsmod.blocks.ModBlocks;
import com.wuppy.samsmod.entity.EntityExampleTNTPrimed;

import cpw.mods.fml.relauncher.Side;
import cpw.mods.fml.relauncher.SideOnly;

@SideOnly(Side.CLIENT)
public class RenderExampleTNTPrimed extends RenderTNTPrimed
{
    private RenderBlocks blockRenderer = new RenderBlocks();

    public RenderExampleTNTPrimed()
    {
        this.shadowSize = 0.5F;
    }

    public void renderPrimedTNT(EntityExampleTNTPrimed par1EntityTNTPrimed,
➥double par2, double par4, double par6, float par8, float par9)
    {
        GL11.glPushMatrix();
        GL11.glTranslatef((float)par2, (float)par4, (float)par6);
        float f2;

        if ((float)par1EntityTNTPrimed.fuse - par9 + 1.0F < 10.0F)
        {
            f2 = 1.0F - ((float)par1EntityTNTPrimed.fuse - par9 + 1.0F) / 10.0F;

            if (f2 < 0.0F)
            {
```

```
            f2 = 0.0F;
        }

        if (f2 > 1.0F)
        {
            f2 = 1.0F;
        }

        f2 *= f2;
        f2 *= f2;
        float f3 = 1.0F + f2 * 0.3F;
        GL11.glScalef(f3, f3, f3);
    }

    f2 = (1.0F - ((float)par1EntityTNTPrimed.fuse - par9 + 1.0F) /
100.0F) * 0.8F;
        this.bindEntityTexture(par1EntityTNTPrimed);
        this.blockRenderer.renderBlockAsItem(ModBlocks.exampleTnt, 0,
par1EntityTNTPrimed.getBrightness(par9));

        if (par1EntityTNTPrimed.fuse / 5 % 2 == 0)
        {
            GL11.glDisable(GL11.GL_TEXTURE_2D);
            GL11.glDisable(GL11.GL_LIGHTING);
            GL11.glEnable(GL11.GL_BLEND);
            GL11.glBlendFunc(GL11.GL_SRC_ALPHA, GL11.GL_DST_ALPHA);
            GL11.glColor4f(1.0F, 1.0F, 1.0F, f2);
            this.blockRenderer.renderBlockAsItem(Blocks.tnt, 0, 1.0F);
            GL11.glColor4f(1.0F, 1.0F, 1.0F, 1.0F);
            GL11.glDisable(GL11.GL_BLEND);
            GL11.glEnable(GL11.GL_LIGHTING);
            GL11.glEnable(GL11.GL_TEXTURE_2D);
        }

        GL11.glPopMatrix();
    }

    /**
     * Actually renders the given argument. This is a synthetic bridge
method, always casting down its argument and then
     * handing it off to a worker function, which does the actual work.
In all probability, the class Render is generic
     * (Render<T extends Entity) and this method has signature public
void doRender(T entity, double d, double d1,
     * double d2, float f, float f1). But JAD is pre 1.5 so doesn't do that.
     */
    public void doRender(Entity par1Entity, double par2, double par4, double par6,
float par8, float par9)
```

```
    {
        this.renderPrimedTNT((EntityExampleTNTPrimed)par1Entity, par2, par4,
➥par6, par8, par9);
    }
}
```

The entity has to be registered like any other entity and requires a render registry in the `ClientProxy` like this:

```
RenderingRegistry.registerEntityRenderingHandler(EntityExampleTNTPrimed.class,
➥new RenderExampleTNTPrimed());
```

Changing Mob Behavior

There are some easy tricks that can be used to edit vanilla mob behavior. Below you can find an example that makes cave spiders spawn everywhere below the height of 40 instead of just at spawners in mineshafts.

The following code is used in the mod class within the `preInit` method:

```
EntityRegistry.registerModEntity(EntityCaveSpiderCustom.class,
➥"cavespidercustom", 0, this, 80, 3, true);

for (int i = 0; i < BiomeGenBase.getBiomeGenArray().length; i++)
{
        if (BiomeGenBase.getBiomeGenArray()[i] != null)
        {
                EntityRegistry.addSpawn(EntityCaveSpiderCustom.class, 4, 3, 5,
➥EnumCreatureType.monster, BiomeGenBase.getBiomeGenArray()[i]);
        }
}
```

The following `Render` class will be used in the `ClientProxy`:

```
RenderingRegistry.registerEntityRenderingHandler(EntityCaveSpiderCustom.class,
➥new RenderSpider());
```

Listing A.11 displays the `EntityCaveSpiderCustom` class.

LISTING A.11   The `EntityCaveSpiderCustom` Class

```
package com.wuppy.samsmod.entity;

import net.minecraft.entity.monster.EntityCaveSpider;
import net.minecraft.world.World;

public class EntityCaveSpiderCustom extends EntityCaveSpider
```

```
{
        public EntityCaveSpiderCustom(World par1World)
        {
                super(par1World);
        }


        @Override
        public boolean getCanSpawnHere()
        {
                if(this.posY < 40.0)
                        return true;
                else
                        return false;
        }
}
}
```

This mob will look and act exactly like the `EntityCaveSpider` even though it is actually a different entity. It is a very specific example, but the same concept can be used for many different things.

Clothes

It is possible to make your armor look like clothing. You can do this by creating normal armor and then adding some custom code. First, the worn armor texture should be cut up into four pieces—a single piece for each single part, instead of one for the helmet, chestplate, and boots and one for the leggings. This should also be coded in the `getArmorTexture` method.

Listing A.12 shows the method you will have to add to your `ItemArmor` file to make it look like clothing.

LISTING A.12   The getArmorModel Method for Clothes

```
@Override
@SideOnly(Side.CLIENT)
public ModelBiped getArmorModel(EntityLivingBase entityLiving,
➥ItemStack itemstack, int armorSlot)
{
        ModelBiped armorModel = null;
        if (itemstack != null)
        {
                if (itemstack.getItem() instanceof ItemElsaArmor)
                {
                        float f = 0.12F;

                        armorModel = new ModelBiped(f);
```

```
                    ItemStack itemstack2 = ((EntityPlayer) entityLiving).
➥inventory.getCurrentItem();
                    armorModel.heldItemRight = itemstack2 != null ? 1 : 0;
                    armorModel.isSneak = entityLiving.isSneaking();
                    if (itemstack2 != null && ((EntityPlayer) entityLiving).
➥getItemInUseCount() > 0)
                    {
                            EnumAction enumaction = itemstack2.
➥getItemUseAction();
                            if (enumaction == EnumAction.block)
                            {
                                    armorModel.heldItemRight = 3;
                            }
                            else if (enumaction == EnumAction.bow)
                            {
                                    armorModel.aimedBow = true;
                            }
                    }
                }
        }
        return armorModel;
}
```

Armor Effects

The following code in Listing A.13 is an example of a custom armor effect. In this case, the armor will change water to ice and lava to obsidian whenever you are wearing the boots.

LISTING A.13 `onArmorTick` for Block Changes

```
@Override
public void onArmorTick(World world, EntityPlayer player, ItemStack itemStack)
{
        if (itemStack.getItem() instanceof ItemExampleArmor)
        {
            if (armorType == 3)
            {
                    int x = (int) player.posX;
                    int y = (int) player.posY - 1;
                    int z = (int) player.posZ;

                    Block block = world.getBlock(x, y, z);

                    // water
                    if (block == Blocks.water || block == Blocks.flowing_water)
                    {
```

```
                    world.setBlock(x, y, z, Blocks.ice);
            }
            if (world.getBlock(x + 1, y, z) == Blocks.water ||
➥world.getBlock(x + 1, y, z) == Blocks.flowing_water)
            {
                    world.setBlock(x + 1, y, z, Blocks.ice);
            }
            if (world.getBlock(x - 1, y, z) == Blocks.water ||
➥world.getBlock(x - 1, y, z) == Blocks.flowing_water)
            {
                    world.setBlock(x - 1, y, z, Blocks.ice);
            }
            if (world.getBlock(x, y, z + 1) == Blocks.water ||
➥world.getBlock(x, y, z + 1) == Blocks.flowing_water)
            {
                    world.setBlock(x, y, z + 1, Blocks.ice);
            }
            if (world.getBlock(x, y, z - 1) == Blocks.water ||
➥world.getBlock(x, y, z - 1) == Blocks.flowing_water)
            {
                    world.setBlock(x, y, z - 1, Blocks.ice);
            }

            // lava
            if (block == Blocks.lava || block == Blocks.flowing_lava)
            {
                    world.setBlock(x, y, z, Blocks.obsidian);
            }
            if (world.getBlock(x + 1, y, z) == Blocks.lava ||
➥world.getBlock(x + 1, y, z) == Blocks.flowing_lava)
            {
                    world.setBlock(x + 1, y, z, Blocks.obsidian);
            }
            if (world.getBlock(x - 1, y, z) == Blocks.lava ||
➥world.getBlock(x - 1, y, z) == Blocks.flowing_lava)
            {
                    world.setBlock(x - 1, y, z, Blocks.obsidian);
            }
            if (world.getBlock(x, y, z + 1) == Blocks.lava ||
➥world.getBlock(x, y, z + 1) == Blocks.flowing_lava)
            {
                    world.setBlock(x, y, z + 1, Blocks.obsidian);
            }
            if (world.getBlock(x, y, z - 1) == Blocks.lava ||
➥world.getBlock(x, y, z - 1) == Blocks.flowing_lava)
            {
                    world.setBlock(x, y, z - 1, Blocks.obsidian);
            }
```

```
            }
        }
}
```

Creating a Custom Dimension

There are only three dimensions in Minecraft, and adding a custom one can make a mod very interesting and large. However, for a dimension, you need a lot of code.

The mod class code required for a custom dimension should look like this:

```
public static int dimension = 5;

DimensionManager.registerProviderType(dimension, WorldProviderExample.class,
➧false);
DimensionManager.registerDimension(dimension, dimension);
```

It is suggested to make the dimension ID configurable for compatibility with other mods.

WorldProviderExample

The WorldProvider contains several important settings for your dimension. Mainly, it sets the WorldChunkManager, which is a class that mostly handles biomes. In this case, WorldChunkManagerHell is used, which means the dimension will only have a single biome. You can make a custom WorldChunkManager, but this is very complicated and only a few people got this working.

LISTING A.14   The WorldProviderExample Class

```
package com.wuppy.samsmod.dimension;

import net.minecraft.util.ChunkCoordinates;
import net.minecraft.world.WorldProvider;
import net.minecraft.world.biome.BiomeGenBase;
import net.minecraft.world.biome.WorldChunkManagerHell;
import net.minecraft.world.chunk.Chunk;
import net.minecraft.world.chunk.IChunkProvider;

public class WorldProviderExample extends WorldProvider
{
        public void registerWorldChunkManager()
        {
                this.worldChunkMgr = new WorldChunkManagerHell(
➧BiomeGenBase.beach, 0.1F);
                this.dimensionId = SamsMod.dimension;
```

```java
}

@Override
public String getSaveFolder()
{
      return "DIM-Example";
}

@Override
public String getWelcomeMessage()
{
      return "Entering The Example Dimension";
}

@Override
public String getDepartMessage()
{
      return "Leaving The Example Dimension";
}

@Override
public boolean canRespawnHere()
{
      return true;
}

@Override
public IChunkProvider createChunkGenerator()
{
      return new ChunkProviderExample(worldObj, worldObj.getSeed(),
➥true);
}

@Override
public String getDimensionName()
{
      return "Example";
}

/**
 * Gets the hard-coded portal location to use when entering this dimension.
 */
@Override
public ChunkCoordinates getEntrancePortalLocation()
{
      return null;
}
```

```
        @Override
        public boolean canDoLightning(Chunk chunk)
        {
                return true;
        }

        @Override
        public boolean canDoRainSnowIce(Chunk chunk)
        {
                return false;
        }
}
```

ChunkProviderExample

The ChunkProviderExample as shown in WorldProviderExample is a huge class that generates your dimension for you. It places the bedrock, stone, dirt, sand, grass, water, and almost everything else you see in a Minecraft world. This is a very important class in your dimension as it will define what it looks like. The class for the custom dimension can be found in Listing A.15.

LISTING A.15 ChunkProviderExample

```
package com.wuppy.samsmod.dimension;

import static net.minecraftforge.event.terraingen.InitMapGenEvent.EventType.
➥CAVE;
import static net.minecraftforge.event.terraingen.InitMapGenEvent.EventType.
➥MINESHAFT;
import static net.minecraftforge.event.terraingen.InitMapGenEvent.EventType.
➥RAVINE;
import static net.minecraftforge.event.terraingen.InitMapGenEvent.EventType.
➥SCATTERED_FEATURE;
import static net.minecraftforge.event.terraingen.InitMapGenEvent.EventType.
➥STRONGHOLD;
import static net.minecraftforge.event.terraingen.InitMapGenEvent.EventType.
➥VILLAGE;
import static net.minecraftforge.event.terraingen.PopulateChunkEvent.Populate.
➥EventType.ANIMALS;
import static net.minecraftforge.event.terraingen.PopulateChunkEvent.Populate.
➥EventType.DUNGEON;
import static net.minecraftforge.event.terraingen.PopulateChunkEvent.Populate.
➥EventType.ICE;
import static net.minecraftforge.event.terraingen.PopulateChunkEvent.Populate.
➥EventType.LAKE;
import static net.minecraftforge.event.terraingen.PopulateChunkEvent.Populate.
➥EventType.LAVA;
```

```java
import java.util.List;
import java.util.Random;

import net.minecraft.block.Block;
import net.minecraft.block.BlockFalling;
import net.minecraft.entity.EnumCreatureType;
import net.minecraft.init.Blocks;
import net.minecraft.util.IProgressUpdate;
import net.minecraft.util.MathHelper;
import net.minecraft.world.ChunkPosition;
import net.minecraft.world.SpawnerAnimals;
import net.minecraft.world.World;
import net.minecraft.world.WorldType;
import net.minecraft.world.biome.BiomeGenBase;
import net.minecraft.world.chunk.Chunk;
import net.minecraft.world.chunk.IChunkProvider;
import net.minecraft.world.gen.MapGenBase;
import net.minecraft.world.gen.MapGenCaves;
import net.minecraft.world.gen.MapGenRavine;
import net.minecraft.world.gen.NoiseGenerator;
import net.minecraft.world.gen.NoiseGeneratorOctaves;
import net.minecraft.world.gen.NoiseGeneratorPerlin;
import net.minecraft.world.gen.feature.WorldGenDungeons;
import net.minecraft.world.gen.feature.WorldGenLakes;
import net.minecraft.world.gen.structure.MapGenMineshaft;
import net.minecraft.world.gen.structure.MapGenScatteredFeature;
import net.minecraft.world.gen.structure.MapGenStronghold;
import net.minecraft.world.gen.structure.MapGenVillage;
import net.minecraftforge.common.MinecraftForge;
import net.minecraftforge.event.terraingen.ChunkProviderEvent;
import net.minecraftforge.event.terraingen.PopulateChunkEvent;
import net.minecraftforge.event.terraingen.TerrainGen;
import cpw.mods.fml.common.eventhandler.Event.Result;

public class ChunkProviderExample implements IChunkProvider
{
    /** RNG. */
    private Random rand;
    private NoiseGeneratorOctaves field_147431_j;
    private NoiseGeneratorOctaves field_147432_k;
    private NoiseGeneratorOctaves field_147429_l;
    private NoiseGeneratorPerlin field_147430_m;
    /** A NoiseGeneratorOctaves used in generating terrain */
    public NoiseGeneratorOctaves noiseGen5;
    /** A NoiseGeneratorOctaves used in generating terrain */
    public NoiseGeneratorOctaves noiseGen6;
    public NoiseGeneratorOctaves mobSpawnerNoise;
    /** Reference to the World object. */
```

```
    private World worldObj;
    /** are map structures going to be generated (e.g. strongholds) */
    private final boolean mapFeaturesEnabled;
    private WorldType field_147435_p;
    private final double[] field_147434_q;
    private final float[] parabolicField;
    private double[] stoneNoise = new double[256];
    private MapGenBase caveGenerator = new MapGenCaves();
    /** Holds Stronghold Generator */
    private MapGenStronghold strongholdGenerator = new MapGenStronghold();
    /** Holds Village Generator */
    private MapGenVillage villageGenerator = new MapGenVillage();
    /** Holds Mineshaft Generator */
    private MapGenMineshaft mineshaftGenerator = new MapGenMineshaft();
    private MapGenScatteredFeature scatteredFeatureGenerator = new
➡MapGenScatteredFeature();
    /** Holds ravine generator */
    private MapGenBase ravineGenerator = new MapGenRavine();
    /** The biomes that are used to generate the chunk */
    private BiomeGenBase[] biomesForGeneration;
    double[] field_147427_d;
    double[] field_147428_e;
    double[] field_147425_f;
    double[] field_147426_g;
    int[][] field_73219_j = new int[32][32];
    private static final String __OBFID = "CL_00000396";

    {
        caveGenerator = TerrainGen.getModdedMapGen(caveGenerator, CAVE);
        strongholdGenerator = (MapGenStronghold) TerrainGen.getModdedMapGen(
➡strongholdGenerator, STRONGHOLD);
        villageGenerator = (MapGenVillage) TerrainGen.getModdedMapGen(
➡villageGenerator, VILLAGE);
        mineshaftGenerator = (MapGenMineshaft) TerrainGen.getModdedMapGen(
➡mineshaftGenerator, MINESHAFT);
        scatteredFeatureGenerator = (MapGenScatteredFeature)
➡TerrainGen.getModdedMapGen(scatteredFeatureGenerator, SCATTERED_FEATURE);
        ravineGenerator = TerrainGen.getModdedMapGen(ravineGenerator, RAVINE);
    }

    public ChunkProviderExample(World par1World, long par2, boolean par4)
    {
        this.worldObj = par1World;
        this.mapFeaturesEnabled = par4;
        this.field_147435_p = par1World.getWorldInfo().getTerrainType();
        this.rand = new Random(par2);
        this.field_147431_j = new NoiseGeneratorOctaves(this.rand, 16);
        this.field_147432_k = new NoiseGeneratorOctaves(this.rand, 16);
```

```
        this.field_147429_l = new NoiseGeneratorOctaves(this.rand, 8);
        this.field_147430_m = new NoiseGeneratorPerlin(this.rand, 4);
        this.noiseGen5 = new NoiseGeneratorOctaves(this.rand, 10);
        this.noiseGen6 = new NoiseGeneratorOctaves(this.rand, 16);
        this.mobSpawnerNoise = new NoiseGeneratorOctaves(this.rand, 8);
        this.field_147434_q = new double[825];
        this.parabolicField = new float[25];

        for (int j = -2; j <= 2; ++j)
        {
            for (int k = -2; k <= 2; ++k)
            {
                float f = 10.0F / MathHelper.sqrt_float((float)(j * j +
k * k) + 0.2F);
                this.parabolicField[j + 2 + (k + 2) * 5] = f;
            }
        }

        NoiseGenerator[] noiseGens = {field_147431_j, field_147432_k,
field_147429_l, field_147430_m, noiseGen5, noiseGen6, mobSpawnerNoise};
        noiseGens = TerrainGen.getModdedNoiseGenerators(par1World,
this.rand, noiseGens);
        this.field_147431_j = (NoiseGeneratorOctaves)noiseGens[0];
        this.field_147432_k = (NoiseGeneratorOctaves)noiseGens[1];
        this.field_147429_l = (NoiseGeneratorOctaves)noiseGens[2];
        this.field_147430_m = (NoiseGeneratorPerlin)noiseGens[3];
        this.noiseGen5 = (NoiseGeneratorOctaves)noiseGens[4];
        this.noiseGen6 = (NoiseGeneratorOctaves)noiseGens[5];
        this.mobSpawnerNoise = (NoiseGeneratorOctaves)noiseGens[6];
    }

    public void func_147424_a(int p_147424_1_, int p_147424_2_, Block[]
p_147424_3_)
    {
        byte b0 = 63;
        this.biomesForGeneration = this.worldObj.getWorldChunkManager().
getBiomesForGeneration(this.biomesForGeneration, p_147424_1_ * 4 - 2,
p_147424_2_ * 4 - 2, 10, 10);
        this.func_147423_a(p_147424_1_ * 4, 0, p_147424_2_ * 4);

        for (int k = 0; k < 4; ++k)
        {
            int l = k * 5;
            int i1 = (k + 1) * 5;

            for (int j1 = 0; j1 < 4; ++j1)
            {
                int k1 = (l + j1) * 33;
```

```
        int l1 = (l + j1 + 1) * 33;
        int i2 = (i1 + j1) * 33;
        int j2 = (i1 + j1 + 1) * 33;

        for (int k2 = 0; k2 < 32; ++k2)
        {
            double d0 = 0.125D;
            double d1 = this.field_147434_q[k1 + k2];
            double d2 = this.field_147434_q[l1 + k2];
            double d3 = this.field_147434_q[i2 + k2];
            double d4 = this.field_147434_q[j2 + k2];
            double d5 = (this.field_147434_q[k1 + k2 + 1] - d1) * d0;
            double d6 = (this.field_147434_q[l1 + k2 + 1] - d2) * d0;
            double d7 = (this.field_147434_q[i2 + k2 + 1] - d3) * d0;
            double d8 = (this.field_147434_q[j2 + k2 + 1] - d4) * d0;

            for (int l2 = 0; l2 < 8; ++l2)
            {
                double d9 = 0.25D;
                double d10 = d1;
                double d11 = d2;
                double d12 = (d3 - d1) * d9;
                double d13 = (d4 - d2) * d9;

                for (int i3 = 0; i3 < 4; ++i3)
                {
                    int j3 = i3 + k * 4 << 12 | 0 + j1 * 4 << 8 |
➥k2 * 8 + l2;

                    short short1 = 256;
                    j3 -= short1;
                    double d14 = 0.25D;
                    double d16 = (d11 - d10) * d14;
                    double d15 = d10 - d16;

                    for (int k3 = 0; k3 < 4; ++k3)
                    {
                        if ((d15 += d16) > 0.0D)
                        {
                            p_147424_3_[j3 += short1] = Blocks.stone;
                        }
                        else if (k2 * 8 + l2 < b0)
                        {
                            p_147424_3_[j3 += short1] = Blocks.water;
                        }
                        else
                        {
                            p_147424_3_[j3 += short1] = null;
                        }
```

```
                                        }

                                        d10 += d12;
                                        d11 += d13;
                                }

                                d1 += d5;
                                d2 += d6;
                                d3 += d7;
                                d4 += d8;
                        }
                }
            }
        }
    }

    public void replaceBlocksForBiome(int p_147422_1_, int p_147422_2_,
➥Block[] p_147422_3_, byte[] p_147422_4_, BiomeGenBase[] p_147422_5_)
    {
        ChunkProviderEvent.ReplaceBiomeBlocks event = new ChunkProviderEvent.
➥ReplaceBiomeBlocks(this, p_147422_1_, p_147422_2_, p_147422_3_,
➥p_147422_4_, p_147422_5_);
        MinecraftForge.EVENT_BUS.post(event);
        if (event.getResult() == Result.DENY) return;

        double d0 = 0.03125D;
        this.stoneNoise = this.field_147430_m.func_151599_a(this.stoneNoise,
➥(double)(p_147422_1_ * 16), (double)(p_147422_2_ * 16), 16, 16, d0 *
➥2.0D, d0 * 2.0D, 1.0D);

        for (int k = 0; k < 16; ++k)
        {
            for (int l = 0; l < 16; ++l)
            {
                BiomeGenBase biomegenbase = p_147422_5_[l + k * 16];
                biomegenbase.genTerrainBlocks(this.worldObj, this.rand,
➥p_147422_3_, p_147422_4_, p_147422_1_ * 16 + k, p_147422_2_ * 16 + l,
➥this.stoneNoise[l + k * 16]);
            }
        }
    }

    /**
     * loads or generates the chunk at the chunk location specified
     */
    public Chunk loadChunk(int par1, int par2)
    {
        return this.provideChunk(par1, par2);
```

```
    }

    /**
     * Will return back a chunk, if it doesn't exist and it's not an MP client,
➥it will generate all the blocks for the
     * specified chunk from the map seed and chunk seed
     */
    public Chunk provideChunk(int par1, int par2)
    {
        this.rand.setSeed((long)par1 * 341873128712L + (long)par2 *
➥132897987541L);
        Block[] ablock = new Block[65536];
        byte[] abyte = new byte[65536];
        this.func_147424_a(par1, par2, ablock);
        this.biomesForGeneration = this.worldObj.getWorldChunkManager().
➥loadBlockGeneratorData(this.biomesForGeneration, par1 * 16, par2 * 16, 16, 16);
        this.replaceBlocksForBiome(par1, par2, ablock, abyte,
➥this.biomesForGeneration);
        this.caveGenerator.func_151539_a(this, this.worldObj, par1, par2,
➥ablock);
        this.ravineGenerator.func_151539_a(this, this.worldObj, par1, par2,
➥ablock);

        if (this.mapFeaturesEnabled)
        {
            this.mineshaftGenerator.func_151539_a(this, this.worldObj,
➥par1, par2, ablock);
            this.villageGenerator.func_151539_a(this, this.worldObj, par1,
➥par2, ablock);
            this.strongholdGenerator.func_151539_a(this, this.worldObj, par1,
➥par2, ablock);
            this.scatteredFeatureGenerator.func_151539_a(this, this.worldObj,
➥par1, par2, ablock);
        }

        Chunk chunk = new Chunk(this.worldObj, ablock, abyte, par1, par2);
        byte[] abyte1 = chunk.getBiomeArray();

        for (int k = 0; k < abyte1.length; ++k)
        {
            abyte1[k] = (byte)this.biomesForGeneration[k].biomeID;
        }

        chunk.generateSkylightMap();
        return chunk;
    }

    private void func_147423_a(int p_147423_1_, int p_147423_2_, int p_147423_3_)
```

```
    {
        double d0 = 684.412D;
        double d1 = 684.412D;
        double d2 = 512.0D;
        double d3 = 512.0D;
        this.field_147426_g = this.noiseGen6.generateNoiseOctaves(this.field_
➡147426_g, p_147423_1_, p_147423_3_, 5, 5, 200.0D, 200.0D, 0.5D);
        this.field_147427_d = this.field_147429_l.generateNoiseOctaves(this.field_
➡147427_d, p_147423_1_, p_147423_2_, p_147423_3_, 5, 33, 5, 8.555150000000001D,
➡4.277575000000001D, 8.555150000000001D);
        this.field_147428_e = this.field_147431_j.generateNoiseOctaves(this.field_
➡147428_e, p_147423_1_, p_147423_2_, p_147423_3_, 5, 33, 5, 684.412D, 684.412D,
➡684.412D);
        this.field_147425_f = this.field_147432_k.generateNoiseOctaves(this.field_
➡147425_f, p_147423_1_, p_147423_2_, p_147423_3_, 5, 33, 5, 684.412D, 684.412D,
➡684.412D);
        boolean flag1 = false;
        boolean flag = false;
        int l = 0;
        int i1 = 0;
        double d4 = 8.5D;

        for (int j1 = 0; j1 < 5; ++j1)
        {
            for (int k1 = 0; k1 < 5; ++k1)
            {
                float f = 0.0F;
                float f1 = 0.0F;
                float f2 = 0.0F;
                byte b0 = 2;
                BiomeGenBase biomegenbase = this.biomesForGeneration[j1 +
➡2 + (k1 + 2) * 10];

                for (int l1 = -b0; l1 <= b0; ++l1)
                {
                    for (int i2 = -b0; i2 <= b0; ++i2)
                    {
                        BiomeGenBase biomegenbase1 = this.biomesForGeneration[j1
➡+ l1 + 2 + (k1 + i2 + 2) * 10];
                        float f3 = biomegenbase1.rootHeight;
                        float f4 = biomegenbase1.heightVariation;

                        if (this.field_147435_p == WorldType.AMPLIFIED && f3 >
➡0.0F)
                        {
                            f3 = 1.0F + f3 * 2.0F;
                            f4 = 1.0F + f4 * 4.0F;
                        }
```

```
                       float f5 = this.parabolicField[l1 + 2 + (i2 + 2) * 5] /
➥(f3 + 2.0F);

                    if (biomegenbase1.rootHeight > biomegenbase.rootHeight)
                    {
                        f5 /= 2.0F;
                    }

                    f  += f4 * f5;
                    f1 += f3 * f5;
                    f2 += f5;
                }
            }

            f /= f2;
            f1 /= f2;
            f = f * 0.9F + 0.1F;
            f1 = (f1 * 4.0F - 1.0F) / 8.0F;
            double d12 = this.field_147426_g[i1] / 8000.0D;

            if (d12 < 0.0D)
            {
                d12 = -d12 * 0.3D;
            }

            d12 = d12 * 3.0D - 2.0D;

            if (d12 < 0.0D)
            {
                d12 /= 2.0D;

                if (d12 < -1.0D)
                {
                    d12 = -1.0D;
                }

                d12 /= 1.4D;
                d12 /= 2.0D;
            }
            else
            {
                if (d12 > 1.0D)
                {
                    d12 = 1.0D;
                }

                d12 /= 8.0D;
            }
```

```
            ++i1;
            double d13 = (double)f1;
            double d14 = (double)f;
            d13 += d12 * 0.2D;
            d13 = d13 * 8.5D / 8.0D;
            double d5 = 8.5D + d13 * 4.0D;

            for (int j2 = 0; j2 < 33; ++j2)
            {
                double d6 = ((double)j2 - d5) * 12.0D * 128.0D / 256.0D
/ d14;

                if (d6 < 0.0D)
                {
                    d6 *= 4.0D;
                }

                double d7 = this.field_147428_e[l] / 512.0D;
                double d8 = this.field_147425_f[l] / 512.0D;
                double d9 = (this.field_147427_d[l] / 10.0D + 1.0D) / 2.0D;
                double d10 = MathHelper.denormalizeClamp(d7, d8, d9) - d6;

                if (j2 > 29)
                {
                    double d11 = (double)((float)(j2 - 29) / 3.0F);
                    d10 = d10 * (1.0D - d11) + -10.0D * d11;
                }

                this.field_147434_q[l] = d10;
                ++l;
            }
        }
    }
}

/**
 * Checks to see if a chunk exists at x, y
 */
public boolean chunkExists(int par1, int par2)
{
    return true;
}

/**
 * Populates chunk with ores etc etc
 */
public void populate(IChunkProvider par1IChunkProvider, int par2, int par3)
{
```

```
    BlockFalling.fallInstantly = true;
    int k = par2 * 16;
    int l = par3 * 16;
    BiomeGenBase biomegenbase = this.worldObj.getBiomeGenForCoords(k +
➥16, l + 16);
    this.rand.setSeed(this.worldObj.getSeed());
    long i1 = this.rand.nextLong() / 2L * 2L + 1L;
    long j1 = this.rand.nextLong() / 2L * 2L + 1L;
    this.rand.setSeed((long)par2 * i1 + (long)par3 * j1 ^ this.worldObj.
➥getSeed());
    boolean flag = false;

    MinecraftForge.EVENT_BUS.post(new PopulateChunkEvent.Pre(par1IChunkProvider,
➥worldObj, rand, par2, par3, flag));

    if (this.mapFeaturesEnabled)
    {
        this.mineshaftGenerator.generateStructuresInChunk(this.worldObj,
➥this.rand, par2, par3);
        flag = this.villageGenerator.generateStructuresInChunk(this.worldObj,
➥this.rand, par2, par3);
        this.strongholdGenerator.generateStructuresInChunk(this.worldObj,
➥this.rand, par2, par3);
        this.scatteredFeatureGenerator.generateStructuresInChunk(this.worldObj,
➥this.rand, par2, par3);
    }

    int k1;
    int l1;
    int i2;

    if (biomegenbase != BiomeGenBase.desert && biomegenbase !=
➥BiomeGenBase.desertHills && !flag && this.rand.nextInt(4) == 0
            && TerrainGen.populate(par1IChunkProvider, worldObj, rand, par2,
➥par3, flag, LAKE))
    {
        k1 = k + this.rand.nextInt(16) + 8;
        l1 = this.rand.nextInt(256);
        i2 = l + this.rand.nextInt(16) + 8;
        (new WorldGenLakes(Blocks.water)).generate(this.worldObj,
➥this.rand, k1, l1, i2);
    }

    if (TerrainGen.populate(par1IChunkProvider, worldObj, rand, par2,
➥par3, flag, LAVA) && !flag && this.rand.nextInt(8) == 0)
    {
        k1 = k + this.rand.nextInt(16) + 8;
        l1 = this.rand.nextInt(this.rand.nextInt(248) + 8);
```

```
        i2 = l + this.rand.nextInt(16) + 8;

        if (l1 < 63 || this.rand.nextInt(10) == 0)
        {
            (new WorldGenLakes(Blocks.lava)).generate(this.worldObj,
➥this.rand, k1, l1, i2);
        }
    }


    boolean doGen = TerrainGen.populate(par1IChunkProvider, worldObj, rand,
➥par2, par3, flag, DUNGEON);
    for (k1 = 0; doGen && k1 < 8; ++k1)
    {
        l1 = k + this.rand.nextInt(16) + 8;
        i2 = this.rand.nextInt(256);
        int j2 = l + this.rand.nextInt(16) + 8;
        (new WorldGenDungeons()).generate(this.worldObj, this.rand,
➥l1, i2, j2);
    }

    biomegenbase.decorate(this.worldObj, this.rand, k, l);
    if (TerrainGen.populate(par1IChunkProvider, worldObj, rand, par2,
➥par3, flag, ANIMALS))
    {
    SpawnerAnimals.performWorldGenSpawning(this.worldObj, biomegenbase,
➥k + 8, l + 8, 16, 16, this.rand);
    }
    k += 8;
    l += 8;


    doGen = TerrainGen.populate(par1IChunkProvider, worldObj, rand, par2,
➥par3, flag, ICE);
    for (k1 = 0; doGen && k1 < 16; ++k1)
    {
        for (l1 = 0; l1 < 16; ++l1)
        {
            i2 = this.worldObj.getPrecipitationHeight(k + k1, l + l1);

            if (this.worldObj.isBlockFreezable(k1 + k, i2 - 1, l1 + l))
            {
                this.worldObj.setBlock(k1 + k, i2 - 1, l1 + l,
➥Blocks.ice, 0, 2);
            }

            if (this.worldObj.func_147478_e(k1 + k, i2, l1 + l, true))
            {
                this.worldObj.setBlock(k1 + k, i2, l1 + l,
➥Blocks.snow_layer, 0, 2);
```

```
                }
            }
        }


        MinecraftForge.EVENT_BUS.post(new PopulateChunkEvent.Post(
➥par1IChunkProvider, worldObj, rand, par2, par3, flag));


        BlockFalling.fallInstantly = false;
    }

    /**
     * Two modes of operation: if passed true, save all Chunks in one go.
➥If passed false, save up to two chunks.
     * Return true if all chunks have been saved.
     */
    public boolean saveChunks(boolean par1, IProgressUpdate par2IProgressUpdate)
    {
        return true;
    }

    /**
     * Save extra data not associated with any Chunk.  Not saved during
➥autosave, only during world unload.  Currently
     * unimplemented.
     */
    public void saveExtraData() {}

    /**
     * Unloads chunks that are marked to be unloaded. This is not
➥guaranteed to unload every such chunk.
     */
    public boolean unloadQueuedChunks()
    {
        return false;
    }

    /**
     * Returns if the IChunkProvider supports saving.
     */
    public boolean canSave()
    {
        return true;
    }

    /**
     * Converts the instance data to a readable string.
     */
    public String makeString()
```

```java
    {
        return "RandomLevelSource";
    }


    /**
     * Returns a list of creatures of the specified type that can
➥spawn at the given location.
     */
    public List getPossibleCreatures(EnumCreatureType par1EnumCreatureType,
➥int par2, int par3, int par4)
    {
        BiomeGenBase biomegenbase = this.worldObj.getBiomeGenForCoords(par2, par4);
        return par1EnumCreatureType == EnumCreatureType.monster &&
➥this.scatteredFeatureGenerator.func_143030_a(par2, par3, par4) ?
➥this.scatteredFeatureGenerator.getScatteredFeatureSpawnList() :
➥biomegenbase.getSpawnableList(par1EnumCreatureType);
    }


    public ChunkPosition func_147416_a(World p_147416_1_, String p_147416_2_,
➥int p_147416_3_, int p_147416_4_, int p_147416_5_)
    {
        return "Stronghold".equals(p_147416_2_) && this.strongholdGenerator
➥!= null ? this.strongholdGenerator.func_151545_a(p_147416_1_, p_147416_3_,
➥p_147416_4_, p_147416_5_) : null;
    }


    public int getLoadedChunkCount()
    {
        return 0;
    }


    public void recreateStructures(int par1, int par2)
    {
        if (this.mapFeaturesEnabled)
        {
            this.mineshaftGenerator.func_151539_a(this, this.worldObj, par1,
➥par2, (Block[])null);
            this.villageGenerator.func_151539_a(this, this.worldObj, par1,
➥par2, (Block[])null);
            this.strongholdGenerator.func_151539_a(this, this.worldObj, par1,
➥par2, (Block[])null);
            this.scatteredFeatureGenerator.func_151539_a(this, this.worldObj,
➥par1, par2, (Block[])null);
        }
    }
}
```

Custom Biomes

Custom biomes can really make a mod stand out. The following code has to be added for a biome to work:

```
public static BiomeGenBase example = new BiomeGenExample(52).setBiomeName(
➡"Example");
BiomeManager.addSpawnBiome(example);
```

LISTING A.16   Displays `BiomeGenExample`

```
package com.wuppy.samsmod;

import java.util.Random;

import net.minecraft.block.Block;
import net.minecraft.block.material.Material;
import net.minecraft.init.Blocks;
import net.minecraft.world.World;
import net.minecraft.world.biome.BiomeGenBase;
import net.minecraft.world.gen.feature.WorldGenAbstractTree;
import net.minecraft.world.gen.feature.WorldGenDesertWells;
import net.minecraft.world.gen.feature.WorldGenMegaJungle;
import net.minecraft.world.gen.feature.WorldGenShrub;
import net.minecraft.world.gen.feature.WorldGenTrees;

public class BiomeGenExample extends BiomeGenBase
{
    public BiomeGenExample(int par1)
    {
        super(par1);
        this.spawnableCreatureList.clear();
        this.topBlock = Blocks.grass;
        this.fillerBlock = Blocks.dirt;
        this.spawnableCreatureList.clear();
        this.spawnableMonsterList.clear();
        this.spawnableWaterCreatureList.clear();

        this.theBiomeDecorator.cactiPerChunk = 0;
        this.theBiomeDecorator.deadBushPerChunk = 3;

        this.flowers.clear();
        this.addFlower(Blocks.red_flower,    4,  3);
        this.addFlower(Blocks.red_flower,    5,  3);
        this.addFlower(Blocks.red_flower,    6,  3);
        this.addFlower(Blocks.red_flower,    7,  3);
        this.addFlower(Blocks.red_flower,    0, 20);
```

```
        this.addFlower(Blocks.red_flower,    3, 20);
        this.addFlower(Blocks.red_flower,    8, 20);
        this.addFlower(Blocks.yellow_flower, 0, 30);
    }

    @Override
    public void decorate(World par1World, Random par2Random, int par3, int par4)
    {
        super.decorate(par1World, par2Random, par3, par4);

        if (par2Random.nextInt(1000) == 0)
        {
            int k = par3 + par2Random.nextInt(16) + 8;
            int l = par4 + par2Random.nextInt(16) + 8;
            WorldGenDesertWells worldgendesertwells = new WorldGenDesertWells();
            worldgendesertwells.generate(par1World, par2Random, k,
➥par1World.getHeightValue(k, l) + 1, l);
        }
    }
}
```

Custom AI

If you have a mob, you want it to be unique. An easy way to make your mob unique is to add some custom AI for it. This can either be completely custom, which can be quite difficult, or adaptations of already existing AI. You will now see two examples of custom AI code, which can be used in quite a few situations. This should give you an insight in how to make your own AI as well as two useful AIs you could use.

Fleeing When Hurt

The following piece of AI in Listing A.17 will make a mob fly when it is hurt, which is, in this case, set to two hearts.

LISTING A.17   `EntityAIFleeOnHurt`

```
package com.wuppy.samsmod.ai;

import net.minecraft.entity.EntityCreature;
import net.minecraft.entity.ai.EntityAIBase;
import net.minecraft.entity.ai.RandomPositionGenerator;
import net.minecraft.util.Vec3;

public class EntityAIFleeOnHurt extends EntityAIBase
{
```

```java
private EntityCreature theEntityCreature;
private double speed;
private double randPosX;
private double randPosY;
private double randPosZ;

public EntityAIFleeOnHurt(EntityCreature par1EntityCreature, double par2)
{
    this.theEntityCreature = par1EntityCreature;
    this.speed = par2;
    this.setMutexBits(1);
}

/**
 * Returns whether the EntityAIBase should begin execution.
 */
@Override
public boolean shouldExecute()
{
    if (this.theEntityCreature.getHealth() > 4F)
    {
        return false;
    }
    else
    {
        Vec3 vec3 = RandomPositionGenerator.findRandomTarget(this.
theEntityCreature, 5, 4);

        if (vec3 == null)
        {
            return false;
        }
        else
        {
            this.randPosX = vec3.xCoord;
            this.randPosY = vec3.yCoord;
            this.randPosZ = vec3.zCoord;
            return true;
        }
    }
}

/**
 * Execute a one-shot task or start executing a continuous task
 */
@Override
public void startExecuting()
{
```

```
        this.theEntityCreature.getNavigator().tryMoveToXYZ(this.randPosX,
➥this.randPosY, this.randPosZ, this.speed);
    }

    /**
     * Returns whether an in-progress EntityAIBase should continue executing
     */
    @Override
    public boolean continueExecuting()
    {
        return !this.theEntityCreature.getNavigator().noPath();
    }
}
```

Attacking By Night

The following piece of AI in Listing A.18 will make sure that the entity using this AI will only hurt the target when it is night. This is an adaptation of `EntityAIAttackOnCollide`.

LISTING A.18   `EntityAIAttackOnCollideNight`

```
package com.wuppy.samsmod.ai;

import net.minecraft.entity.EntityCreature;
import net.minecraft.entity.EntityLivingBase;
import net.minecraft.entity.ai.EntityAIBase;
import net.minecraft.pathfinding.PathEntity;
import net.minecraft.pathfinding.PathPoint;
import net.minecraft.util.MathHelper;
import net.minecraft.world.World;

@SuppressWarnings("rawtypes")
public class EntityAIAttackOnCollideNight extends EntityAIBase
{
    World worldObj;
    EntityCreature attacker;

    /**
     * An amount of decrementing ticks that allows the entity to attack
➥once the tick reaches 0.
     */
    int attackTick;

    /** The speed with which the mob will approach the target */
    double speedTowardsTarget;
```

```
    /**
     * When true, the mob will continue chasing its target, even if
➥it can't find a path to them right now.
     */
    boolean longMemory;

    /** The PathEntity of our entity. */
    PathEntity entityPathEntity;
    Class classTarget;
    private int field_75445_i;

    private int failedPathFindingPenalty;

    public EntityAIAttackOnCollideNight(EntityCreature par1EntityCreature,
➥Class par2Class, double par3, boolean par5)
    {
        this(par1EntityCreature, par3, par5);
        this.classTarget = par2Class;
    }


    public EntityAIAttackOnCollideNight(EntityCreature par1EntityCreature,
➥double par2, boolean par4)
    {
        this.attacker = par1EntityCreature;
        this.worldObj = par1EntityCreature.worldObj;
        this.speedTowardsTarget = par2;
        this.longMemory = par4;
        this.setMutexBits(3);
    }

    /**
     * Returns whether the EntityAIBase should begin execution.
     */
    @SuppressWarnings("unchecked")
    @Override
    public boolean shouldExecute()
    {
        EntityLivingBase entitylivingbase = this.attacker.getAttackTarget();

        if (entitylivingbase == null)
        {
            return false;
        }
        else if (!entitylivingbase.isEntityAlive())
        {
            return false;
        }
        else if (this.classTarget != null &&
```

```java
➡!this.classTarget.isAssignableFrom(entitylivingbase.getClass())))
        {
            return false;
        }
        else if(this.worldObj.isDaytime())
        {
            return false;
        }
        else
        {
            if (-- this.field_75445_i <= 0)
            {
                this.entityPathEntity =
➡this.attacker.getNavigator().getPathToEntityLiving(entitylivingbase);
                this.field_75445_i = 4 + this.attacker.getRNG().nextInt(7);
                return this.entityPathEntity != null;
            }
            else
            {
                return true;
            }
        }
    }

    /**
     * Returns whether an in-progress EntityAIBase should continue executing
     */
    @Override
    public boolean continueExecuting()
    {
        EntityLivingBase entitylivingbase = this.attacker.getAttackTarget();
        return entitylivingbase == null ? false : (!entitylivingbase.
➡isEntityAlive() ? false : (!this.longMemory ? !this.attacker.
➡getNavigator().noPath() : this.attacker.isWithinHomeDistance(
➡MathHelper.floor_double(entitylivingbase.posX), MathHelper.floor_double(
➡entitylivingbase.posY), MathHelper.floor_double(entitylivingbase.posZ))));
    }

    /**
     * Execute a one-shot task or start executing a continuous task
     */
    @Override
    public void startExecuting()
    {
        this.attacker.getNavigator().setPath(this.entityPathEntity,
➡this.speedTowardsTarget);
        this.field_75445_i = 0;
    }
```

```
/**
 * Resets the task
 */
@Override
public void resetTask()
{
    this.attacker.getNavigator().clearPathEntity();
}


/**
 * Updates the task
 */
@Override
public void updateTask()
{
    EntityLivingBase entitylivingbase = this.attacker.getAttackTarget();
    this.attacker.getLookHelper().setLookPositionWithEntity(entitylivingbase,
30.0F, 30.0F);

    if ((this.longMemory || this.attacker.getEntitySenses().canSee(
entitylivingbase)) && --this.field_75445_i <= 0)
    {
        this.field_75445_i = failedPathFindingPenalty + 4 + this.attacker.
getRNG().nextInt(7);
        this.attacker.getNavigator().tryMoveToEntityLiving(entitylivingbase,
this.speedTowardsTarget);
        if (this.attacker.getNavigator().getPath() != null)
        {
            PathPoint finalPathPoint = this.attacker.getNavigator().
getPath().getFinalPathPoint();
            if (finalPathPoint != null && entitylivingbase.getDistanceSq(
finalPathPoint.xCoord, finalPathPoint.yCoord, finalPathPoint.zCoord) < 1)
            {
                failedPathFindingPenalty = 0;
            }
            else
            {
                failedPathFindingPenalty += 10;
            }
        }
        else
        {
            failedPathFindingPenalty += 10;
        }
    }

    this.attackTick = Math.max(this.attackTick - 1, 0);
```

```
        double d0 = (double)(this.attacker.width * 2.0F * this.attacker.width
➥* 2.0F + entitylivingbase.width);

        if (this.attacker.getDistanceSq(entitylivingbase.posX, entitylivingbase.
➥boundingBox.minY, entitylivingbase.posZ) <= d0)
        {
            if (this.attackTick <= 0)
            {
                this.attackTick = 20;

                if (this.attacker.getHeldItem() != null)
                {
                    this.attacker.swingItem();
                }

                this.attacker.attackEntityAsMob(entitylivingbase);
            }
        }
    }
}
```

Using Your Custom AI

Your custom AI code can be used exactly the same as any other piece of AI. There is no need to register it in any way. The following line of code uses `EntityAIFleeOnHurt` just like any other `EntityAI`:

```
this.tasks.addTask(0, new EntityAIFleeOnHurt(this, 1.1D));
```

Spawning Particles

Sometimes you want to spawn particles around your blocks or items to make them look better. Listing A.19 shows a method called `randomDisplayTick`, which is a method for blocks used to spawn custom particles. There are similar methods for entities and items.

LISTING A.19 Spawning Custom Particles

```
@SideOnly(Side.CLIENT)
@Override
public void randomDisplayTick(World par1World, int par2, int par3,
➥int par4, Random par5Random)
{
        super.randomDisplayTick(par1World, par2, par3, par4, par5Random);

        if (par5Random.nextInt(2) == 0)
```

```
    {
        double var1 = (double) ((float) par2 + par1World.rand.nextFloat());
        double var2 = (double) ((float) par3 + par1World.rand.nextFloat());
        double var3 = (double) ((float) par4 + par1World.rand.nextFloat());
        par1World.spawnParticle("smoke", var1, var2, var3, 0.0D, 0.0D, 0.0D);
        par1World.spawnParticle("flame", var1, var2, var3, 0.0D, 0.0D, 0.0D);
    }
}
```

Playing Sounds

It's often a good idea to have certain sound effects with your items, blocks, or entities. The following line of code will play a sound:

```
worldObj.playSound(x, y, z, "step.wood", 1F, 1F, true);
```

The full list of sound names can be found here at http://minecraft.gamepedia.com/Sounds.json.

Using a Model for an Item

Sometimes, you want your item to look a little fancier than just a normal flat image. In this case, you could try to use a custom model for your item. To do this, you need a custom `Render` class, which is shown in Listing A.20.

LISTING A.20   RenderExampleItem

```
package com.wuppy.samsmod;

import net.minecraft.client.Minecraft;
import net.minecraft.item.ItemStack;
import net.minecraft.util.ResourceLocation;
import net.minecraftforge.client.IItemRenderer;

import org.lwjgl.opengl.GL11;

public class RenderExampleItem implements IItemRenderer
{
    private ModelExample model;

    public RenderExampleItem ()
    {
        model = new ModelExample();
    }

    @Override
```

```java
    public boolean handleRenderType(ItemStack item, ItemRenderType type)
    {
            return true;
    }


    @Override
    public boolean shouldUseRenderHelper(ItemRenderType type, ItemStack item,
➡ItemRendererHelper helper)
    {
            return true;
    }


    @Override
    public void renderItem(ItemRenderType type, ItemStack item,
➡Object... data)
    {
            GL11.glPushMatrix();

            GL11.glScalef(-1F, -1F, 1F);

            switch (type)
            {
                    case INVENTORY:
                            GL11.glTranslatef(0, 0.12F, 0);
                            break;
                    case EQUIPPED:
                            GL11.glTranslatef(-0.8F, -0.2F, 0.7F);
                            break;
                    case EQUIPPED_FIRST_PERSON:
                            GL11.glTranslatef(0, -0.7F, 0.7F);
                            break;
                    default:
            }

            Minecraft.getMinecraft().renderEngine.bindTexture(new
➡ResourceLocation("textures/entity/zombie/zombie.png"));
            model.render(null, 0.0F, 0.0F, -0.1F, 0.0F, 0.0F, 0.0625F);

            GL11.glPopMatrix();
    }
}
```

This `Render` class can use any kind of model; just make sure you set it in the constructor. The texture used in this situation is the zombie texture, but you can use any texture you want. You may have to change some of the values in the render and GL11 methods for your model to look nice.

You have to register this `Render` class with the item you want to render this way using the following line of code:

```
MinecraftForgeClient.registerItemRenderer(SamsMod.exampleItem, new
➥RenderExampleItem());
```

Index

How can we make this index more useful? Email us at indexes@samspublishing.com

How can we make this index more useful? Email us at indexes@samspublishing.com

How can we make this index more useful? Email us at indexes@samspublishing.com